The American History Series

SERIES EDITORS
John Hope Franklin, *Duke University*
Abraham S. Eisenstadt, *Brooklyn College*

D1500824

Arthur S. Link

GENERAL EDITOR FOR HISTORY

John Ferling
WEST GEORGIA COLLEGE

Struggle for a Continent

The Wars of Early America

HARLAN DAVIDSON, INC.
ARLINGTON HEIGHTS, ILLINOIS 60004

Copyright © 1993
Harlan Davidson, Inc.
All Rights Reserved

This book, or parts thereof, must not be used or reproduced in any manner without written permission. For information, address the publisher, Harlan Davidson, Inc., 3110 North Arlington Heights Road, Arlington Heights, Illinois 60004-1592.

Library of Congress Cataloging-in-Publication Data

Ferling, John
    Struggle for a continent : the wars of early America / John Ferling
       p. cm.—(The American history series)
    Includes bibliographical references and index.
    ISBN 0-88295-896-8
      1. United States—History—Colonial period, ca. 1600–1775.
2. United States—History, Military—To 1900. I. Title.
II. Series: American history series (Arlington Heights, Ill.)
E188.F4 1993
973—dc20
                                               92-32469
                                                  CIP

Cover illustration: "On the Warpath" by Howard Pyle. Copyright © 1901 Brown County Library, Green Bay, Wisconsin.

Manufactured in the United States of America
97 96 95 94 93 1 2 3 4 5 EB

FOREWORD

Every generation writes its own history for the reason that it sees the past in the foreshortened perspective of its own experience. This has surely been true of the writing of American history. The practical aim of our historiography is to give us a more informed sense of where we are going by helping us understand the road we took in getting where we are. As the nature and dimensions of American life are changing, so too are the themes of our historical writing. Today's scholars are hard at work reconsidering every major aspect of the nation's past: its politics, diplomacy, economy, society, recreation, mores and values, as well as status, ethnic, race, sexual, and family relations. The lists of series titles that appear at the back of this book will show at once that our historians are ever broadening the range of their studies.

The aim of this series is to offer our readers a survey of what today's historians are saying about the central themes and aspects of the American past. To do this, we have invited to write for the series scholars who have made notable contributions to the respective fields in which they are working. Drawing on primary and secondary materials, each volume presents a factual and narrative account of its particular subject, one that affords readers a basis for perceiving its larger dimensions and importance. Conscious that readers respond to the closeness and immediacy of a subject, each of our authors seeks to restore the past as an actual present, to revive it as a living reality. The individuals and groups who figure in the pages of our books appear as real people who once were looking for survival and fulfillment. Aware that historical subjects are often matters of controversy, our authors present their own findings and conclusions. Each volume closes with an extensive critical essay on the writings of the major authorities on its particular theme.

The books in this series are designed for use in both basic and advanced courses in American history, on the undergraduate and graduate levels. Such a series has a particular value these days, when the format of American history courses is being altered to accommodate a greater diversity of reading materials. The series offers a number of distinct advantages. It extends the dimensions of regular course work. Going well beyond the confines of the textbook, it makes clear that the study of our past is, more than the student might otherwise understand, at once complex, profound, and absorbing. It presents that past as a subject of continuing interest and fresh investigation. The work of experts in their respective fields, the series, moreover, puts at the disposal of the reader the rich findings of historical inquiry. It invites the reader to join, in major fields of research, those who are pondering anew the central themes and aspects of our past. And it reminds the reader that in each successive generation of the ever-changing American adventure, men and women and children were attempting, as we are now, to live their lives and to make their way.

John Hope Franklin
A. S. Eisenstadt

CONTENTS

ACKNOWLEDGMENTS

Many individuals contributed to the completion of this study. Inasmuch as it was written as I grappled with heavy teaching assignments, I am indebted to Albert S. Hanser for consistently providing schedules that afforded blocks of time for research, reflection, and writing. In addition, through a grant bestowed by the Learning Resources Committee of West Georgia College, I was able to spend several days at the Massachusetts Historical Society and Boston Public Library working through manuscripts and other materials that otherwise would have been unavailable to me.

The librarians and staff at the Irvine Sullivan Ingram Library assisted in numerous ways. I am especially grateful to Nancy Farmer, who secured book after book for me through interlibrary loans.

I am grateful to Karen Ordahl Kupperman and Don Higginbotham, who read all or considerable portions of the original draft of the manuscript, and who made numerous helpful suggestions. Readers for the publisher also provided enormous assistance in rounding the manuscript into its final form.

Finally, I am grateful to the editors of this series, John Hope Franklin and Abraham S. Eisenstadt, for many useful suggestions. Maureen Gilgore Hewitt's unflagging patience and encouragement helped through some difficult times of revising and rewriting, and Claudia Wood's assistance in the final editing seemed nothing short of miraculous.

John Ferling

CHRONOLOGY OF EVENTS

July 1584	First English exploration of Roanoke Island.
June 1585	First English colony planted at Roanoke Island.
June 1586	Lane attacked Dasemunkepeuc. Wingina killed. The first Roanoke colony abandoned.
July 1587	Second Roanoke colony ("The Lost Colony") founded.
1607	Jamestown established.
1609–1614	First Anglo-Powhatan War.
December 1620	Plymouth colony founded.
1621	Dutch established New Netherland.
1623	Plymouth attacked Wessagusett; Witawamet killed.
March 1622	Opechancanough launched surprise attack against English in Virginia.
1622–1632	Second Anglo-Powhatan War.
1629	Puritan "Great Migration" to New England began.
August 1636	John Endicott's campaign on Block Island. Pequot War began.
May 1637	Under John Mason English attacked Pequot's Mystic River Fort.
1643–1646	Kieft's War in New Netherland.

March 1644	Opechancanough launched second surprise attack.
1644–1646	Third Anglo-Powhatan War.
August 1664	New Netherland capitulated to England.
1666	Iroquois humbled following fifteen-year war with France.
July 1675	War erupted with Susquehannocks and Doegs in Virginia.
May 1676	Nathaniel Bacon destroyed Occaneechee tribe.
June 1676	King Philip's War broke out in New England.
December 1676	The New England army attacked the Narragansetts in the Great Swamp in Rhode Island.
February 1677	Attack on Lancaster; Mary Rowlandson's captivity began.
August 1677	Philip killed by Benjamin Church's unit.
1683	New France attacked Iroquois.
1687	New France under Devonville attacked Senecas.
1689	King William's War (War of the League of Augsburg) declared.
February 1690	Schenectady attacked by Frontenac's forces.
April 1690	Phips led expedition against French in Acadia (Nova Scotia).
August 1690	Fitz-John Winthrop's campaign against French in Montreal began.
October 1690	Phips failed to take Quebec.
1692	Benjamin Church's campaign into Penobscot territory.
1696	Church's expedition into Acadia.
1697	Peace of Ryswick ended King William's War.
1701	Queen Anne's War (War of the Spanish Succession) began.
Autumn 1702	South Carolina failed in siege of Spanish Saint Augustine.

August 1703	French and Indians launched attack across the Maine frontier.
February 1704	French and Indians attacked Deerfield, Massachusetts.
May 1704	Benjamin Church expedition against Minas and Chignecto.
May 1707	New England campaign to take Acadia failed.
August 1707	Second New England campaign to take Acadia failed.
1707–1708	Dudley, Vetch, et al. urged British assistance to destroy New France.
Summer 1709	Northern provinces raised armies to attack New France; Great Britain canceled project.
Autumn 1710	Anglo-American forces siezed Acadia (Nova Scotia).
August 1711	Anglo-American forces (under Hovenden Walker) failed to take Quebec.
1711–1712	Tuscarora War on the North Carolina frontier.
1713	Peace of Utrecht.
1715–1721	Yamassee War in South Carolina.
1723	Dummer's War on Massachusetts frontier.
1732	Colony of Georgia created.
1739	War of Jenkins' Ear declared.
Spring 1740	Oglethorpe's siege of Saint Augustine failed.
April 1741	Anglo-American campaign at Cartagena failed.
July 1742	Montiano failed to take Saint Simons Island.
1744	King George's War (War of the Austrian Succession) declared.
Spring 1745	Anglo-American forces (under Pepperrell and Warren) successfully besieged Louisbourg.
1748	Treaty of Aix-la-Chapelle.
1753	George Washington's mission to Fort Le Boeuf.
June 1754	Washington's Virginia regiment attacked French force; Albany Plan of Union proposed.
July 1754	Washington surrendered at Fort Necessity.
July 1755	Braddock defeated at Monongahela.

September 1755	Battle of Lake George.
1756	Seven Years' War (French and Indian War or The Great War for Empire) declared; Montcalm and Loudoun assumed command.
August 1756	French seized Oswego; Pitts became prime minister.
September 1756	Pennsylvania destroyed Kittanning villages.
August 1757	French and Indians seized Fort William Henry.
January 1758	Loudoun recalled; succeeded by Abercromby.
June 1758	British under Amherst took Louisbourg.
July 1758	Abercromby's attack on Fort Ticonderoga repulsed.
August 1758	Fort Frontenac fell to force led by Bradstreet.
November 1758	Fort Duquesne fell to Anglo-American force under Forbes.
August 1759	Forts Ticonderoga and Saint Frédéric fell to British force led by Amherst.
September 1759	Battle of Quebec; Wolfe and Montcalm perished.
September 1760	Montreal surrendered to British under Amherst.
1763	Treaty of Paris.

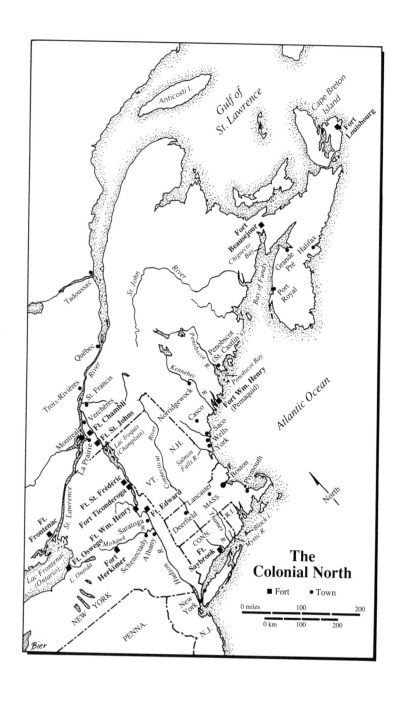

Anticosti I.

Gulf of
St. Lawrence

Cape Breton
Island

**Fort
Louisbourg**

**Fort
Beauséjour**

Chignecto Bay

Grande
Pré

Halifax

Port
Royal

Bay of Fundy

Tadoussac

St. John
River

Québec

Penobscot (St. Castin's)

Penobscot R.

Penobscot Bay

Fort Wm. Henry
(Pemaquid)

Kennebec R.

Norridgewock

Casco

Saco

Wells

York

Trois-Rivières

St. Francis

Verchères

Ft. Chambli

Ft. St. Johns

Lac Iroquis
(Champlain)

Connecticut River

N.H.

Salmon
Falls R.

Boston

Plymouth

Montreal

La Prairie

St. Lawrence

Ft. St. Frédéric

Fort Ticonderoga

Ft. Wm. Henry

VT.

Ft. Edward

Lancaster

MASS.

Deerfield

R.I.

**Ft.
Frontenac**

Saratoga R.

Ft. Oswego

Mohawk

**Fort
Herkimer**

Schenectady

Albany

Hudson R.

Thames R.

Block I.

Mystic R.

CONN.

**Ft.
Saybrook**

Lac Frontenac
(Ontario)

L. Oneida

NEW
YORK

New
York

PENNA.

N.J.

Atlantic Ocean

North

The
Colonial North

■ Fort   ● Town

0 miles   100   200

0 km   100   200

Bier

INTRODUCTION

In December 1606, under a wintry sky, George Percy boarded the *Susan Constant,* the one-hundred-ton flagship of an expedition bound from London to a region in North America that the English called Virginia. The ships would sail at night to hide their departure from Spanish spies. Percy and the nearly 150 men with whom he sailed were on a mission to plant an English colony in America.

An English blueblood with a taste for adventure, Percy had soldiered for England in Ireland and in the Netherlands since 1599. Service in Virginia attracted him because several soldier-friends had volunteered to make the voyage and be-cause—this was his primary motive—he found the prospect of danger in America to be irresistible. This hotspur did not have long to wait before his yearning for risk was fulfilled.

On the day that land was sighted, Percy was a member of the reconnaissance party sent ashore at today's Lynnhaven Bay. Seventeen men clambered into small boats and rowed to the beach. Wearing armor and carrying shields, they clanked as they climbed out of their crafts, waded through the shallow, warm summer surf, struggled unsteadily across sand dunes, and finally started into the dense forest that lay spread before them. Percy and his compatriots explored for eight hours. The woods were thick and tangled and the air humid in this green, enveloping environment. Toward evening the men started back to the beach. Suddenly Indians sprang from behind large trees and attacked them. The assailants had crept "on all fours like bears," Percy said later, then had concealed themselves. The English were caught by surprise. One member of the search party was shot in the hand by an arrow. Another was shot in the gut. The fight ended when the English, after only a few seconds of conflict, fired on the Indians with their muskets. The attackers quickly broke off the battle and fled into the woods.

Percy survived that military engagement, but it was a foretaste of what lay ahead. Later Percy wrote: "There were never Englishmen left in a foreign country in such misery as we were in this new discovered Virginia." Men died of disease, starvation, and injuries inflicted by Indians. None would have survived, Percy also declared, had not God "put a terror in the savages' hearts." The terror of which Percy spoke was the retaliation of English soldiers, men like himself. Percy once described an action that he carried out against an Indian village near Jamestown.

Then drawing my soldiers into battle [readiness] . . . we marched toward the town. An Indian guide with me named Kempes, who was led in shackles, brought us the right way near the town. So then I commanded every leader to set fire to the savages' houses that none might escape. . . . And then we fell on them and put some 15 or 16 [sentries and Indian warriors] to the sword. . . . My Lieutenant captured the queen and her children, as well as one male Indian. . . . I had his head cut off, and then I dispersed my soldiers to burn their houses and cut down their corn growing about the town. . . .
[After the operation was completed and] we marched out with the queen and her children to our boats, my soldiers began to complain because these Indians had been spared. . . . It was agreed [at a meeting of the officers] to put the children to death. This was done by throwing them overboard and shooting out their brains in the water.

Percy somehow survived five years in Virginia, although at least one-half of his shipmates on the *Susan Constant* were dead within eighteen months of their arrival. He returned to England in 1612, where he quietly lived out the remainder of his years.

About a century after Percy's death, Adam Stephen, a Scotsman, immigrated in 1748 to the Virginia that his predecessor had fought to establish. Unlike Percy, Stephen hailed from humble roots; his father was either an artisan or merchant in a small, rural village. Stephen received a fine education, however. His immigration to America at the age of twenty-seven did not occur until completion of his medical studies at the University of Edinburgh. Economic opportunity enticed Stephen. He believed he could establish a more prosperous medical practice in America, and he hoped to use his profits to invest in land along Virginia's steadily advancing frontier.

Within five years Stephen dwelled in a two-story log house on a two-thousand acre estate along the Opequon Creek in the bucolic northern Shenandoah Valley, hundreds of miles northwest of the James River region where Percy lived and fought. Although Stephen was an established physician and an esteemed member of his community, his social and economic status remained well below that of the great planters of Virginia.

Stephen's life changed suddenly in 1754. War erupted along Virginia's frontier. In February the governor asked for volunteers to serve in a Virginia army; he set aside two hundred thousand acres of land near the Ohio River that was to be divided among those who bore arms. Stephen volunteered and was commissioned a captain. The prospect of hazardous duty appealed to him; so did the lure of free land.

Stephen soldiered for eight years. Like Percy he fought against Indians. Unlike Percy he fought against the French as well. He was thrust into dangerous situations repeatedly. Twice Stephen was wounded in action. He was a good amateur soldier—an effective leader, a tough disciplinarian, and a good recruiter. English professionals who served with him described him as a "gentleman" of a "good & soldier-like appearance." He rose steadily until he held the rank of lieutenant colonel and was second in command in his unit.

Upon leaving Virginia's army in 1762 Stephen received five thousand acres in bounty lands, and soon he moved into a large stone house. He was chosen for numerous local offices, positions customarily reserved for the most respected citizens. Following the war Colonel Stephen—as his neighbors continued to address him—was the most esteemed resident of Berkeley County, Virginia.

Warfare in early America fulfilled the desires of Percy and Stephen. Percy's emotional needs to experience danger and to test himself were satiated; Stephen accepted military service as an acceptable price to pay for socioeconomic advancement. For countless others, however, the wars that erupted with disconcerting frequency in early America would have an altogether different meaning.

Young William Polson, also a Scottish immigrant to Virginia, left a wife, Rebecca, and an infant child at home when he joined the same army as Adam Stephen. He likely harbored many of the same aspirations as Stephen. But fifteen months after he donned his handsome buff and blue officer's uniform, Lieutenant Polson died of a bullet wound in a dark forest hundreds of miles from his family.

In 1676 Mary Rowlandson was a six-year-old child when war came to the small New England town in which she lived. She was wounded in the first minutes of an Indian attack, shot through the stomach. Taken captive by her assailants, she died after nine days and was buried in a shallow grave in unfamiliar woodlands far from her home.

John Hawks was a farmer who moved to another New England frontier town in 1673. Two years after he and his family arrived, Indians destroyed the town during King Philip's War. Hawks and his family escaped the attack and returned following the war to help rebuild the village. One of their children, John, Jr., remained in the town after he grew to adulthood. He eventually married and raised his own children in this same town. In 1704 war returned to the village. One snowy February night Indians struck. The attack came without warning. John Hawks, Jr., hurried his wife and three children into a cellar to hide. The family experienced a nightmare. The attackers set fire to the dwelling; in no time every exit was blocked. Trapped in the basement, every member of John Hawks's family smothered to death.

But the English were not the only victims in these wars. Men, women, and children among the native peoples of America often found their ancestral lands and their culture remorselessly threatened by the steady encroachment of European settlement. They, too, took up arms. Like their adversaries, some Indians exhibited considerable bravery and courage, some were brutal and barbaric and treacherous, some must have fought more from compulsion than true commitment, some were innocents trapped by bewildering forces beyond their control or comprehension, and many died by the hand of a hated assailant, deaths no less lonely and painful than those experienced by English soldiers and settlers.

The history of early European settlement in North America often is presented as a grand and glorious story of settlers immigrating in search of freedom or economic opportunities. In the wilderness of America, according to many accounts, these immigrants refashioned the habits of the Old World; in time something new and better emerged—a "new man, the American," as Michel de Crèvecoeur, a French immigrant, styled the citizens of the United States in 1782.

This story omits much, however. Certainly it ignores the European struggle for hegemony in America. The conquest of America is not a pretty story. It is replete with prejudice, deceit, rapacity, cruelty, destruction, and death. The history of England's conquest of eastern North America is a history of warfare, not unbroken conflict, but periodic struggle. Hostilities erupted with such frequency, however, that one can barely find a generation of Anglo-Americans between 1607 and 1763 whose lives were not somehow touched by war.

Two broad phases are discernible in these recurrent wars. Before 1689 the English settlers and various native peoples who lived near the Atlantic seaboard often fell into conflict. These were grim clashes, what the twentieth century would term total warfare, life and death struggles in which the very existence of the society of each side was at stake. After 1689 the wars usually arose from the competing interests of the great European imperial powers: Great Britain, France, and Spain. Usually their rivalries and wars drifted across the Atlantic and engulfed their settlers and Indian allies in bloody conflicts far removed from the royal courts, imposing government offices, and sumptuous drawing rooms where the hostilities had originated.

The brunt of this warfare fell upon ordinary citizens to a degree that was unimaginable in Europe. While wars in Europe were contested between professional armies, citizen-soldiers composed the provincial armies. Generations of colonial volunteers and conscriptees laid aside their plows and stepped away from their workbenches to bear arms. War reshaped the daily lives of settlers, aroused unfathomable anxieties, and brought terrible pain and loss.

When warfare occurs with considerable frequency, as it did in early America, it impacts society's institutions and attitudes. Entrepreneurs and workers alike feel the effect of battles waged on distant frontiers. In such circumstances, war shapes the character and identity of a people. By the end of the colonial era, for instance, some Americans believed that an American army could hold its own against the best armies of Europe. Through repeated tests America's citizenry had, as John Adams once suggested, acquired "courage, experience, discipline, and hardiness."

The first settlers to English North America, mostly pacific farmers devoid of military experience, crossed the Atlantic expecting to find the peaceful "paradise of this world," what John Winthrop, the Puritan governor of Massachusetts, called the "Lord's garden," a "whole continent fruitful and convenient for the use of man." The last generation of colonists still saw America as a benighted land. "Freedom is offered to us," said an orator in 1776 at the commemorative service of the Boston Massacre. That freedom, he went on, which had been "driven from the other regions of the globe . . . wishes to find an asylum in the wilds of America." But that orator and his contemporaries believed liberty could be preserved only if they bore arms with "determined bravery." The Revolutionary generation was summoned to arms as had been so many of their American forebears. It saw itself as composed of "embattled farmers," as Ralph Waldo Emerson later described this generation. Congressman John Adams told them that "Every Body must and will, and shall be a soldier." A poem, which drew "a picture of the American soldier," described the colonists as "by nature brave" and capable of winning their objectives. A song sung by New York soldiers proclaimed that "The rising world shall sing of us a thousand years to Come / And tell our Children's Children the Wonders we have Done." And in the fateful days of April 1775, with still another American war once again inescapable, the men of Concord, Massachusetts, the men who would begin this fight, did what generations of uncertain, untested citizen-soldiers before them had done: they prayed with their pastor on the eve of battle for the firmness and resolve to "conduct [themselves] in such a Manner as to reflect Honor on the military Character."

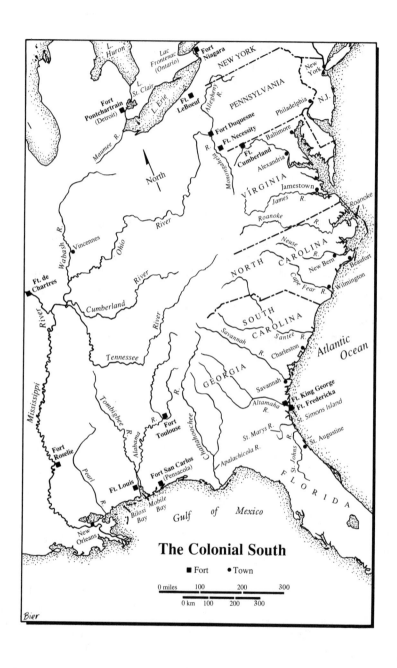

The Colonial South

■ Fort   ● Town

0 miles   100   200   300

0 km   100   200   300

CHAPTER ONE

The European Invasion of America

The Opening Clashes

The English arrived in southern waters in 1584. One typically warm midsummer day that year lookouts on two small English vessels, a bark of about sixty tons and a tiny pinnace only half that size, sighted the barrier islands off North Carolina. Soon a large party put ashore; most wore armor and all carried calivers, a heavy handgun. First, the men engaged in a ritual in which they took possession of this new land for their monarch, Queen Elizabeth. Next, they explored briefly, laboring under the weight of the armaments and shields as they floundered across the sandy soil and groped through the dense foliage. They discovered abundant game and fowl, summer grapes whose pungent odor filled the air, and thick forests that abounded with a variety of hardwoods and pines. The English spotted cypress, sweet gum, and dogwood trees, as well as what they believed surely must be the "highest and reddest cedars of the world." After a few hours they pitched tents in preparation for their first night ashore.

As they worked in these final hours of daylight, the English experienced their first contact with the Indians who dwelled in the region. Three Indians in a small canoe suddenly appeared. Each wore a loincloth of animal skin. Each was tattooed and adorned with armlets and chains of shells. The three Indians were armed but friendly. Later that evening perhaps fifty other Indians arrived, bringing fish that they gave to the strangers; the English responded with gifts of hats, shirts, and trinkets.

The English remained for about thirty days, traversing the woods, examining several islands, exploring rivers, and trading with the Indians. In August the tiny English shallops departed, their cargo holds laden with the skins, dyes, conch, and pearls they had acquired, and their commander charmed with the "most pleasant" environment and the "goodly people" that he had discovered.

The English who landed in America that year had been sent by Sir Walter Raleigh to reconnoiter a part of the New World with which England was unfamiliar. Raleigh possessed a Crown patent to colonize in North America; though free to locate his colony wherever he pleased, he hoped to situate his enterprise along the same latitude as the southern Mediterranean, where the climate would be hospitable and exotic commodities might be grown, then shipped to England. More important, perhaps, he sought a southerly base from which to plunder ships traveling between Spain and its Caribbean colonies.

Included among the thirty-five or so men who comprised Raleigh's expedition to discover a suitable site were specialists—a cartographer, a mineralogist, a surveyor, even an artist. The leaders, however, were veteran soldiers. Philip Amadas was a gentryman who had served in the English army; Arthur Barlowe had soldiered under Raleigh in the Irish wars in 1580–81. What the English had learned in their usurpation of Ireland would be of inestimable value in the adventures that lay ahead in America.

The English had commenced their colonization of Ulster and Munster only a few years before. Their conquest, such as it was, had been accomplished with considerable violence, bloody work that had been justified on the grounds that the indigenous population allegedly was idle, filthy, licentious, barbarous, and pagan. A great number of Irish perished, including civilians who were systematically executed under martial law; at Smerwick, for instance, Raleigh supervised the execution of six hundred people following the surrender of a besieged garrison. The Irish campaigns served as a period of apprenticeship for the English soldiers. Not only would many veterans of Irish battlefields eventually serve in America, but the English justified the subjugation of the American Indians with the same reasoning they used in the suppression of the Irish.

The English colonizers who turned to America had diverse motives. Some looked forward to the establishment of self-sufficient plantations that could supply England, enriching both investors and the parent state. Some anticipated a lucrative trade with the natives, while still others expected the colonies merely to facilitate further exploration, in the course of which the Northwest Passage or precious minerals might be found. Like Raleigh, some sought to establish bases for plundering Spanish ships. Whatever the goal, no colonial planner could ignore how the Indians fit into the scheme.

The first generation of Englishmen who settled in America arrived with preconceived views of the Indians. Since Christopher Columbus's depiction of them, following his first voyage of discovery, innumerable published reports and unpublished tales regarding the Indians had circulated, including the chronicles of subsequent explorers, narratives of the alleged behavior of the natives within Spanish and French colonies, and relations of encounters between English mariners and Indians dating back to early in the sixteenth century. Not surprisingly, the English harbored a varied image of the Indians.

Almost all articulate Englishmen agreed that all humans, including the American Indians, were descended from a single man and woman, as revealed in Genesis. Most would have agreed with the writer who maintained that the Indians' "outsides say they are men, their actions say they are reasonable." Nevertheless, most Englishmen believed that the Indians differed from the Europeans in two profound ways. The English looked upon themselves as "civilized" and upon the natives as "wild." "Savage" became their favorite description of Indian behavior, the term equated with animal-like ferocity. Indeed, many Englishmen compared the behavior of the Indians with that of wolves, a beast much feared and despised in this agrarian era. A second crucial difference stemmed from the fact that the English were Christians and the natives worshipped numerous gods. For centuries Christians had been taught that all nonbelievers were blasphemers and idolaters, a view shared by most Elizabethans and a belief that ultimately led many settlers to see the Indians as ignoble savages, the very incarnation of the devil. Therefore, many English accounts described the native peoples as abhorrent, primitive "bruit beasts."

The earliest English in North America also perceived many desirable qualities in the natives. Writers lauded the Indians as loving, cheerful, sharing, trustworthy, dignified, and courteous people who were led by sober and astute *werowances,* or chiefs. In addition, the Indians were seen as a "peaceable, lowly, mild, and gentle People" who were quite tractable. This latter view was the overwhelming conclusion drawn by members of the Amadas and Barlowe mission. They discovered the Carolina Algonquians to be generous and friendly, "void of all guile and treason," as Barlowe wrote, a people who could be manipulated to the ends desired by the English.

Whatever their outlook, many in England understood the need for cooperation with the native peoples of America, for England's tiny New World outposts could not long endure the Indians' hatred and fury. Many Englishmen were confident that their colonists could coexist peacefully with the Native

Americans; if the Indians were treated courteously, and if trade flourished, peace would prevail.

Almost everyone recommended dispatching soldiers to the colonies. Richard Hakluyt the elder, a leading publicist for colonization, thought a military presence essential to protect against Spanish attacks and to make the Indians more pliant. For him, the aims of colonization were: "1. To plant Christian religion. 2. To trade. 3. To conquer." He thought the subordination of the natives could be achieved only through force. His cousin, also named Richard Hakluyt, another advocate of settling the New World, took a similar tack, as did the forthright Sir George Peckham, who held title to lands in New England. The Indians could be expected to commit treacherous acts, Peckham advised; in such an event, he added, the English should "do whatsoever is necessary" to protect themselves.

The English did not know precisely what to expect when they returned to America in June 1585. They planned to establish a military outpost as a precursor to colonization. The leader of the expedition was Sir Richard Grenville. Scion of an old and powerful family, Grenville had served as a sheriff and a judge, sat in Parliament, and fought in Hungary and in Ireland. Serving under him was Ralph Lane, a professional soldier recalled from Ireland for this assignment. The company of 107 planters included about 50 to 60 soldiers, as well as an armorer skilled in repairing muskets and perhaps a gunsmith. One of the first activities was to construct a polygonal, or star-shaped, fort surrounded by a palisade and to mount cannon.

The colonists brought supplies, but they expected to trade with the natives for much of their food. Their reliance on the local people became even more pronounced when the *Tiger,* one of five ships that made the crossing, was damaged and lost most of its food stores. This dependency, combined with their expectation of Indian treachery, profoundly shaped the English experience that followed.

Relations between the natives and the newcomers deteriorated soon after the English arrived. Ethnocentricity on both sides undoubtedly contributed. Matters were not improved when Indians succumbed to diseases brought by the strangers. Isolated incidents of conflict must also have heightened tensions. But two factors above all others destroyed whatever chance existed for peace. One was the English insistence that the Indians provide them with food. During the first three months of the colony, the Roanoke Indians appear to have exchanged adequate quantities of food in return for English copper utensils; thereafter, as food shortages occurred among their own people, the Indians were less forthcoming, prompting the English to shift from making requests for food to issuing demands.

The Indians were further alienated by the behavior of the English commanders. The English manifested the same bullying, undiplomatic manner that they had learned in Ireland. While exploring the mainland two weeks after their arrival, Grenville discovered that a silver cup was missing. Suspecting the Indians of thievery, he demanded the return of the vessel from them; when the natives did not comply, he razed their town and cornfields. Later, when the English first explored Albermarle Sound, Lane initiated his expedition by holding the chief's son hostage as security against an Indian attack.

In February 1586, after nine months with the intruders, the Roanokes ceased all food shipments to the English and made plans for a surprise attack. When a native informant revealed their intentions to the English, Lane decided upon a preemptive strike. The English were confident of success. In their view, Indian culture was so primitive that the natives were "not to be feared," as one colonist wrote. Lane boasted that ten English soldiers could easily fight off one hundred native warriors. This characteristic English bravado stemmed from their reliance on firearms, principally flintlock and matchlock muskets and pistols. The English muskets were accurate up to about eighty yards, and their soft bullets could cause massive damage. The explosion that occurred when these firearms were discharged, as well as the horrendous wounds inflicted by the seemingly invisible bullets, gave the English an actual and a psychological advantage. Against this firepower, the natives not only lacked armor, but they bore simple arms—truncheons, knives, spears, and of course, the bow, a weapon fashioned from supple maple, locust, or witch hazel that fired arrows tipped with stone, copper, bone, antlers, or wildfowl talons.

The English monopoly on firearms did not assure success, however. Muskets were notoriously inaccurate weapons, and they were unserviceable in wet weather. Under the best conditions these weapons were cumbersome; even the most skilled soldier could fire only two shots a minute. Against this, a skilled bowman could fire up to twelve arrows a minute, and with greater range and accuracy than a musketeer could wield his weapon. In addition, the Indians made excellent use of the natural environment, fighting from behind rocks and trees, and often fleeing into the stygian forests, within which the effectiveness of European arms was even further reduced. As several generations of English soldiers discovered, the Indians refused to fight according to the conventions of European warfare, where belligerents played out their grim proceedings at close range in open surroundings. Instead the Indians fought the English as they had previously fought one another, resorting to ambushes, hit-and-run operations, and guerrilla attacks upon both soldiers and civilians. Well into the eighteenth century the English excoriated the Indians for such "cowardly" behavior, but the natives would have been mad to abandon these tactics that were best suited to their weaponry.

Lane's reasons for deciding on a surprise attack are clear. He knew that he could not win a protracted war. Indeed, the destruction of the colonists' fishing weirs—which the natives undertook in April—threatened the survival of the colony. In a surprise attack, however, the English would dictate the terms. More important, such an assault might result in the immediate subjugation of the natives.

Colonel Lane planned a night assault on the Indian village of Dasemunkepeuc, situated on the mainland across Croatoan Sound. Dasemunkepeuc was selected because it was the residence of Wingina, leader of the Roanoke Indians. When the arriving English were discovered by the Indians, however, Lane improvised. Waiting until the next morning, June 1, he and twenty-seven soldiers entered the village under the pretext of wishing to confer with Wingina. The chief fell into the trap; he sat with his English visitors and began a discourse. A few minutes after the parley began, Lane cried out, "Christ our Victory," the signal for his men to open fire. Several Indians were hit. Wingina was struck, too, though not fatally; he tried to escape into the woods, but he was shot again, this time in the buttocks. Unable to flee further, Wingina was overpowered and decapitated.

The attack was the final act of the first English outpost in America. Within the week Francis Drake, the privateer, arrived. Drake expected to use Roanoke Island as his North American base, but upon finding the colonists anxious to return home, he bore the entire assemblage back to England. The venture had collapsed after less than a year, the victim of God's anger, the younger Hakluyt soon wrote, because of the "outrages committed by some of them against the native inhabitants." Hakluyt seemed to understand that a swashbuckling military manner, combined with a rapacious, parasitic attitude toward the natives, would inevitably produce irremediable strains in the relationship between the settlers and the natives.

Whether Raleigh understood this as well is not clear, but when he sent over his next—and final—expedition the following spring, it differed in significant ways, perhaps due to financial exigency. Raleigh had already lost a vast fortune on North American colonization. In 1587 he dispatched at least 110 colonists, including fourteen families, lured to America by a promise of legal title to hundreds of acres. Soldiers accompanied the colonists, yet unlike his previous venture Raleigh now sought to establish a self-sustaining province, one that might exist peaceably among the Indians.

The prospects for peace diminished immediately, however. A colonist was killed by Indians before the colony was three days old. That provocation elicited an English reprisal, although in their fury and ineptitude the colonial soldiers attacked natives who were not responsible for the murder of the colonial official. What occurred next remains a mystery. The governor of the endeavor hurried home to procure supplies, only to discover that England was at war with Spain; three years elapsed before he returned to Roanoke Island, which he found abandoned. The houses had been abandoned and the smaller guns removed, the ruins were overgrown with vegetation. An immediate search for the colonists along the mainland and on nearby islands was unsuccessful, as were numerous searches over a much wider area, even into the Chesapeake. The settlers, left alone in America for years, probably made an orderly departure, perhaps relocating amid Indians whose attitudes had not been poisoned by the ferocious, volcanic events of the recent past.

Struggle on the Chesapeake

After two attempts, the English had failed to establish a colony. Nearly two decades elapsed before they sought to plant another outpost. When peace with Spain was restored, the English started anew at Jamestown in 1607. The Virginia Company, the joint-stock company licensed to establish the colony, planned a permanent community in North America, the first village in a perpetual, expanding society. Land had not been important in Raleigh's initial Roanoke Island settlement, but it would be crucial in the Virginia settlement, and the land appropriated belonged to the natives.

The English realized that their goal of acquiring land would create conflict with the natives. The Virginia Company prudently included some professional soldiers and army veterans among the 144 colonists who sailed late in 1606. The leaders of the colony, a majority of whom were men with military backgrounds, brought a vast array of weapons, certain, as the company's instructions stated, that the natives would fear only cannon and muskets. The precautions were warranted. On the day that land was sighted, a reconnaissance party sent ashore at Cape Henry was attacked.

A few days later the leaders of the expedition settled on a site for their outpost, a point in the tidal marshlands on the James River peninsula. Described by an Englishman writing three years later, Jamestown began with pomp and dispatch:

The Trumpet sounding, the Admiral struck sail and before the rest of the Fleet anchored, the colonists disembarked, and every man brought his particular store and furniture, together with the general provisions, ashore. . . . For their security, a quantity of ground was surveyed, which they began to fortify, and thereon, in the name of God, to raise a fortress, with the ablest and speediest means they could.

For good reason construction of the fortress began without delay. Forays into the Chesapeake, such as the 1584 Amadas and Barlowe expedition, had revealed that these Indians were less receptive to strangers than the tribes on Roanoke Island. In addition, these Indians were more united than those to the south. About thirty tribes with a total population of approximately seventy-five hundred recognized Powhatan (called Wahunsonacock by his followers) as their principal chief; his domain stretched from the James to the Potomac and into the interior for about eighty miles. Because of these realities the leaders of the colony selected a site with defensive considerations in mind. Jamestown was situated almost sixty miles up the James River for security against a Spanish attack; in addition, its peninsular location—Jamestown was laid out on what was almost an island—offered some protection against an assault by the Indians.

Illness was a more dangerous foe during the first two years of Jamestown's existence than Powhatan's warriors. Only thirty-eight of the original settlers were still alive one year later; almost all of the dead had been victims of disease, of what one early colonist described as such "cruel diseases as Swellings, Fluxes, [and] Burning Fevers," most likely typhoid fever, dysentery, and malaria.

The Indians had responded cordially to the newcomers, offering tobacco and corn as a gesture of their friendliness. Whether because Powhatan misinterpreted the magnitude of the threat posed by the intruders, or, as is far more likely, because he hoped to use the English as a source of weapons and as an ally against his traditional Indian adversaries farther to the west, the chieftain clearly sought amicable relations with the Jamestown settlers. With the disasters at Roanoke Island fresh on their minds, the English also hoped for peace and spoke of avoiding "raging cruelties" that would estrange the natives.

But the peace was an uneasy one. That first summer two hundred natives attacked James Fort, killing two colonists. While some of Powhatan's followers attributed the assault to a recalcitrant, minor tribe within his jurisdiction, it is more likely that Powhatan ordered the attack as a deliberate test of arms. Other incidents occurred, the best remembered of which took place just before Christmas. The Indians ambushed a party led by Capt. John Smith as it explored the James; they killed several English and captured Smith, one of the soldiers hired by the Virginia Company.

Captain Smith, only twenty-seven years old, had packed adventure upon adventure into his few adult years. The son of a substantial farmer, he had received a grammar school education in preparation for a mercantile career. But a sedentary life held no allure for this young man. At age fifteen he sped away to Europe to begin a life of soldiering. He fought for three years with the Protestant Dutch against Catholic Spain; later, he served in the Austrian army that fought against the Turks in Hungary. His courage in combat led to his rapid promotion, but his luck ran out at Regall. When his army was defeated, Smith was captured, marched five hundred miles to Turkey, and held in slavery. He escaped by killing his master and fleeing on a stolen horse, riding hundreds of miles to reach Christian Europe and freedom. By 1606 Smith was back in England, but he longed for still more adventure; mercenary employment in America intrigued him. He signed on with the

Virginia Company and arrived with the first colonists. During his first seven months in America, Smith served as a negotiator with the Indians and led several expeditions into the interior. Smith was exploring in the region of present Hampton when he was captured in December 1607. Perhaps as never before, Smith must have presumed that there would be no escape from this captivity.

In his subsequent histories of early Virginia Smith described this episode as another incident in which he had cheated death. He claimed that upon Powhatan's orders he was to be executed, but just as his executioners "being ready with their clubs to beat out his brains, Pocahontas the King's dearest daughter . . . got his head in her arms, and laid her own head upon his to save him from death: whereupon the Emperor was contented he should live." Not all historians now believe that Smith's life was in danger; some scholars think that Pocahontas was participating in an elaborate ceremony in which Smith was adopted and made a werowance, or commander, under Powhatan. Soon after Pocahontas's intervention, Smith was released from captivity.

Smith's adventure was one of many incidents that occurred during this period. But war did not break out. Clearly, neither side desired actual war. Powhatan, perceiving no threat for the small English outpost, preferred commerce to war. The English leaders must have known that they could not have survived a war; beset by limited supplies and epidemic disease, Jamestown depended upon the willingness of the Indians to provide sufficient food.

On occasion, however, the colonists used force to procure food. When Captain Smith became president of the colony about eighteen months after Jamestown was established, he began an aggressive campaign of intimidation. He brashly demanded food and peace from the Indians; when he did not get what he wanted, he razed their fields and homes. Smith's strategy succeeded. Bloodshed was reduced, food was plentiful, and death from disease within the colony declined sharply.

Inspired by Smith's success, the Virginia Company institutionalized the measures he had pursued. The colony was placed on a semimilitary footing; the services of veteran officers were procured (company officials pulled strings to secure their release from assignments elsewhere), and ordinary colonists were considered half-soldiers, half-civilians. In addition, Captain Smith's successors were directed by the company officials in London to achieve a military occupation of the Chesapeake: the various tribes were to be reduced to vassals and compelled to furnish food, furs, dyes, and labor to the intruders. It was a reversion to the very scheme that had destroyed the settlement at Roanoke Island twenty-five years before. Jamestown nearly experienced the same fate.

Predictably, the Indians resisted their neighbors' new policies, inaugurating in 1609 what has been called the First Anglo-Powhatan War. The English knew this would be a ghastly conflict; they had observed Indian wars and realized what would follow. John Smith, who once had watched the Powhatans fight a rival tribe, knew the Indians used not only bows and arrows as weapons, but "the horn of a Deer put through a piece of wood in the form of a pickaxe" and hatchets made of iron. Smith marveled at the Indians' skill with the bow, as well as their strength, agility, heartiness, and facility for coping with the wilderness. In warfare, he added, the Indians sought victory through "treacheries or surprises." When they fought they "painted and disguised themselves in the fiercest manner." He later described the Powhatans' battle against an Indian adversary:

Upon the first flight of arrows they gave such horrible shouts and screeches, as so many infernal hell hounds could not have made. When they had spent their arrows, they joined together, charging again and again. . . . As they got the advantage they caught their enemy by the hair of the head, and down he came. He then beat the brains out of his enemy with his wooden sword.

The First Anglo-Powhatan War, as anticipated, was a grim affair. Each side abandoned restraint and committed terrible atrocities. Captain Smith had once warned Powhatan of "the cruelty we use upon our enemies." His successors now offered an awesome display of English brutality. English raiding parties captured and murdered women and children. They burned Indian villages, destroyed religious icons and sacred sites, desecrated the corpses of earlier native leaders, and stole whatever was valuable, especially food, pearls, and copper jewelry. On at least one occasion the English decapitated two victims. The Indians, in turn, sought to poison the English, used naked women to lure their unwary foes into ambushes, flayed unfortunate captives alive, and scalped their victims, a part of Indian warfare that the Europeans had encountered as far south as South America, as far north as Canada.

The Jamestown colony suffered horribly during the first year of the war. In addition to the high mortality rate caused by malaria, typhoid bacteria, and other diseases, many colonists perished at the hands of the Indians. An entire forage party of seventeen men vanished; soon thereafter, thirty-four of fifty members of a company sent to barter with Powhatan for food were killed. The settlers at Jamestown grew desperate. In a colony that had never been able to feed itself, there were not enough healthy men to simultaneously fight a war and produce food. Starvation set in. Desperate colonists consumed dogs, cats, snakes, even shoe leather; one instance of cannibalism occurred. Twelve months into the war Virginia's population had declined from five hundred to only sixty. In June 1610 the colony was abandoned entirely, only to be saved when the vessel bearing the departing colonists turned back when it met with a relief expedition that included three hundred new colonists. Additional colonists came during the next four years, but in 1614 only 350 settlers (of perhaps 2,200 that had shipped out for Virginia since 1607) remained alive within the colony.

But the natives paid as well. Confronted with an enemy that was superior in firepower (the English had accumulated an arsenal of twenty-four cannon and over three hundred pistols and muskets by the time the war began), three tribes among the Powhatans suffered heavy losses, and two tribal centers were eradicated. When armed musketeers despoiled the Pamunkeys, one of the larger tribes under Powhatan, and when Pocahontas was captured and held as ransom for peace, Powhatan accepted a humiliating settlement and soon abdicated his post. Other nearby tribes, such as the Chickahominies, followed suit, not wishing to be isolated against the English.

The colony soon prospered as never before. Food was more plentiful. Four new outposts were established within two years of the peace and more than a dozen others sprang up by 1622. Virginia's English population likewise swelled, to about 1,250 by 1622. Then in March disaster struck. The Indians attacked suddenly in a massive surprise assault, touching off the Second Anglo-Powhatan War.

The attack was planned by Opechancanough, Powhatan's successor and werowance of the Pamunkey Indians. His people's situation had deteriorated since Powhatan's subjugation in 1614. Soon thereafter the colonists discovered a profitable staple crop—tobacco; an extraordinary growth in population and a land boom ensued. With every Indian in Powhatan's old confederacy now threatened by the expansive colony, Opechancanough evidently concluded that his society's survival hinged upon the extirpation of the colony.

While the murder of an esteemed native served as the immediate catalyst for Opechancanough to act, the time was propitious to attack the hated intruders. Not only had the English discounted the tribes of Virginia's tidewater region as a formidable adversary, but the wily Opechancanough had lulled the English with declarations of peace. In addition, the English seemed especially vulnerable, for the tobacco-growing settlers were dispersed as never before.

The settlers sustained a devastating blow on the first day of the Second Anglo-Powhatan War. On a late March morning the Indians, as was customary, entered several of the outposts to conduct trade; abruptly, they produced weapons—in some instances English firearms that they had been stockpiling covertly—and attacked the unsuspecting colonists. By the end of this green, spring day, nearly 350 settlers, about one in four of Virginia's English inhabitants, were dead and most of the upriver settlements had been wiped out. Seventy-five residents of Martin's Hundred, just seven miles from Jamestown, perished, and only hurried warnings by friendly Indians saved Jamestown itself. Fifteen years after the settlement's founding, during which time approximately five thousand colonists had migrated to Virginia, only about one-fifth that number remained alive in the colony.

But Opechancanough failed to achieve his goal of forcing the intruders back to their homeland, and his people soon paid a terrible price for his failure. Crown and company officials now sought nothing less than the expulsion of the natives from their midst, the very conquest that the elder Hakluyt had foreseen as early as 1585. The Virginia Company dispatched nearly fifteen hundred muskets and pistols to Virginia, while local officials unlocked the armory and distributed firearms to the citizenry, an unprecedented step in this era. For the next two years total war raged. The Virginians waged a war of attrition, referring to their strategy as "food fights." Raiding parties of up to three hundred armor-clad, heavily armed men destroyed fishing weirs and canoes, torched Indian villages and fields, and carried the natives' food back to the colonists. But the English did not confine their targets to food. They killed every Indian they could locate regardless of age or sex. In June 1623 a party under Captain William Tucker pursued a strategy identical to that employed by Captain Lane at Dasemunkepeuc almost forty years earlier; Tucker's party entered a Powhatan village "under color to make peace" and negotiate a prisoner release, but once in the town he and his men opened fire, killing forty inhabitants. Tucker enjoyed even greater success later in a Potomac River village. He came to parley, he said, and he brought wine to lighten the proceedings. The cask contained poisoned wine, however. Approximately two hundred Indians died from the tainted beverage, and fifty or more others, who attempted to flee upon realizing the English treachery, were gunned down. The soldiers "brought home part of their heads" as trophies.

Miraculously, Opechancanough eluded capture, but many werowances were taken and untold numbers of their subjects perished, mostly from malnutrition, disease, and starvation. Despite their losses the Indians fought back as best they could, often using English muskets in their attacks upon the isolated and the unwary. Only one pitched battle occurred, a two-day engagement at Pamunkey in 1624 between an intertribal force of eight hundred braves and sixty English musketeers. In that encounter the English withstood repeated assaults; battered and exhausted, the Indians eventually withdrew and, according to a Virginia soldier, from a distance watched "dismayedly . . . while their Corn was cut down."

Hostilities continued for another eight years, until a truce was negotiated in 1632. Although many English had perished in Opechancanough's surprise attack and in countless subsequent ambushes and raids, it is difficult not to believe that the English had won this long war. Not only had English firepower been superior to that of the Indians, but the natives found it difficult to replace their food supplies. The Indian population, moreover, had declined at an alarming rate. The pre-Jamestown population in the Chesapeake tidelands that ranged from the James to the Potomac probably totaled about forty thousand; fewer than five thousand Indians were left by the early 1630s.

England's massive retaliation in this conflict grew in part from the biases toward the Indians that it had harbored all along. But the English policy after the Second Anglo-Powhatan War also should be seen both as a departure and a turning point. Until 1622, many had envisioned an English empire in America in which Indian tribes and settlers would live in harmony, perhaps even intermarrying. Now, however, the English condemned Indians as savages who must be moved aside, removed from the presence of the English. Edward Waterhouse, secretary of the Virginia Company, set the tone: "Our hands which before were tied with gentleness . . . are now set at liberty by the treacherous violence of the Savages," he wrote. "Now their cleared grounds in all their villages . . . shall be inhabited by us." Waterhouse's prophesy proved correct. Within slightly more than a decade of Opechancanough's attack, Virginia's English population had reached five thousand, and the colony had been divided into eight counties. The ancient homeland of the Powhatans had passed under the jurisdiction of Virginia sheriffs, constables, clerks, coroners, and Anglican churchwardens.

The peace that came to Virginia in 1632 was fragile and often punctured by skirmishes and reprisals. Resolving never to be caught off guard again, Virginia established a militia company in each county and constructed a string of fortifications up the James River and northward to the York River. Some counties punished imprudent citizens who traveled without their arms and powder. By 1642 the governor had ordered a threefold increase in militia training. Virginia's authorities obviously feared the renewal of total war. Their worst nightmares became reality in April 1644, with the beginning of the Third Anglo-Powhatan War.

Increasingly hemmed in by the growing colony and realizing that their cultural heritage was imperiled by the English, the Indians once again responded to Opechancanough's calls for mobilization and war, foolhardy as such a notion now had become. Opechancanough knew of the English Civil War that had broken out two years before; he may have chosen this moment to strike because he believed that this time, unlike 1622, the colonists would be unaided by the parent state. What seems indisputable, however, is that by 1644 Opechancanough believed that war offered the only hope of halting the final destruction of what remained of the Indians' way of life in Tidewater Virginia.

Virginians had never presumed that their militia units could repel a surprise attack. They hoped, instead, that their military posture would deter an assault. When the blow fell, therefore, the Indians were initially successful. In a series of surprise attacks up and down the line of English settlement, more than five hundred colonists—approximately one in twelve Virginians—perished, and several of the outlying settlements were eradicated. Considering that Opechancanough had fewer warriors than in 1622 and that he was attacking a people who had built strong defenses, his daring strike achieved amazing results. Nevertheless, by June the Virginians launched a counteroffensive. Once again, the Indians paid dearly. Their towns and crops disappeared in smoke, and the English sold many captives into slavery. In 1646, Opechancanough, now so old and infirm that he had to be transported on a litter, was captured by a party of Virginia cavalry; he was murdered by a soldier while in captivity in Jamestown.

The Third Anglo-Powhatan War ended shortly thereafter with the surrender of the natives. The Indians ceded to the English the region south of the York River from the fall line to the Chesapeake. In addition, the English sundered the unity of the Powhatan tribes, and each became the subject of the Crown. The natives' freedom of movement was severely circumscribed, and the Indians agreed to pay an annual indemnity in beaver skins. The first two wars had threatened the survival of the colony. The third conflict produced considerable suffering, but the existence of Virginia was never in jeopardy. In the end, it was the Indians who were the principal losers. An Anglican parson who visited Virginia in its early years had reported that Indian shamans often warned their people that one day "bearded men . . . should come and take away their country." Within two generations of the founding of Jamestown, that was the fate of the Powhatans.

Conflict in New England

Nearly forty years elapsed between the initial settlements in the Chesapeake and the arrival of the first permanent colonists to New England. The English who first settled above Virginia, beginning with the plucky voyagers aboard the *Mayflower* in 1620, were mostly Puritans, religious dissidents who fled the corruption and oppression they believed to be stalking their homeland, and who moved to America in the hope of reforming the world through their godly example. They harbored the same preconceived attitudes toward the Indians that had existed in the minds of the first settlers in Virginia; few migrants to New England would have disagreed with William Bradford, the governor of Plymouth colony, who confessed to having arrived expecting to meet a "savage people, who are cruel, barbarous, and most treacherous."

The situation in New England was combustible from the start. Not only were the Puritans fully aware of the history of hostilities experienced by the Virginians, but by 1620 some tribes in New England that had previously met with Europeans had good reason to question the amiability and good intentions of the new intruders. English explorers, fishermen, even other colonists, had preceded the Puritans to New England. Friction was common in these early contacts with the natives; fights had flared, blood had been shed, men had been kidnapped. An attempt to found a colony in Maine in 1607 quickly failed, in part because, as one observer noted, the settlers "beat, maltreated and misused [the Indians] outrageously," ultimately provoking a devastating attack by the natives. The European fishermen, operating from jerry-built, temporary villages on the New England coast, sometimes cheated and mistreated the Indians. They spread diseases among the natives, often with catastrophic results. Epidemics of smallpox, yellow fever, and typhoid fever decimated entire tribes, reducing the native population by about one-third and prompting one English resident of Massachusetts to remark in 1622 that so many bones and skulls littered the forests that "it seemed to me a new found Golgotha."

Conflict came quickly. Hostilities occurred on the first day that the Puritans made contact with the Indians. A party of Nausets on Cape Cod attacked suddenly, evidently hoping to discourage settlement in their neighborhood. The English did move on, eventually selecting a site in Plymouth Harbor, an area inhabited by the Wampanoags. Cordial relations developed between the newcomers and the natives. Trade flourished, and much cooperation ensued between the mutually distrustful peoples. Massasoit, the chief of the Wampanoags, chose the same course as Powhatan. Although he easily could have destroyed the new settlement—50 percent of the colonists died from disease, exposure, and the complications of malnutrition during that first winter—Massasoit instead sought peace, apparently because he hoped for English assistance against his foes, the Narragansetts to the west, the Massachusetts in the north. His policy succeeded in the short run. The English pledged their assistance and soon English soldiers fought alongside their new friends. In 1623, just after learning of Opechancanough's surprise attack in Virginia, the Puritans believed Massasoit's warning that the Massachusetts tribe was plotting an assault upon Plymouth. The infant colony took preventive action. A Plymouth force led by Capt. Miles Standish, a professional soldier who had accompanied the colonists to America, struck suddenly at Wessagusett on Massachusetts Bay. The tribe was routed and its chief, Witawamet, slain; his severed head was returned to Plymouth for public display. Thereafter the Massachusetts referred to the English as "wotowquenange"—their term for cutthroats.

The Massachusetts "could not imagine, from whence these [English] men should come," one colonist remarked. What they did know by 1630 was that these strangers were aswarm in their midst. That was the year that the Puritan migration began in earnest. One thousand English immigrants descended upon the Massachusetts Bay region that year; twenty times that number came during the next dozen years. Only a few hundred of the Massachusetts tribe remained, the survivors of a terrible plague unintentionally introduced by Europeans a few years earlier.

The Massachusetts Indians had no choice but to pursue a pacific policy toward the Puritan settlers. Accommodation, moreover, might procure English assistance against their tribal adversaries, the Tarrantines, or Abnakis, who inhabited parts of present-day Maine and New Hampshire. The Puritans, on the other hand, had to have been delighted at their good fortune for having landed in the midst of a depopulated tribe. Aware of earlier English experiences in America, they came prepared for the likelihood of war. The Massachusetts Charter of 1628 commanded the settlers "to encounter, expulse, repel, and resist by force of arms" any attempt to destroy the settlement. Moreover, the voyagers aboard the *Arbella,* the flagship of the Puritans' Great Migration, were admonished to "neglect not walls, and bulwarks, and fortifications for your own defence." The Puritans took the advice. While they never contemplated the establishment of a military regime such as that mandated by the Virginia Company for Jamestown, they selected sites for settlement with an eye on protection, often choosing defensible bluffs, then enclosing the community inside a palisade. The immigrants also listened when they were warned to "store yourselves with all sorts of weapons for war." The first settlers in the Massachusetts Bay colony brought along five artillery pieces, as well as skilled artisans who were to build gun carriages and search for the alloys and nitrates used in making soft lead bullets, metal shells, and ammunition.

The Puritans also hired professional soldiers, mostly veterans of England's recent wars in the Low Countries, men who were to provide immediate assistance and to organize a militia system. The English militia heritage stretched back to the ancient Anglo-Saxon tradition that all able-bodied freemen were to be considered potential soldiers and could be made to participate in the common defense in times of emergency. By the seventeenth century, by law and tradition, England's militia system had evolved into a defensive military system for the purpose of meeting short-term military emergencies.

The first militia company in Massachusetts Bay was established shortly after the arrival of the *Arbella,* and within five years the colony sported fourteen companies organized into three regiments. All fit males between ages sixteen and sixty were expected to serve, except public officials, Indians, African Americans, and those who provided essential services. As in Plymouth, each male—whether a freeman or a servant— was compelled to own and maintain his own weapons.

In Massachusetts, militia companies comprised sixty-five to two hundred men, but normally a company seldom exceeded seventy-five men. Two-thirds of the men were musketeers; the remainder, with the exception of a drummer or two and perhaps even a couple trumpeters, carried pikes. Later in the seventeenth century troops of cavalry, or mounted soldiers, emerged as well. The soldiers elected their company officers, which included a captain, a lieutenant, and an ensign. Regimental officers (the ranks of major, lieutenant colonel, and colonel) were selected by provincial officials. The first Puritan military law mandated militia exercises every Saturday, although in time muster days were required just eight times each year; toward the end of the century the militia in many areas mustered only twice annually. Drill consisted of learning how to march, how to stand at attention, how to carry one's weapon, how to move as a unit on the battlefield and how to reload and fire quickly. Drill also included review and inspection; target practice; training with pikes, the sharp-pointed weapon still used by European armies; and finally a mock battle. A drill day also gave officers the opportunity to learn how many of their men were fit and available for duty and to see that their soldiers had adequately maintained their weapons. Exercises usually ended by early afternoon. In New England a parson brought the drills to a close with a long prayer, after which the remainder of the day was filled with social activities, including much drinking and dancing, for wives and younger women often came to the drill site to watch their husbands and friends prepare for war.

The militiaman drilled regularly, although peace prevailed during the first years. The Indian population was so small that the huge influx of immigrants who appropriated land that once had belonged to the natives initially provoked few problems. Although some Puritans believed they held claim to New England by the right of discovery and some enunciated the theory of *vacuum domicilium*—that is, that the property inhabited by the Indians was legally "vacant" because the natives had not "subdued" and properly utilized the soil as God had com-

manded (Genesis 1:28)—the authorities in Massachusetts actually purchased land from the Native Americans. Indeed, at
first the Massachusetts tribe appears to have been delighted
with the possibility of selling its surplus land for metal tools,
English clothing, and jewelry. The result was a long period of
tranquil relations with the Indians, at least by contrast with
the experience of the Virginians.

As wave after wave of Puritan immigrants disembarked
in America and erected settlements at the best sites near Massachusetts Bay, available land within this first, thin frontier
grew scarce. Explorers soon were active to the west, seeking
both suitable locations for habitation and a lucrative trade with
the Indians along the southern New England coast. Their ex-
cursions led them to the Pequot Indians, a tribe with villages
along the Thames River in southeastern Connecticut; the Pequot's dominion extended approximately fifteen miles to
either side of the river. Later, Puritan spokesmen claimed that
the Pequots were a fearsome, bellicose people who had recently
invaded New England, driving other tribes from the Thames
Valley and expropriating their land. The claim is questionable;
the Pequots were probably native to New England.

The earliest contacts between Puritans and Pequots were
cordial. The earliest known description of these natives by an
English settler characterized them as "affable" and honest. It
was not long, however, before relations soured. By the early
1630s, the Pequots began to feel pressure from the European
migration. The Dutch, from their nearby colony of New Netherland, had established a post at present-day Hartford; Plymouth colonists were ensconced at Windsor, and several
hundred Massachusetts residents had moved to the Connecticut Valley. Strains became evident. For a time in 1634 it
appeared that peace might be shattered when John Stone, a
trader from Virginia, and eight of his party were murdered by
Pequots or members of a subordinate tribe. Puritan leaders
grieved little for Stone, an Anglican outsider who had refused
to abide by the Puritan code of conduct during his brief residence in Plymouth and Boston. Nevertheless, the Pequots had

to be punished for killing Englishmen, according to John Winthrop, the governor of Massachusetts. English tempers were soothed, however, when the Indians agreed to pay an indemnity of wampum (strings of shell beads) and beaver and otter skins and to hand over the assassins to Massachusetts. Hostilities were avoided for two years, during which time trade developed between the two peoples.

The Pequots neither paid the full indemnity nor delivered the killers of Stone. Moreover, in 1636 the Pequots were suspected of having killed another trader, John Oldham, whose mutilated body was found off Block Island, adjacent to the Connecticut–Rhode Island coast. The Massachusetts Bay colony responded to Oldham's murder with a show of force. It sent ninety armed volunteers into Pequot country, a force commanded by John Endicott, a soldier from Devon, England, who immigrated to New England in 1628 and served as the first governor of Massachusetts Bay. The object of the expedition was to apprehend the killers of Stone and Oldham and to punish these refractory natives.

Oldham's violent death presented the Puritans with a golden opportunity to subjugate a tribe that occupied a region coveted by the swelling horde of English immigrants. The leaders of Massachusetts colony evidently believed they could accomplish their ends with little trouble, as the Pilgrims had when they assisted Massasoit in humbling his rivals. English arrogance stemmed from the belief that the natives fought in a "feeble manner" that did not "deserve the name of fighting," as a Connecticut militia officer remarked. In time, the English learned that such a notion was erroneous, for it was based on watching Indians fight one another. Clashes between native tribes could be "very cruel and bloody," as one of Raleigh's men had observed, but their battles were decidedly more limited than conventional warfare in Europe. The object of Indian warfare was vengeance, not conquering territory or eradicating another tribe. "Their Wars are far less bloody, and devouring than the cruel Wars of Europe," Roger Williams, the Puritan clergyman, remarked. It seemed logical that a demonstration of European prowess would cow the Pequots.

Endicott seemed the perfect man to humble the Indians. He manifested a rock-hard disposition; a veteran soldier who had lived in America for nearly a decade, he had been known to use his fists on or draw his sword against colonists who did not heed his commands. Without doubt, he possessed the temperament for carrying out his orders. He had been commanded to be merciless, to kill all the men on Block Island and to seize as hostages all the women and children; the English would hold these captives as a leverage to attain their indemnity and those responsible for killing Stone and Oldham.

Although Endicott's force entered Indian country spoiling for a fight, he failed to secure his objectives. When the Indians fled into the dark swamps and thickets that dotted Block Island, Endicott knew that he lacked the means to flush them out. Instead, he destroyed their wigwams and burned their corn, then sailed for the Connecticut mainland. But like their counterparts on Block Island and in Virginia, these Indians refused to engage in warfare in the European manner. They melted into the woods, from whence they quietly watched as the English spent two days despoiling their property and food supplies. When Endicott retreated he had accomplished little else than arousing the fury of the Pequots.

The Pequots, a proud people and a far stronger tribe than the Massachusetts had been, fought back. They laid siege to the Puritan trading post of Saybrook at the mouth of the Connecticut River and later carried out a reprisal against Wethersfield, an upriver settlement. By April 1637, eight months after the Endicott expedition, thirty colonists in Connecticut— 5 percent of the province's population—had perished, several the victims of torture, which included dismemberment and burning at the stake. At Saybrook, for instance, the natives, according to a contemporary account, seized one unfortunate captain, "tied him to a stake, flayed his skin off, put hot embers between the flesh and skin, cut off his fingers and toes, and made hatbands of them."

The Puritan leadership did not sit by idly in the face of this bloodshed. The Massachusetts Bay colony reorganized its militia units into three regiments; Plymouth and Connecticut stepped up military training, the latter imposing heavy fines upon those who missed a drill. Meanwhile, a frantic effort ensued to win the loyalty, or at least the neutrality, of the various native tribes in the region. The Mohegans and the Connecticut River tribes posed no problems; they encouraged war against the Pequots, their neighbors and rivals. Both the Pequots and the Puritans courted the powerful Narragansetts, however. The Massachusetts Bay Puritans induced Roger Williams, a dissenting preacher whom they had recently expelled, to meet with Miantonomo, the Narragansett sachem, or chief. It was a dangerous undertaking. Williams sailed from Providence "all alone, in a poor canoe, and . . . through a stormy wind, with great seas" to reach the chief. Evidently Williams was more persuasive than his competitors. The Narragansetts severed all ties with the Pequots and agreed to cooperate with the English; in return, the Massachusetts Bay colony promised perpetual peace and friendship.

In 1637 the three Puritan colonies, Massachusetts Bay, Rhode Island, and Connecticut, declared war against the Pequots and mobilized their fighting forces, but the provinces failed to cooperate. Anxious to claim Pequot lands through the right of conquest and prodded into immediate action by an Indian raid on Wethersfield, the Connecticut militia led the fighting in this war. Connecticut raised an army of ninety men under Capt. John Mason, a veteran of the wars in the Netherlands, a man described by a contemporary as "full of Martial Bravery and Vigour." He was joined by nineteen Massachusetts volunteers and hundreds of Indian allies, mostly Mohegans, but also Narragansetts and Eastern Niantics.

Mason's objective was a Pequot fort on the Mystic River. He had been directed by the Connecticut authorities to make a frontal attack on the principal Pequot stronghold at the entrance to Pequot Harbor. He dismissed that directive; not only was such an assault too risky, but surprise was more likely to be achieved by attacking the Mystic River village. Mason had been instructed "not to do this work of the Lord's revenge slackly." He abided this command. From the outset, he planned to destroy the village and everyone in it. Some of the European-trained officers who accompanied him expressed reservations until the army's chaplain, after a night of prayer, countenanced the operation.

During the night of May 25, in weather that was unseasonably hot, Mason's army moved quietly to the periphery of the Pequot village, a circular, palisaded fort. The Indians had neglected to post sentries. His soldiers quietly ringed the fort; Mason placed his Indian allies in an outer circle beyond the hamlet. Once everyone was stationed, the attackers nervously awaited the signal to strike. Breathing rapidly, sweating profusely, barely able to swallow, the men listened intently. Suddenly a dog barked. Alerted at last, a native cried out: "Owanux!" ("Englishmen!").

The English stormed the fort, surging inside and unleashing a deadly fire into the scores of residences. Some Indians stumbled half-asleep from their habitations and were gunned down. Most resisted, however, taking refuge behind shrubs or in their wigwams and fighting valiantly. Their stubborn resistance surprised the English. "We had formerly concluded to destroy them by the Sword and save the Plunder," Mason later acknowledged, but after the first minutes of the fight he altered his plan. "We should never kill them after that manner," Mason decided. "We must Burn them." Consequently he gave the order to torch the fortress. Mason described the scene that followed:

When it was thoroughly kindled, the Indians ran as Men most dreadfully Amazed. And indeed such a dreadful Terror did the Almighty let fall upon their Spirits that they would fly from us and run into the very Flames where many of them perished. . . . The fire was kindled on the northeast side to windward and it swiftly overran the Fort, to the Amazement of the Enemy, and great Rejoicing of ourselves. Some of them climbed to the Top of the Palisade; others ran into the very Flames; many of them pelted at us with their Arrows;

and we repaid them with our small arms. The most courageous of the Indians, we estimated about forty in all, issued forth and perished by the Sword. . . . Thus were they now at their Wit's End, who not many Hours before exalted in their great Pride, threatening and resolving the utter Ruin and Destruction of all the English, Exulting and Rejoicing with Songs and Dances. But God above them, who laughed at the Enemies of his People [the English], made them a fiery Oven. Thus were the Stout Hearted spoiled. . . . Thus did the Lord judge among the Heathen, filling the Place with dead Bodies!

The English had made no allowance for age or sex. Almost everyone inside the fort had been killed, and those who escaped the white-hot inferno were caught and killed by the English or the Mohegans, whom Mason had posted in the rear. In a matter of minutes, seven hundred Pequots were slaughtered; seven were captured and about half a dozen were thought to have escaped. Two English perished, one the victim of an errant shot by a comrade.

New Englanders celebrated when they learned of this massacre. The terrible fate of the Pequots was seen as a victory occasioned by God's will. The governor of Plymouth touted the conquest as a "revenge so sweete." With regard to the sight of the natives "frying in the fire, and the streams of blood quenching the same," the governor rejoiced in the "sweet sacrifice" made possible by the English soldiery.

This cataclysmic defeat at Mystic broke the will of the Pequots to continue the struggle. Many sought asylum in the Mohawk country west of the Hudson River, while others fled to Long Island or hid with neighboring tribes. Nearly two hundred surrendered to the Narragansetts, hoping for better treatment than they might receive from the English. Still, the English did not rest. Fresh troops from Massachusetts and Connecticut scoured the countryside for survivors. They were ordered to "utterly root them out." Troops using dogs flushed out many Pequots; some were shot down in cold blood. Captured sachems were beheaded. Nor did the English shrink from committing atrocities. One colonist described the capture of a Pequot warrior. The prisoner, he wrote, boasted that the

English "dared not kill a Pequot. . . . But it availed this savage nothing. They [his captors] tied one of his legs to a post, and twenty men, with a rope tied to the other, pulled him in pieces."

The last act of this ghastly war was played out after the Narragansetts surrendered to the English most of the Pequots who had fled into their midst. The New England authorities parceled out the elderly, the females, and the younger males to friendly tribes to do with as they pleased, but they executed most of the twenty or so able-bodied men. English terrorism was well-calculated. Not only were the Pequots deliberately destroyed, but "the Indians everywhere [were] so terrified," according to the governor of Massachusetts, that additional war was unlikely any time soon. By autumn of 1637, the Pequots had ceased to exist as a tribe and Connecticut exercised jurisdiction over the conquered territory.

Before 1637, the New England Indians had never seen a large colonial army in action. What they witnessed in the Pequot War horrified them. The army was "too furious, and slays too many," a colonist quoted a Narragansett as having exclaimed after observing the wanton nature of the Puritan assault. The unrestrained barbarism of the Puritan armies was not unusual for European warfare in this era. The military manuals that circulated in Europe spelled out antiseptic conventions of warfare. Sometimes armies abided by these dictates, sparing women and children, refusing to plunder and destroy civilian property, and exchanging prisoners; on occasion the officers behaved in a benignly chivalrous manner. The reality of war, however, seldom resembled the ritualistic prescripts sketched in the manuals. The English conquest of Ireland, the grim, destructive fighting in the Spanish Netherlands in the late sixteenth and early seventeenth centuries, and the Thirty Years' War—all ideologically inspired conflicts in which the combatants were driven by fervent emotional convictions—were waged with the same vicious brutality as that manifested by Masons' Puritan army.

Other factors also contributed to the severity of New England warfare. First, the Puritans obviously hoped to avoid what they believed to have been the mistakes of their brethren to the south. "Too much lenity of the English towards the Virginian savages, had almost been the destruction of the whole plantation," one Puritan noted; New England did not intend to permit the Pequots to retaliate. Second, the English believed—as Captain Mason observed—that the Indians sought nothing less than "the utter Ruin and Destruction of all the English." The English understood full well that they were locked in a life-and-death struggle with an adversary that sanctioned surprise attack, thrusts against civilians, and the ritualistic torture of captives; therefore, each soldier should view any means to victory as justifiable. Lt. Lion Gardener, for instance, remarked that he would do anything to prevent the day when he might find himself tied to a stake, whereupon "my flesh [would be] roasted and thrust down my throat." Third, the yawning cultural differences between the Europeans and the Indians contributed to the barbarism of the New England response. New Englanders believed that they "may as well go to War with Wolfes and Bears" as with the natives, and they were taught by their leaders that the Indians "act like wolves & are to be dealt withall as wolves." No place for civility existed in their warfare with the Indians.

The ruthlessness of the Puritan armies was not questioned in New England. The Puritans saw the hand of God in their remarkable victory. The settlers had reason to gloat, for after the Pequot experience every New England tribe south of present-day Maine acknowledged the authority of the New England governments.

Conflict in the Middle Colonies

The human tragedies that had been played out in Virginia's dense, humid forests and across New England's frontier soon were repeated in the Middle Atlantic region. Dutch traders and settlers were the first Europeans to enter the area now called New York, arriving in 1621, the year after the Pilgrims came ashore at Plymouth.

The Dutch immediately initiated a lucrative fur trade with the natives. In exchange for the products of European technology, particularly its firearms, the Indians provided the Dutch with furs for the eager European market. The Mohegans, who lived near Albany, were their first great trading partners. This lucrative trade encouraged New Netherland to maintain cordial relations with the natives; moreover, the want of a staple crop constrained Dutch immigration to America, thus limiting the steady encroachment of settlers onto Indian lands, incursions that had helped trigger hostilities in New England and Virginia.

Nevertheless, the presence of the Dutch soon had a significant impact upon the Indians. Subsistence hunting for beaver gave way to a relentless search for valuable pelts; when the territory of the Mohegans was denuded, the Dutch sought a new purveyor of furs. They eventually chose the Mohawk Indians, the easternmost tribe of the Iroquois, a powerful northeastern confederacy whose domain extended from the Adirondack Mountains to the Great Lakes, and the traditional adversary of the Mohegans. Similarly driven by a relentless quest for gain, the Mohawks soon clashed with the Huron tribes who dwelled above the Great Lakes and who had become the principal supplier of furs to the French in Canada. Although they resided a world away from the gleaming towers of European civilization, these native peoples were soon enmeshed in the struggle between Paris and Amsterdam for economic hegemony.

New Netherland's friendly liaison with the Mohawks differed from the relationship between the Dutch and the smaller tribes who lived near New Amsterdam. All too soon the pattern that had produced trouble between the English and the Indians was replicated in this province. After two decades of minimal growth, Dutch immigration increased after 1638, and violent incidents between the settlers and the Algonquian tribes in the lower Hudson became commonplace. When death or destruction of property resulted, New Netherland, like Massachusetts, often demanded that the perpetrators be surrendered and subjected to Dutch justice. The Indians customarily refused to comply. After one such incident early in 1643, the Dutch governor, Willem Kieft, ordered retaliatory attacks on two Wecquaesqeek encampments near New Amsterdam. The slaughters that resulted resembled the Puritan extirpation of the Pequot's Mystic River fort. Men and women were killed, as were "Young children, some them snatched from their mothers . . . [and] cut in pieces before the eyes of their parents," according to the testimony of a Dutch official.

Other tribes fought back, and the Dutch frontier became a bloody killing ground during the next three years. Many settlers perished in the course of Kieft's War (1643–46), but their numbers were inconsequential compared with the death toll suffered by the natives. Close to one thousand Indians died in this struggle.

The Indians were not the only group humbled by the Dutch. In 1655, New Netherland dispatched six hundred men in seven ships to strike down embryonic Swedish settlements on the Delaware River. Forts Casimir and Christina fell. Dutch influence spread south toward present-day Philadelphia. But time was short for the Dutch empire in mainland America.

A growing Anglo-Dutch commercial rivalry had already prompted a naval war between the two nations in 1652. The end of the English Civil War and the Restoration of Charles II in 1660 freed England to expand its possessions in North America; the new monarch moved quickly to seize New Netherland. He promised his brother James, Duke of York, the region from Delaware Bay to the west bank of the Connecticut River; the gift included New Amsterdam and the Hudson River. Charles, whose largess knew no bounds, also threw in Long Island, Martha's Vineyard, Nantucket, and parts of Maine. James immediately organized an invasion force under Col. Richard Nicolls. Late in August 1664 Nicolls's armada of four warships landed at Gravesend Bay. He quickly communicated his intent to the Dutch: "I demand the Town, situated upon the Island commonly known by the Name of Manhattan with all the forts thereunto belonging." Devoid of a naval arm of his own, Peter Stuyvesant, the Dutch governor, spent nearly two weeks negotiating with the invaders. In the end, he capitulated. The British conquered the region without a shot having been fired.

If the Dutch experience with the natives was sadly reminiscent of previous events in New England and the Chesapeake, the "Holy Experiment" of the Quakers to the south proved to be a refreshing change. The victims of religious persecution in England, Quakers followed William Penn in a large migration to Pennsylvania that began in the 1680s. Their attitudes toward war and the native population differed markedly from those of their predecessors. Not only were they pacifists, but they viewed the Indians as children of God for whom Christ had died. Penn and his followers believed that the Indians were entitled to their lands in America, territory that the English must purchase to enjoy. In an early letter to the Indians, Penn communicated his feelings, addressing the natives as he might have spoken to a friendly, articulate Englishman. "I desire to enjoy [Pennsylvania] with your Love and Consent, that we may always live together as Neighbors and friends," he said.

During land negotiations with the Delawares, the largest of the small tribes in the region, the Quakers exchanged wampum, blankets, tools, mirrors, clothing, weapons, and alcohol for land. Penn sought to regulate trade with the Indians, including the sale of rum, and he traveled among the natives, learning their culture and language. Harmony prevailed to such an extent that some Indians who had suffered under the English in Maryland, North Carolina, and Virginia moved to Pennsylvania.

This unprecedented reign of peace was due mostly to the religious convictions of the early Quaker migrants, but good fortune also played a role. As the fur trade remained centered north of Pennsylvania, relatively little commerce developed between Quakers and Indians, thus reducing the chances for misunderstanding and conflict. In addition, the Pennsylvania tribes with whom Penn dealt were quite unlike the Pequots or Powhatan Indians; previously weakened by disease likely spread by the Dutch and Swedes, these Indians were largely the peaceful vassals of the Iroquois, who were closely tied to the English.

After 1700, when Penn departed America for the final time, and particularly after his incapacitation due to illness in 1712, discord grew more pronounced. Religious fervor among the second and third generation of Quaker settlers declined. A heavy influx of land-hungry Scotch-Irish and German migrants crowded the Indians. Fraud and intimidation now frequently characterized land transactions. Although open warfare did not erupt, by 1735 eastern Pennsylvania was as devoid of its previous Indian population as was the James River peninsula two generations into Virginia's stormy history. In this instance, these tribes had been pushed to the interior of Pennsylvania, or, where possible, they had migrated to the tramontane West.

The Final Round

As the Quakers began their experiment in friendly accommodation with the natives, violent warfare once again exploded along the frontiers of Virginia and Massachusetts. The Third Powhatan War had culminated in 1646 with the demarcation of Virginia into white and red zones. The Chesapeake tribes were guaranteed the territory north of the York River, the English settlers the region below that river. Tranquillity prevailed for about fifteen years; a profitable fur trade developed between the two sections. Inevitably, however, a growing white population looked covetously upon the lands enjoyed by the Indians. Due to heavy immigration and a decline in the mortality rate, the colony grew by 150 percent between 1653 and 1663. A large proportion of this population consisted of former indentured servants, strong young men who had forfeited their freedom for several years in the hope of gaining land in Virginia. The Indians, meanwhile, faced dislocations of their own. When the English supplanted the Dutch in 1664, the northern fur trade changed, causing ripples that can only be imagined. One result was that some tribes were forced from their traditional homelands; the Susquehannocks, for instance, were compelled to move to Virginia from their lands at the head of the Chesapeake Bay.

Incidents occurred with regularity in the late 1650s, mostly the result of provocations by armed white settlers who acted with impunity toward the natives. Soon the House of Burgesses, alarmed at the growing number of incidents between the settlers and the natives, ordered all Virginians to carry arms when they left home to attend public meetings, but the government did little to inhibit the reckless expansionism that lay at the heart of the problem. Given the volatility of this situation, it is not surprising that open war came once again to Virginia, but that so much time elapsed before it began.

The catalyst that sparked this round of conflict occurred in the green Potomac River valley in July 1675. A feud between a Stafford County planter and members of the Doeg tribe over the alleged pilfering of hogs resulted in bloodshed on both sides; the spilling of white men's blood prompted the mobilization of the local militia company. The militiamen soon marauded into Maryland, where they killed ten Doegs and, by mistake, fourteen Susquehannocks. A now all-too-familiar pattern ensued. Stung by their losses, the Indians retaliated, whereupon Virginia and Maryland raised still larger militia forces. Late in September a combined colonial force totaling nearly one thousand men laid siege to a Susquehannock-Doeg fort on Matapoint Creek. Five sachems who emerged to parley were overpowered and summarily executed. The Indians replied in kind. As Virginia's woods turned to red and ochre that fall, no frontier family could sleep soundly, lest a band of armed Indians strike from the silent forest. In one daring raid early in 1676, thirty-six persons living along the upper Rappahannock River paid with their lives for the folly of the previous summer, and many estates, together with their lush fields of grain, were burned.

In most respects these unfortunate events resembled the tragedies that had befallen earlier residents on previous frontiers. But there was a difference. This episode had little central direction. Virginia's Gov. William Berkeley, nearly seventy years old, a veteran of wars in England and Virginia, and a friend of the king, had served as governor for most of the past thirty-five years. He had not sent Virginia's soldiers into action. Berkeley appears neither to have wanted war nor to have known how to avoid it. Worse, he did not know how to wage the war that he found all about him in 1676.

Two options for the subjugation of the natives were available to Berkeley. He could have pursued an offensive war, ruthlessly killing Indians and spoiling the food supplies of the enemy. Such a course brought success after 1622 and 1644. Berkeley rejected this course in favor of a more defensive posture. He ordered residents in exposed areas to congregate in strong houses, heavily fortified structures in which considerable firepower could be amassed. He prevented shipments of arms to Indians, and he halted vigilante actions by whites. Trade with friendly tribes within Virginia continued, in the hope of preserving their neutrality. Finally, the heart of his plan involved the construction of a string of nine palisaded forts at the head of Virginia's major rivers. Each fort was to be garrisoned by about forty to fifty men; the territory between the forts was to be secured by a force of 125 cavalrymen.

The frontiersmen scoffed at Berkeley's design. If it was workable at all, success would come with painstaking slowness. Already more than three hundred Virginians had perished, many after enduring excruciating torture, and many farms had been laid waste. There was not much sympathy for the friendly Indians within Virginia, some of whom were suspected of complicity in the atrocities that had occurred in the wilderness. Finally, some thought—unfairly, it appears—the governor's strategy fraught with dishonesty, a means by which he could continue to profit from the Indian trade, as well as a scheme to augment the frontier lands owned by favored great planters. Not surprisingly, Berkeley soon lost control of the whirlwind sweeping his province.

Defiance came from within Virginia's militia system. Responding to rumors that a large force of natives was moving downriver, the militia commissioners of Charles City and Henrico counties petitioned to send their militia units above the falls of the James, where the Indians could be confronted and stopped before they reached the English settlements. Berkeley refused. The seething militiamen marched anyway, led by a Henrico planter, Nathaniel Bacon. Their intent, Bacon told the governor, was to stop "those barbarous Enemies" who had invaded the settlers' lands and "barbarously murdered" their families. Bacon, a tall, slender young man with long black hair and a face that seemed always to be filled with anxiety, styled himself "General of the Volunteers." He first led his followers through several Pamunkey villages in the east, then he and his men stormed about the frontier. No invasion force of Indians was discovered. Undaunted, Bacon and his men swept into Occaneechee territory, the domain of a tribe thought to be friendly. Despite an amicable reception, Bacon ordered an assault. Virtually the entire tribe was destroyed.

Unaccustomed to such defiance, Governor Berkeley declared Bacon a rebel. But Bacon's treachery had made him a hero on the frontier. With an army that swelled rapidly to five hundred men, he occupied the capital and demanded permission to carry the war to the natives. He wanted an additional one thousand men; half his army would strike up the James and York rivers, while the remainder would pacify northern Virginia, he said. Berkeley and the assembly capitulated. Within three weeks, close to fifteen hundred soldiers carried the war into the most remote corners of the frontier, though without much success. The Indians, as usual, vanished into the woods at the sight of their adversary. After three weeks of flailing about the wilderness, Bacon had killed fewer than twenty Indians—a majority of whom were women and children—and captured about sixty. He had better luck against his own government. Governing "by the consent of the people," as he put it, Bacon proclaimed the governor a traitor. In the brief civil war that followed Bacon's army burned Jamestown. One month later, however, Bacon was dead of the "Bloody Flux" and "Lousey Disease," probably a combination of exposure and dysentery.

By the time of Bacon's demise, more than a year after the eruption of hostilities, peace returned to the frontier, although incidents were reported as late as the following February. Three months later commissioners for the Crown, accompanied by three warships and 1,130 English troops—a far greater ratio of English soldiers to colonial population than the Crown would have in America during the War of Independence a hundred years later—arrived in Virginia. The army was sent to suppress the rebellion, not to pacify the Indians. Charles II had wasted no time. Not only had royal authority been challenged, but the civil war threatened Virginia's tobacco exports, which annually yielded about one hundred thousand pounds for the king. The army's commander, Col. Herbert Jeffreys, took control of Virginia immediately upon his arrival at Middle Plantation (later Williamsburg). Domestic tranquillity was restored and a peace treaty was concluded with the neighboring tributary Indian tribes. On the one hand, the pact's wording and the statements made by the commissioners were tantamount to a confession that Virginia's land-hungry settlers had provoked the recent war from the "wish and aim at an utter extirpation of the Indians." On the other hand, the treaty recognized the subordination of the tribes left in the Tidewater and Piedmont regions of the colony. These remnants of what had once been Powhatan's Confederacy were restricted to small tracts of land. Their survival as individuals was guaranteed, but their tribal identity was decimated. They now faced a future of utter subordination to the whims of white Virginia. The resolution of Indian affairs in Virginia by 1677 was strikingly similar to that reached in southern New England during the same period.

While Virginia's frontier blazed in the mid-1670s, the New England colonists also were at war, ending a generation of uneasy peace. In 1643, six years after the destruction of the Pequots, the colonies of Massachusetts, Plymouth, New Haven, and Connecticut had formed the New England Confederation, a military alliance directed against the Dutch at New Netherland as well as at various neighboring Indian tribes.

Little time elapsed before the colonies were confronted with a crisis. In 1645, the Narrangansetts, after an outrage committed by the Mohegans, requested permission from the English to retaliate. When consent was denied and the Narragansetts attacked anyway, the New England Confederation raised an army of 220 men to force submission. Isolated as the Pequots had been less than a decade earlier, the Narragansetts had no choice but to capitulate. They were saddled with heavy fines, some of which they paid by ceding land near the present Connecticut–Rhode Island border. Nearly a decade later a similar episode occurred, only this time the Narragansetts acted in concert with their neighbors the Eastern Niantics against the Mohegans. Another English show of force—an army of more than three hundred men was raised—once again obliged the natives to cry peace. Under the settlement that followed this 1654 crisis, the Eastern Niantics surrendered land in Connecticut to the English.

The power of the New England colonies increased over the next generation. The population of these colonies grew at a remarkable rate, doubling between 1650 and 1675, when approximately fifty thousand English resided in the region. As this population seeped into the backcountry, some tribes, including the Wampanoags who lived in southern Massachusetts and Rhode Island, found themselves confronted with the same dilemma that Opechancanough and his people had once faced in Virginia. To submit to the encroaching settlers threatened the natives with the loss of their identity as a people; to move from their ancestral homeland to an uncertain future on a new frontier was hardly more attractive. Other factors stoked a growing bitterness toward the English within the Wampanoag tribe. In 1664, Plymouth leaders had compelled Metacomet, or King Philip as the English called the Wampanoag sachem, to agree never to dispose of any of his lands without their consent; seven years later, in retaliation for the Wampanoags allegedly menacing the recently opened settlement of Swansea, the leaders of Plymouth fined the tribe, sought to disarm it, and coerced Philip into a formal recognition of English sovereignty. It was soon clear to most Wampanoags—and particularly to the younger, more defiant generation—that independence could be secured only through resistance. Many believed that a resort to arms, although dangerous and unpredictable, could succeed. Unlike the Pequots, many tribes in southern New England now possesssed firearms and the skill not only to manufacture bullets, but to repair flintlock muskets.

The catalyst for action came in 1675 when Plymouth executed three Wampanoags on a charge of murdering a Christian Indian, John Sassamon. Following the hanging of the alleged killers of Sassamon, the cauldron boiled over. Retaliatory incidents occurred. Houses were plundered and burned, and a week after the initial raids the first blood was drawn. Other disasters followed, yet these early assaults occurred so desultorily that they suggest isolated vigilante responses by individual warriors. It is conceivable that Philip still sought to avoid war, but, if so, he was fast losing control to individuals who refused to submit to English authority. More likely he simply sought to avoid war in the summer of 1675, perhaps because he had not yet pieced together an effective alliance system among the disunited, often fractious, tribes.

Whether or not he sought conflict, Philip was at war within a week of the first pillaging. Within that time Plymouth and Massachusetts Bay rushed militia units to the frontier. After a month more than 350 soldiers, together with a few Indian allies, had been activated, but they were ineffective against the hit-and-run tactics of the natives. Nor were their offensive actions fruitful. Expeditions in June and July into Mount Hope peninsula and Pocasset swamp country turned up almost no Indians. Emboldened by the Puritans' lack of success, several other tribes soon joined Philip. By the end of the summer the English grasped the full meaning of this war. Houses in villages in a wide arc from the Merrimack River northeast of Boston to the Plymouth frontier lay in smoldering ruins. Before the first sharp bite of the New England autumn, settlements on the Connecticut River had been struck, and three of the eight towns in western Massachusetts had been abandoned.

The first effective English military action was directed not against the Wampanoags but against the Narragansetts, the largest and most powerful tribe in New England. Prodded by intelligence that the Narragansetts would openly join with the Wampanoags early in 1676, the New England Confederation raised an army of one thousand men. The New England army was unlike that which Bacon soon commanded in Virginia. Whereas Bacon used entire militia companies for his campaign, New England's army consisted of men conscripted from their trainband units. The difference arose because the laws of the New England colonies prohibited militiamen from being sent outside their colony. Thus, colonies assigned each town a manpower quota based on its population. The selection process was left to the towns, but most villages appear to have acted similarly. Men who provided essential services (pastors and physicians, for instance) were not chosen; young bachelors were first to be called. As a result, the army was composed mostly of young, single militiamen, although some husbands and fathers also were forced into its ranks. About 25 percent of the militiamen entered this army. The remainder were left at home to provide a corps of armed resistance in the event of an Indian attack. Following a special day of prayer, the army plunged deep into southern Rhode Island.

This great Puritan army was commanded by the governor of Plymouth, Josiah Winslow, whom some thought too frail for such an undertaking. But he was assisted by tough, vigorous subalterns, some of whom saw this war as an opportunity for personal profit, including the acquisition of both slaves and land. This army was readied for an American-style warfare. Eschewing the heavy suits of body armor worn by the first

English soldiers in America, these men wore thick leather jerkins and lighter padded coats, and they were armed almost exclusively with firearms. The commanders retained the discipline and traditional tactical concepts taught by the European military manuals, but they had adapted to fighting in the American wilderness. This army was willing to use stealth, to "creep . . . on their bellies," as one officer put it, rather than march into combat as they might do on a European battlefield. Nor did the leaders disdain ambush, an Indian tactic that had once been denounced as cowardly by the English. Determined to secure an enduring peace and adequate security, as had been achieved through the decimation of the Pequots, this army was prepared to wage total war, a life-and-death, give-no-quarter struggle in which women, children, and the elderly were as much a target as the fiercest Indian warrior.

The objective of Winslow's army was the Great Swamp, just east of the Chippuxet River. An Indian turncoat, Indian Peter, guided the New England soldiers. It was not uncommon for Indians to assist the English. Since the outset of hostilities some friendly Indians had laid down their arms to demonstrate their peaceful intentions, and they willingly assisted the English. This aid was heartily welcomed by the Puritan leaders, whose ignorance of wilderness warfare often resulted in excessive caution, a proclivity for stumbling into ambushes, and a grievous inability to find the enemy. In King Philip's War the Mohegans provided protection against surprise attacks, frequently discovering and flushing out parties of hostile Indians. Connecticut grew so dependent on its Indian auxiliaries that the provincial council routinely ordered its soldiers home when their native allies wearied of fighting. The council exhorted its citizenry to cooperate with friendly Indians, explaining that it is "not safe for us and the health of the colony's interest to break with them."

Indian Peter's role commenced on the second day of the operation. The previous day the armies of Massachusetts and Plymouth had endured a long, tiring march under a paltry winter sun; at day's end they rendezvoused at an old trading post once operated by Roger Williams. The next morning, in weather that had turned dark and stormy, the combined armies plodded onward past brown, barren forests; up one hill and down another; around cold, blue ponds; through damp, bone-chilling swamps. Snow fell most of the day; the men, their hands and feet soon numb, pushed on quietly, eating uncooked victuals as they advanced. Their target was a secret village into which more than one thousand Narragansetts had fled for the winter. The Narragansetts occupied a fortified city situated on a small island in the Great Swamp; here, behind a masonry wall with block houses and flankers competently laid out, the Indians lived in a five-acre village.

The English reached the stockade late in the afternoon, just as the Indians prepared for dinner. They attacked immediately, before darkness descended. The assault was a spontaneous, helter-skelter affair devoid of design. The first attack failed, but a second attempt succeeded when a Massachusetts company discovered a gap in the wall of the fortress. Soldiers penetrated the breach. After a furious battle, the English torched the wigwams. Some inhabitants were shot as they fled; others died in the inferno, trapped in their homes. "[T]hey and their food fried together," one English observer noted laconically. In the last gray light of day on December 19, 1675, the Great Swamp Fight ended. The encounter resulted in a massacre, similar to that at Mystic River Fort nearly forty years before. Roughly three hundred Narragansett warriors and an equal number of women and children perished. In addition the English killed the native blacksmith and destroyed the forge he had used to repair the Indians' firearms. But the English paid, too. Eighty or more soldiers—about 20 percent of the army—were killed or wounded. One-half of the company commanders were casualties.

In February and March 1676, the Wampanoags, now joined by tribes who had entered the war in response to the English army's brutality and aggression, resumed the offensive. The town of Medfield, only twenty miles from Boston, was hit, and nearly fifty houses were destroyed. Weymouth, on the

Atlantic coast, fell victim four nights later. During the next month fighting raged not only in Maine, but in villages from Rhode Island to the upper Connecticut River. Even Providence was raided. The home of Roger Williams, who was now in his mid-seventies, was burned. The best-remembered assault, however, occurred in Lancaster, about thirty miles west of Boston, where Mary Rowlandson, the wife of the local pastor, was taken captive. Following her release several months later she wrote an account of her ordeal, the first of a new literary genre, the captivity narrative, that would titillate American readers during the next two hundred years.

Rowlandson's ordeal began in the early morning hours of February 10, 1676. Since late January the 250 residents of frontier Lancaster had spent their evenings crowded into five log garrison houses that they had constructed at strategic points within the township. They knew the danger was considerable; several nearby towns had been struck. In addition, a Christian Indian of the Nashaway tribe had informed authorities that Lancaster had been targeted for an assault. After the days' work was completed on February 9, Rowlandson and thirty-seven others came to the garrison house to which they had been assigned. They hurriedly ate a light supper and put the children to bed; early on in the cold evening the adults climbed into their beds, most to spend a restless, anxious night. Sentries were on duty all night, squinting into the darkness, straining to see any unusual movement, listening for any strange sounds.

The night passed slowly, uneventfully. Just before daybreak some of the adults began to stir. Soon the first light appeared in the sky, the pinks and grays that ushered in a new day. Most residents thought danger had been averted for a few more hours.

Suddenly, gunshots were heard in the distance. Several inhabitants raced to the windows. Indians were attacking. They had struck at one of the outlying garrison houses. Soon, smoke was seen to the west. After a furious fight the Indians pierced that strong house. The horrified witnesses in Rowlandson's house watched as five of their friends were dragged outside;

three, including a woman and a child, were killed with to-
mahawks. Moments later a man was murdered, and just after
that a man trying to escape into the woods was shot. Once all
the residents of the first strong house had been killed or captured, some of the attackers turned to a second garrison house,
some to the vacant residences, which were looted, then burned.
Many with Rowlandson watched helplessly as their homes
were destroyed.

Slowly and methodically the Indians worked their way
toward Rowlandson's garrison house, the last to be attacked.
Finally, two hours after this grisly day began, her garrison came
under assault. She described what followed:

The house stood upon the edge of a hill; some of the Indians got
behind the hill, others into the barn, and others behind anything that
could shelter them; from all which places they shot against the house,
so that the bullets seemed to fly like hail; and quickly they wounded
one man among us, then another, and then a third. About two
hours . . . they had been about the house before they began to fire it
(which they did with flax and hemp, which they brought out of the
barn). . . . [T]hey fired it once and one inhabitant ventured out and
dowsed it, but they quickly set it afire again, and that took. Now is
the dreadful hour come. . . . Some in our house were fighting for their
lives, others wallowing in their blood, the house on fire over our heads,
and the bloody heathen ready to knock us on the head, if we stirred
out. . . . Then I took my children . . . to go leave the house, but as
soon as we came to the door and appeared, the Indians shot so thick
that the bullets rattled against the house, as if one had taken a handful
of stones and thrown them, so that we were forced back inside. . . . But
we must go, the fire increasing, and coming along behind us roar-
ing. . . . No sooner were we out of the house before my brother-in-
law, wounded in the throat, fell dead. . . . [P]resently . . . the bullets
flying thick, one went through my side and the same through the
bowels and hand of my dear child in my arms. One of my sister's
elder children, William, had then his leg broken, which the Indians
perceiving, they knocked him on the head. Thus were we butchered
by these merciless heathen, standing amazed, with the blood running
down to our heels. . . . Oh the doleful sight.

Twelve who had spent the night with Rowlandson perished that morning. All but one of the others were taken into

captivity. That was Rowlandson's fate. She was kept prisoner for nearly one hundred days, during which she was kept almost constantly on the move. Her worst experiences came early on. To be taken prisoner, to see one's home destroyed and one's family and friends killed, was a terrifying, disorienting experience. Rowlandson later spoke of the first evening of her captivity as "the dolefullest night that ever my eyes saw," and she spoke of her "miserable" and "disconsolate" feelings. Nine days into her captivity her wounded child died. Her own wound, which was superficial, gradually healed, helped along with generous applications of oak leaves pressed against the bullet hole. All in all, Rowlandson's treatment as a prisoner was not particularly harsh. She suffered from lack of food, but so did her captors. She was never physically abused, she was permitted to travel unescorted from one Indian village to another to visit friends and relatives, and she was given additional food, when available, as compensation for sewing and mending the tattered clothing of her captors.

When Rowlandson's ordeal began, Massachusetts had seemed almost powerless against the Indian onslaught. There was not adequate manpower to defend each village. Indeed, the New England Confederation failed even to keep a strong army in the field during that winter. Friction over the size of each colony's troop contribution led Connecticut to recall its men; Plymouth declined to provide a single soldier. Massachusetts posted cavalry units on the frontier, but given the enormity of the war zone, these troopers had only limited success; on more than one occasion the Indians lured these raw, impetuous soldiers into ruinous ambushes.

By April, with planting season looming, morale reached a low point. Refugees streamed to the east, taxes mounted, and minor food shortages and high prices plagued the citizenry. Resistance to the draft became commonplace. The colonies designated days for fasting and prayer; uplifting messages poured from every Puritan pulpit.

By May, as the first mild, green days of spring graced New England, the tide turned. The cumulative effects of nine months of war showed on the natives, especially once the English began to rely more heavily on Indian auxiliaries. Puritan fortunes seemed to rise in direct proportion to the natives' willingness to provide assistance against Philip and his allies. Philip's casualties mounted. Hunger and disease reached acute proportions among some tribes. Here and there, small groups emerged from the forests, no longer full of fight. Late in the month, English spirits were buoyed by a rare smashing victory. Responding to intelligence provided by an escaped captive, a Massachusetts force surprised the enemy at Paskcompscut, above Deerfield on the Fall River. More than one hundred Indians perished. Less than two weeks later a Connecticut force scored a major victory. Soon both provinces had large armies in the field. Indian casualties mounted steadily. During the first two days of July, almost a year to the day since the conflagration had erupted, a Connecticut force killed or captured 238 Narragansetts; not a single Englishman was killed in this operation. Hardly a day passed when fugitive Indians were not apprehended or others—tired, hungry, and disillusioned—simply surrendered.

The end to hostilities came about six weeks later with the death of King Philip. An Indian deserter who said his brother had been murdered by the sachem disclosed the whereabouts of Philip and offered to lead the English to the chieftain's lair, a camp in a tangled swamp near Mount Hope. Although some suspected a trap, Capt. Benjamin Church seized the opportunity. Church was the son of a veteran of the Pequot War. Tall and broad, a sturdy New England farmer who knew his way about the wilderness, Church had answered his province's call to arms nearly a year earlier. Church had been wounded in the Great Swamp Fight, shot in the thigh; another bullet "pierced [my] pocket and wounded a pair of mittens," he later recounted, and still another shot passed through his baggy trousers and underwear but miraculously left him unscathed.

On August 12, 1676, Church and his small company of Plymouth volunteers and Indian auxiliaries crossed the Taunton River under a midnight moon and plunged into the swamp. Their guide expertly led them through the darkness and across the matted, labyrinthine landscape. As the English neared Philip's encampment, Church stationed some men on the periphery to prevent the Indians' escape. His precaution was unnecessary; Philip had not posted a sentry. The Indian leader, together with a few followers, was asleep. The English, straining to move as noiselessly as possible, crept to the edge of the hideout, then without warning opened fire. A few Indians escaped into the woods. Philip was not among them. Startled from his slumber, he attempted to flee, but he did not get far before he was gunned down, shot by one of Church's Indian allies. Philips's chief lieutenant attempted to summon his brethren to fight: "Iootash! Iootash!" "Stand and fight," he exhorted. But for this night the fighting had ended.

Church and his soldiers gathered to observe Philip, whom the English captain described as "a doleful, great, naked, dirty, beast." Church then ordered the body decapitated and quartered; the turncoat who had led the English to Philip was permitted the honor of severing the dead sachem's head. Church then directed that various pieces of Philip be suspended from several trees, although Philip's head was returned to Plymouth, where for years it remained on public display.

Thereafter, resistance withered away, until in October 1676 the New England Confederation proclaimed the conflict at an end. But the grim business of settling old scores proceeded. Lynch mobs prowled the streets of Boston in search of Indians. In the countryside soldiers frequently murdered Indian captives; other prisoners were executed following trials whose outcomes were never in doubt. In Marblehead, summary executions occurred, execrable proceedings in which some of the female inhabitants of the town played a prominent role. Those who perished quickly may have been the most fortunate of the vanquished, for many of the survivors—including Philip's wife and son—were sold abroad into perpetual slavery, although some children were kept in New England as bound servants. Altogether, the natives suffered close to five thousand casualties in this war.

New England paid a heavy price for its victory. Thirteen towns were totally destroyed. Perhaps one-quarter of the villages had sustained heavy damage. The frontier population decreased, and in some places settlement would not reappear for nearly two generations. More than five hundred English soldiers died in this war. Twice that many civilians perished. Indeed, about one in every thirty-five residents of New England died in this war, a death rate—measured proportionally—that exceeded United States' losses in the War of Independence, the Civil War, or World War II. However, a greater percentage of the Virginia population perished in both the Second and Third Anglo-Powhatan Wars.

Undeniably, of course, the Indians paid the heavier price, including those who sided with the English. Throughout southern New England the native peoples were reduced to a second-class status, disarmed, in some jurisdictions prohibited from congregating in large numbers, compelled to surrender tribal homelands, and in Massachusetts forced to reside on one of four reservations or to work for the English as servants.

The bloody struggles in Virginia and New England in 1675–76 brought to a close the warfare between the European settlers and the Indians on America's first frontier. In retrospect, Quaker Pennsylvania's shining example notwithstanding, it appears that conflict and tragedy had been unavoidable. To the Indians the Europeans must have appeared as invaders, intruders who came bearing frightening new arms and spreading catastrophic diseases. They were an alien people who altered the Indians' traditional habits and culture and who pushed relentlessly, remorselessly, into the ancestral lands cherished by one tribe after another. The Europeans arrived with a mixed outlook toward the natives. But their steadily swelling numbers, together with their land hunger, religious prejudices, and cultural biases impeded the best prospects for accommodation. Following Opechancanough's devastating attack on the Virginia settlements in 1622, moreover, all hope that the Indians might be peacefully conciliated and dominated were dashed.

In the conflicts that followed, warriors on both sides borrowed from the adversary. While the Indians continued to use stealth, cunning, and wilderness skill to good advantage against the plodding colonists, they sought European firearms. Although they lacked the technological skills to manufacture these weapons, the Indians gradually learned how to repair defective pieces and to cast bullets. At times, too, the Indians fortified their villages along the European model, employing their own masons to construct stone forts that included sharp flankers. The settlers' armies, meanwhile, gradually learned what professional English officers in the next century would call an "irregular way of war." Although the colonial armies did not abandon martial discipline or the basic tactical concepts commonplace in European warfare, modifications in their practice of warfare evolved during the seventeenth century. Colonists who had initially refused to admit Indians to their militia units actively recruited Indians as scouts and auxiliaries. The Indians were invaluable as the eyes of colonial soldiers who too often were blind in the American wilderness, and provincial armies came to rely heavily on native warriors to locate the enemy and to prevent ambushes. Upon the advice of Indians, Puritan soldiers such as Captain Church learned to move more quickly, to spread their formations to minimize the likelihood of ambush, and to rely more often on the element of surprise. These changes were perhaps inevitable, and they likely were hastened by the gradual displacement of the European professionals who had led Virginia's first military units and trained the initial generation of Puritan settlers. By the time of the Third Anglo-Powhatan War in the Chesapeake and King Philip's War in New England, the colonial officers no longer were mercenaries and career soldiers, but hearty and dedicated amateurs who learned the way of war in the pitiless struggles on America's earliest frontiers.

During the wars of the seventeenth century, the natives possessed two advantages. At the outset of English settlement the Indians almost everywhere enjoyed a considerable numerical superiority; throughout the seventeenth century they possessed superior skills in the use of the American wilderness, a capability that enabled them to live off the land, travel great distances relatively quickly, and often easily elude their pursuers. But the natives were hampered by severe liabilities. They repeatedly failed to overcome their traditional intertribal hostilities, rendering them divided and isolated in the face of their English adversaries. Additionally, the Indians lacked the reserves to replace the huge losses in manpower, weapons, and comestibles that resulted in every major war with the settlers. Finally, from the initial engagements at windswept Roanoke Island to Philip's demise in a forbidding and lonely New England swamp, the English possessed firearms. When the large colonial armies wielded these terrifying weapons, the English enjoyed a distinct advantage over their native adversaries.

The Indians were always capable of inflicting great damage on the English settlers, but in every major war in the seventeenth century the coastal tribes met a cataclysmic fate. By that dark summer night when Captain Church presided over the dismemberment of Philip's body, less than a century had elapsed since the warm day in 1584 when the first English, garbed in armor and wielding cumbersome handguns, had landed on a clean, white Roanoke Island beach. They had come, they had said, to spread Christianity, to trade, and to conquer. Each of the three ends had been advanced, but none so zealously as the last.

CHAPTER TWO

The European Struggle for America: Round One

The Origins of International Conflict

The first threat to the success of the English colonies had been posed by the Indians. A century into England's experience in America a second threat emerged. Supremacy in America, perhaps survival itself, henceforth hinged upon the outcome of the collision between Europe's imperial powers, in concert with their colonists and their Indian allies.

French and Spanish colonists arrived in America before the first Englishmen came ashore at Roanoke Island. Spanish settlers returned to Hispaniola with Columbus on his second voyage in 1493; by 1550, more than a quarter century before Raleigh dispatched his first expedition to explore the Chesapeake, nearly one hundred thousand Spanish lived in the Americas. The French had sought without success to plant colonies in Canada, Brazil, and Florida between 1535 and 1562. Fifty years later, at the time of the settlement of Jamestown, the French came back to Canada. Disappointment dogged their early endeavors, but gradually some rude bases in Acadia survived, the nascence of a French empire in America. Gradually France planted not only small frontier outposts below the Great Lakes and on the marshy, sultry Gulf Coast, but also more substantive sugar colonies in the Caribbean.

An uneasy peace characterized England's relationship with France and Spain during most of the seventeenth century. At first Spain provoked the greatest concern among the English. Sites for colonies were selected with an eye on defense against Spanish attack; at Roanoke, for instance, the cannon in the first fort built by the English were trained toward the sea, for the Spanish were thought to pose a greater threat than the Indians. But the dreaded attack never came, and in the Treaty of Madrid of 1670 Spain recognized England's right to eastern North America above Florida. Détente did not eliminate tensions. English pirates plundered Spanish shipping in New World waters, and the English settlers in South Carolina after 1670 competed with Spanish Florida for the Indian trade it had previously monopolized. Nevertheless, as Spanish interest in North America receded and as Dutch power waned, France emerged as England's greatest colonial rival.

Troubles between France and England surfaced from time to time throughout the century. Much of the contention arose from competing interests in Acadia, a cold and inhospitable land, but a region coveted by both European nations for its furs and rich fishing grounds. In 1613 the English in Virginia, barely able to defend themselves against hunger and the Powhatans, attacked and destroyed the lone French settlement in Acadia. A generation later, the English once again seized Acadia and Quebec, although both were returned to France by Charles I in 1632. Acadia was taken a third time by the English in 1655, but it was subsequently exchanged by royal officials for the French island of Saint Kitts.

Acadia notwithstanding, harmony between France and England had generally prevailed throughout the seventeenth century. By the late stages of the century, however, evidence of an inescapable conflict had surfaced. Both France and England were expansionist powers with designs on extending their possessions in North America. The French king dreamed of building a larger, more self-sufficient American empire, one that would help him achieve his primary goal—the expansion of French hegemony in Europe. But imperial England was similarly expansionist. "The King of England did grasp at all America," one high-placed Frenchman grumbled, and it must have seemed so, as the royal government in London created one English colony after another. In fact, the English had expanded steadily since 1660, taking New Netherland and pushing to new frontiers in New England; its interest in Acadia was readily apparent, as England had become entrenched even in the region above the French settlements on the Saint Lawrence River. In 1668, England first conducted a profitable trade on Hudson Bay. Soon thereafter, through the Hudson's Bay Company, the English erected posts in the area, encroaching upon the French trade with the Indians. The presence, therefore, of two ambitious and expansionist European rivals in close proximity to one another in America created a combustible situation.

That these mighty European powers established their far-flung outposts in lands long inhabited by a variety of native groups only added to the likelihood of conflict. Indeed, in the late seventeenth century it was England's ties to the Iroquois Confederacy that most immediately threatened New France. This powerful confederacy, also known as the Five Nations Confederacy, consisted of five tribes—the Mohawks, Oneidas, Onondagas, Cayugas, and Senecas—who shared kinship ties and a common Iroquoian language, Ganonsyoni. Their domain stretched from the Adirondack Mountains in upper New York to the Great Lakes in Pennsylvania.

Problems between the French and the Iroquois had begun a generation earlier. Early in the history of New France, Samuel de Champlain, the founder of the first French colonies, established close economic ties with the Huron, who lived north of Lake Ontario and who brought furs to the French via the

Ottawa River. Both sides were served nicely by this commerce for two generations, until the Iroquois intruded. Dwelling in the region south and east of Lake Ontario, the Five Nations had opened trade with the Dutch in New Netherland during this period, transporting their furs to Fort Orange, near the point where the Mohawk River enters the Hudson River. Trade flourished until the 1640s, when the supply of beaver in Iroquois territory was exhausted. The Iroquois sought new hunting grounds to the north, inevitably bringing them into conflict with the French, who now stood to lose the profitable commerce they enjoyed with the Hurons to the Dutch. At mid-century, New France went to war with the Iroquois, a long struggle in which both sides resorted to guerrilla tactics. Peace came in 1666, after Louis XIV sent his Canadian governor a regiment of one thousand regulars. The French show of force persuaded the Iroquois to suspend their attempt to monopolize the fur trade above Lake Ontario.

England had conquered New Netherland two years earlier, in 1664, and had assumed the flourishing commerce that its predecessors had established with the Iroquois. Usually acting as a middleman, the powerful Iroquois gathered furs from other tribes, as well as from renegade French frontiersmen. The pelts were transported to old Fort Orange—the English renamed it Albany—where the English consistently offered a good deal; for fewer furs than would be required at Montreal, the Iroquois could obtain more guns, powder, knives, metal utensils, and woolen blankets. A symbiotic relationship quickly emerged: the Iroquois required English goods to maintain hegemony in their sector of the northern frontier; certain powerful Englishmen built fortunes on the Iroquois trade.

The peace that began following the humbling of the Iroquois by France in 1666 unraveled within a generation. In 1680 René-Robert Cavelier de La Salle, seeking to open the Mississippi River valley to the French fur trade, established posts deep down the Illinois River. The Iroquois immediately understood that French expansion posed a grave threat to their existence; if blocked from the western fur trade, they faced certain ruin. The western Iroquois, the Seneca, went on the warpath, attacking the Illinois Indians, France's new trading partner. Soon French access to the entire Great Lakes basin was obstructed.

New France's difficulties were exacerbated by the arrival of a new, aggressive governor in New York. Col. Thomas Dongan arrived in 1683. He was a career military man who had served in Louis XIV's armies, had led the Irish corps for Charles II, and had held executive appointments in England's overseas possessions. Perhaps because of his background, Dongan understood clearly the broad outlines of Anglo-French rivalry, and he comprehended what England must do to augment its position. Dongan knew that the right Indian alliances were essential for gaining supremacy in North America; he also understood that through affiliation with the Iroquois, the English could expand to the west while confining New France to Canada. Iroquois friendship, hence, was crucial for England's future success in America. The leaders of New France understood just as clearly that their prosperity hinged on the evisceration of the Iroquois.

In 1683 New France dispatched an army of more than one thousand men, including some regulars sent over by the imperial government, to bring the Iroquois to heel. The campaign failed egregiously. Four years later, the French tried again. Under the leadership of the governor of New France, the Marquis de Denonville, a three-thousand-man force swept into Seneca territory, killing and plundering in a manner reminiscent of the Virginians during the early Powhatan wars. The Seneca were chastened, but the apparent French success was misleading. Denonville's campaign only drove the Iroquois more firmly into the arms of the English.

By the late 1680s the Iroquois, supplied by the English and capable of putting the strongest military force in America into the field, were on the warpath from one end of Lake Ontario to the other. In August 1689 the extent of their power was revealed. Under cover provided by a hailstorm, fifteen hundred Iroquois launched a surprise attack on Lachine, a village located on the same island as Montreal. The result was the worst butchery in Canada's history. Fifty-nine farms were destroyed and scores of residents killed or captured. Lachine was merely the worst of the horrors of a rapidly spreading war. The French had recently attacked and destroyed three English trading posts on Hudson Bay, a steadily thriving emporium for the English fur trade since 1668. Moreover, hostilities had flared on the frontier in Maine, where both the English and the French coveted the Kennebec River area. Indeed, while the ruins of Lachine still smoldered, the Abnaki tribe, encouraged by the French, laid waste the English coastal port of Pemaquid—modern Bristol—in Maine.

During the summer of 1689, just a few days before the devastation of Lachine, word arrived that war had broken out between England and France, what the Europeans would call the War of the League of Augsburg, what the English colonists would know as King William's War. The European war, in reality a world war, resulted from changes that eroded the old balance of power. In England, a Protestant, William III, had deposed the Roman Catholic–leaning monarch, James II, in the Glorious Revolution of 1688. William III was an implacable foe of the French Sun King, Louis XIV. Thus, anti-French feelings within England were strengthened at the very moment that anxiety had mounted among Englishmen at the prospect of a renascent Roman Catholicism throughout Europe, a resurgence embodied in the magisterial, absolutist king of France.

English misgivings at the intentions of Louis were not misplaced. The French monarch's ambitions were grandiose, including both expansion in Europe and the creation of a grand New France in America. London trembled at the thought of Europe under his sway. In addition, England was anxious at the steady growth of French commercial power, including recent French activities in the Illinois country and on the Mississippi River, which appeared to be a plan to encircle the English colonies that hugged North America's Atlantic seaboard. Nor was it only Englands' apprehension that was aroused. The Sun King's far-flung aspirations created far-flung enemies, and when Louis invaded the Rhineland in the fall of 1688 a coalition of threatened powers mobilized to stop him. England entered the conflict in the spring of the following year.

Even though America's frontiers were ablaze before war erupted in Europe, the continental powers sought to prevent open conflict between their colonies. They failed. Avarice and ambition, combined with religious and cultural bigotry, proved too strong for the maintenance of peace. The war in America remained of secondary importance to the statesmen in Europe, but in time France, England, and ultimately Spain saw in the European struggle opportunities and dangers for their New World empires. From the beginning, the rulers of England had known that force would determine the fate of their colonial enterprise. In 1584, Elizabeth's instructions to Raleigh had been to plant the first English colony in America and to "encounter and expulse, repel and resist as well by sea as by land, and by all other ways whatsoever" those who might imperil the province. A century later the contest that the queen had anticipated in America between Englishmen and their European rivals had erupted.

An Indecisive War

Europe's soldiers came to America slowly. In King William's War the colonies fought largely unaided by their parent states. For the European inhabitants of North America this initial intercolonial war must have seemed merely a continuation of earlier conflicts, as much of their fighting was against Indian adversaries.

The Iroquois and the leaders of New France were the most enterprising warriors during the initial year of this conflict. Well into autumn the Iroquois continued to target French villages and trading posts in the backcountry; many Canadian residents abandoned the frontier and scurried for Montreal and safety—if, indeed, it provided any security. Most *habitants* remained on their farms, praying for deliverance. The experiences of Lachine, where, it was rumored, children had been tortured, then roasted like oxen over an open fire, and later of La Chesneye, a hamlet in which twenty French had perished in an attack on a snowy November morning, filled them with terror.

New France, however, soon took the offensive. A new governor had arrived at Quebec. Denonville had been recalled. Count Louis de Buade de Frontenac, once before the governor of New France, had been reappointed to his old post. Frontenac, the godson of Louis XIII and the grandson of a secretary of state, had soldiered since the age of fifteen; he was a colonel by age twenty-three, a brigadier general after three more years. He suffered several wounds during his service, one of which permanently crippled his right arm. Exuding tenacity and courage, Frontenac soon was considered to be one of France's best soldiers. Time did not tarnish his reputation. In 1669, when he was forty-nine, he was sent by France to save Venice, under attack by the Turks. Three years later, in 1672, the monarch sent him to America for the first time; Frontenac came as governor and lieutenant general of New France. He longed for the power and the action that went with the job, and he welcomed life away from an imperious wife who refused to accompany him to an inhospitable, backwoods settlement on the Saint Lawrence.

Hot-tempered, headstrong, passionate, flamboyant, intelligent, cultivated, vain, often melancholy, and zealous in his aspirations to make New France the glory of his nation and his monarch, Frontenac lasted nearly ten years in Quebec. In 1682, the king summoned him home. Frontenac had been the victim both of innumerable clashes with the clergy and of his penchant for treating the province as if it were his private fiefdom. But he had excelled in his dealings with the Indians, whom he genuinely liked, and no one doubted his ability to lead in a crisis. Simultaneous hostilities with the Indians and the English constituted a crisis indeed, and in 1689 Louis XIV turned again to Frontenac, now age seventy. "I send you back to Canada," the Sun King told him. "I am sure that you will serve me well as you did before, and I ask nothing more of you." Frontenac's landing in Quebec bore little resemblance to the dark circumstances that had existed at the time of his recall years before. Though a chilly October evening, all the citizens of Quebec descended on the waterfront to greet their new governor and to guide him with their torchlights back to his residence in the governor's palace.

Count Frontenac had been sent to America to implement a war plan conceived by his predecessor. Denonville had recognized that New York both incited and supported the Iroquois; in 1688, he had urged the Crown to send over a large French army to crush the natives and conquer the province. Louis XIV applauded the concept, but he objected to the request for troops. Somehow, Frontenac would have to obtain his goal against considerable odds.

The governor-general was undeterred. He had ample native allies and a small but hardy Canadian militia at his disposal; moreover, the English colonies not only were unaccustomed to cooperating with one another, but many—New York, in particular—were beset with domestic distractions, a residue of the Glorious Revolution. Nor were Frontenac's expectations unrealistic. Indeed, with a better conceived strategy he might have accomplished more. Had Frontenac moved decisively against Albany, the principal supply base of the Iroquois, that powerful confederacy might have been knocked from the war, and the English colonists thrown on the defensive. Instead Frontenac divided his forces and struck his enemy at three separate points. He gained a measure of revenge and spread terror along the New York and New England frontiers, but otherwise he accomplished little.

The first blow, delivered in February 1690, fell on Schenectady, the most isolated English settlement in New York. The attack party of 96 Indians and 114 Frenchmen marched for two weeks to reach its destination. A midwinter thaw had set in, making travel easier, although the warmer weather also meant that day after day the men slogged through bone-chilling slush, soaking them to the skin. As the expedition neared Schenectady the weather turned cold again; late on the afternoon of February 8, when the war party reached the outskirts of the village, it was snowing. Throughout the last hours of the day the attackers remained in the thick, dark woods that surrounded the town, watching as the unsuspecting villagers completed their farm chores. Gradually night descended. Within a couple hours the glow from the last candle disappeared.

The village was dark and peaceful. The attackers waited. An hour passed, then another. No sound, no sign of activity came from the village; nor was there any sign of a sentry. The time for the attack had come. Under the black canopy of night the assailants crept forward noiselessly and surrounded each house. Strangely, no dogs barked. Nothing betrayed the war party. They waited only an instant, then the signal was flashed. The assault began. Many residents heard the war whoop of the Indians only seconds before they died; some were hacked or bludgeoned to death, others were shot. In all, sixty perished, twenty-seven males were taken captive, and the village, together with the inadequate stockade that had surrounded it, was burned.

More than a month passed before the second assault force struck, falling upon Salmon Falls in New Hampshire. Under winter skies, a party of fifty French and Abnaki raided the unsuspecting village. More than thirty inhabitants died and about twice as many were taken prisoner. Eight weeks later, in mid-May, Frontenac's men assailed Fort Loyal, situated at Falmouth on Casco Bay in Maine. Following the surrender on the fourth day of the siege, the French stood by while the Indians killed more than one hundred English of all ages; those who survived were carried off into captivity.

If Frontenac's goal had been to spread terror along the breadth of the English frontier, he had succeeded. If he had sought to break the will to resist among the Iroquois and English, he had failed egregiously. What he had achieved was an unprecedented degree of accord among the English.

The news of Schenectady, which spread rapidly across New England, aroused despair and loathing among the English.

Less than fifteen years after King Philip's War, hostilities once again loomed. For the first time in the course of English colonization, Indians had been incited by a European leader to attack another European people. Yet, not all the blame for the Anglo-American response can be laid at the feet of Frontenac. Even before news arrived of the Schenectady massacre, the authorities in Massachusetts had decided to strike at the French in Acadia. For some time the leaders in Massachusetts Bay had been under mounting pressure from both its frontier inhabitants and influential businessmen in the Boston fishing industry to act against the French in Acadia, particularly against Port Royal. Six months before the attacks on Schenectady and Salmon Falls, French frigates from Port Royal had seized several Salem fishing ketches and taken thirty fishermen captive, acts that threatened the survival of Massachusetts's fishing industry. The provincial authorities in Boston decided to act, but only if Great Britain declared war on France. Word that Britain and France were at war arrived in December 1689. Within the week Gov. Simon Bradstreet of Massachusetts expressed his desire "to take revenge upon the French at Nova Scotia"; a week later the assembly voted to raise a force "for the Reducing of Acadia." Lurid images evoked by the tragedies at Schenectady and Salmon Falls—"Women and Children murder'd. Women with Child ripped up, Children had their Brains dashed out," exclaimed the diary of Samuel Sewall, a magistrate in Boston—simply galvanized public opinion in support of an action that had already been decided.

Moving quickly, the province recruited an army of nearly 750 men and located seventeen ships to transport them to the northeast. This was not the customary New England army. The English tradition that forbade sending militiamen to fight outside England had come to America with the first colonists as a prohibition against using trainbands beyond the borders of the colony. Militia units, thus, were not included in this army. This army consisted entirely of volunteers.

Many factors lured men to serve. Religious bigotry was one incentive. Influential clergymen in the colony sometimes encouraged recruiting, instructing the faithful that to bear arms against French Catholics was to do God's work. Ultimately, however, economic inducements appear to have been more persuasive than the allure of religion. The opportunity to share in the victor's spoils acted as a powerful magnet in drawing men into the army. Consequently, more of those who soldiered in this campaign, in contrast to those who had born arms in King Philip's War, were drawn from among Boston's disadvantaged: the unemployed, the low-paid, and the itinerants who were between jobs.

Sir William Phips was appointed to command the invasion force. Despite his noble title, Phips was native-born. The youngest of twenty-six children born to humble parents in Maine, he once had been a shepherd; later, young Phips had been apprenticed as a ship's carpenter and had practiced his trade in Boston. Marriage to a wealthy widow changed his life. Laying aside his artisan's tools, he became a contractor in the shipbuilding industry; with the money he made in that endeavor, Phips financed several expeditions to the West Indies in search of sunken Spanish galleons laden with gold. After six years of failure, he found what he had been looking for off the coast of Hispaniola. Suddenly wealthy and knighted by the Crown for his contribution to the English treasury, Phips became a popular hero and an important Bostonian. When he volunteered to command the Acadia expedition, he was given the assignment, despite his lack of military experience.

Phips scored an easy victory in the spring of 1690, although it was not a conquest of much significance. His expedition departed Boston in late April and returned thirty days later. At Port Royal, the principal French settlement, Phips found an overmatched garrison all too happy to be given the opportunity to surrender. The English then proceeded to destroy the Catholic church, burn the fort, plunder the town, and hurry home. But no one was left to garrison Port Royal, which was soon reclaimed by the French.

Governor Bradstreet clearly looked upon this foray as only a first step. Just after Salmon Falls, he urged a meeting between representatives of several northern colonies to consider an "Attempt upon Canada." As Phips was sailing from Boston, delegates from Connecticut, Plymouth, New York, and Massachusetts gathered in New York to contemplate strategy. The conference quickly adopted a plan offered by Jacob Leisler, the governor of New York. Leisler envisioned strikes at the heart of New France. A combined force of 850 colonials and 2,000 Iroquois would muscle its way toward Montreal through the wilderness above Albany; meanwhile, a joint naval and army force of New Englanders would descend on Quebec via the Saint Lawrence River. Once the English controlled that mighty waterway, Canada, with all its treasures, would belong to Anglo-America.

Planning and preparation consumed the spring and summer, but, finally, in August the two armies moved out. Fitz-John Winthrop, the son of a Connecticut governor, led the western units out of Albany. Winthrop, so homely that his appearance was almost comical (he had a tiny mouth, a long but full nose, and enormous eyes), was the eldest son in an influential family that dwelled on a vast sprawling estate carved from lands taken from the Pequots in 1637, the year before his birth. Drawn by the adventure of war, he had left home before his twentieth birthday to fight in Oliver Cromwell's army in the English Civil War; later Winthrop had been one of Connecticut's highest ranking militia officers during King Philip's War, but he had not experienced combat. Although a civilian, he had dealt with military matters much of his adult life, and when King William's War erupted he answered the call to serve.

From the outset Winthrop's operation faced formidable problems. Only Connecticut met its manpower quota, so that Winthrop's army was but one-fourth its projected size; moreover, his men had few boats with which to traverse Lake Champlain. Matters soon grew even worse. Not only were his already depleted ranks further thinned by an outbreak of dysentery and smallpox, but instead of the nearly two thousand Iroquois allies that he expected to find awaiting him at Lake Champlain, Winthrop discovered only seventy warriors who were willing to accompany the English; they explained that smallpox also had struck their villages. After only three weeks in the field, his supply of pork and biscuit deteriorating quickly, Winthrop ordered a countermarch to Albany without ever embarking on Lake Champlain, much less having seen the rooftops and spires of Montreal.

Phips's expedition weighed anchor at Boston a few days after Winthrop had departed from Albany, but it did not reach Quebec until early October. By then the French had long since learned of Phips's approach. As he awaited the arrival of his adversary, Frontenac must have counted the advantages he would possess in the coming engagement. He already had posted an army of two thousand men, mostly militiamen from all over New France (men who were freed from defending Montreal now that Winthrop had retreated) to welcome the English. In addition to his substantial army, Frontenac occupied a site that was ideally suited by nature for defense. Quebec sat atop a promontory at a point where the Saint Charles River emptied into the Saint Lawrence River. To reach the French fortress at the pinnacle of this rock an attacking army would first have to defeat entrenched defenders along the Saint Charles, then penetrate the fortress itself. The odds against an attacking army were formidably high.

Nevertheless, Phips had some advantages of his own. He had 2,200 men under his command, although some were sailors on board the thirty-four vessels in the fleet, and others were too ill from smallpox to fight. He possessed total naval superiority, as well as enormous firepower. Not only could his men drag field artillery ashore, but his ships were laden with cannon.

Phips's first glimpse of Quebec came on a mellow autumn afternoon. Once he moved into position, Phips first attempted to bluff Frontenac. Through an emissary, he called upon the French governor to lay down his arms without a fight; if he complied, Phips promised, Quebec would be spared. The old man refused to budge. "I have no reply to make to your general other than from the mouths of my cannon and muskets," he haughtily told Phips's messenger. Phips now was left with two options. First, he might initiate a siege. With winter ahead and the soon-to-be frozen Saint Lawrence closed to French relief vessels, a siege might be successful; then again, it might fail, as the New England army was too poorly supplied to sustain itself through a protracted siege. Second, Phips could try an assault, although for that tactic to succeed the English would have to fight their way to the top of the well-defended promontory. Faced with a difficult choice, Phips leaned toward a frontal attack. He planned to land twelve hundred men under Maj. John Walley downriver from Quebec. With assistance from the fleet, Walley's force was to fight its way across the Saint Charles, then, covered by the powerful guns of the English armada, Walley and his men were to storm the fortress high above the Saint Lawrence.

Walley put his men ashore, but that was about as far as he got. Faced with a fierce French resistance, he was unable to cross the Saint Charles River, which lay between his force and Quebec. Phips, meanwhile, had used almost all his ammunition in a futile shelling of Quebec, so that even had Walley broken through there would not have been sufficient powder to provide covering fire for the assault party. After four days enduring cold and hunger, Walley's landing party returned to the fleet (later there were charges that the men had fled ignominiously), ending the first American campaign to take New France.

Whatever Walley's misdeeds, the English failed because they fielded armies of too few men equipped with too few supplies, farmers and laborers who were untrained soldiers, and who were commanded for the most part by men who were inexperienced in waging war. Although the English campaign in 1690 enjoyed considerable popular support, it was implemented by a rapacious elite who anticipated a quick, cheap victory accompanied by the immediate acquisition of great wealth derived first from plunder, then from the riches that would flow from their possession of Canada. Instead the war left the English colonials, and especially Massachusetts, with heavy debts and mounting taxes. Nor did the failure come cheaply in terms of lives. While only thirty men died in the fighting at Quebec, nearly one thousand succumbed to disease or shipwreck in the course of the retreat to Boston.

Following the utter failure of the English campaign in 1690, the French and English in America waged the war as two spent, wary boxers might contest the final rounds of what had begun as a spirited bout: each eschewed a knockout punch in favor of running, jabbing, and occasionally counterpunching. In part, the war slowed to a contest of frontier raids and skirmishes because neither side received much help from home. During a war that rattled on for eight years, London sent over only four Independent Companies—and those for the purpose of reasserting imperial control in New York after the dislocations that followed the Glorious Revolution—and an occasional warship. Frontenac not only received virtually no military aid from the embattled Louis, but the war in Europe and on the high seas frequently made it impossible for France to rescue its colonists from acute food shortages. Within the English provinces support for the war waned following the abysmal failures of 1690. In 1691 the governor of New York proposed the establishment of an intercolonial defense fund, but his idea got nowhere; even New York's assembly refused to appropriate more money for military activities, for many had come to believe that the interests of the province could best be served by remaining neutral in the enduring French-Iroquois feud. Furthermore, the New England colonies were not enthusiastic about helping their neighbor. "I will not send a man or a farthing of money to the assistance of New York and it is a monstrous thought to suppose I should," announced the new governor of Massachusetts, William Phips. When a few colonies met in 1693 to discuss plans for concerted military action, Phips did not attend, and the conference ultimately ended in failure. Finally, colonies whose frontiers did not border on Canada had only a tepid interest in this conflict.

The French and their Indian allies mounted spectacular campaigns after 1690. Early in 1692, Abnaki and Canadian warriors launched raids into Maine and New Hampshire that resulted in the destruction of York and Wells; nearly one-third of the residents of York perished, and large numbers of prisoners were taken from both villages. More blows fell on Maine in 1694 and 1696, punishing assaults that decimated homes and crops and reduced the frontier residents to a frantic state of anxiety. In 1696 the French captured Fort Pemaquid, Massachusetts's stone quadrangle stronghold on the extreme frontier midway between the Kennebec and the Penobscot rivers, a fortress through which the English treated with the Abnakis and enjoyed some success in diverting the French fur trade to Boston. Ultimately, however, these forays were of little consequence, except for the grief and anxiety they caused the inhabitants of the backcountry; certainly, the incursions neither ended English settlement nor added the New England frontier to the dominions of New France.

Of greater consequence were the two French invasions of New York. In 1693, 625 French and Indians invaded Mohawk country. Three villages were obliterated and three hundred captives taken. Most of the prisoners were liberated during the Canadians' return to Montreal by a rescue party sent from Albany. Still, such a blow impacted heavily upon the Mohawks, a sedentary, farming people. The English rushed food to their allies, but the Five Nations' will to fight was weakened, especially when it noticed—and openly questioned—the passivity of so many English colonies. Three years later, Frontenac (now seventy-six years old and so feeble that he could barely walk) personally led an army of two thousand into Onondaga country, near present-day Syracuse. Vast destruction once again resulted. The three French forays into Iroquois territory, beginning with the Denonville incursion nine years before, had seriously weakened the Iroquois, reducing their number of warriors by nearly one-half. The assault by Frontenac was the final straw. Thereafter, the Five Nations came to the bargaining table. At a council held at Montreal in 1701, the Iroquois agreed to remain neutral in the wars of England and France. Simultaneously, however, they reaffirmed their political and economic ties with England.

Frontenac's success, though far from total, was unmatched by the English. While Mohawk country seethed with conflict, Massachusetts sought to pacify the Abnaki in Maine and Acadia. Benjamin Church once again laid aside his plow to lead campaigns into Penobscot territory in 1692 and 1696. Only the first foray achieved anything near success; the Indians in the Kennebec River region deserted the French cause and made peace, although the French regained influence within four years. Church's second expedition, an incursion into Acadia, proved nothing. In the end, Church resorted to bluster, telling the Acadians that if he had to return he would "come with hundreds of savages, and let them loose to kill, scalp, and carry away every French person . . . for they [the French] were the root from which all the branches came that hurt us." Church's ineffectual second campaign only convinced Massachusetts that it lacked the resources to drive the French from Acadia. Soon after Church returned empty-handed to Boston in the autumn of 1696, the Massachusetts assembly informed King William that only a combined Anglo-American naval and land force could seize and secure that forbidding territory. Indeed, Massachusetts knew that the conquest of Quebec, not Acadia, held the key to its security. As Cotton Mather, the Boston pastor, declared: "Canada [is] the Chief Source of New-England's Miseries. . . . Canada must be Reduced."

The war continued on in America until Europe made peace. Louis XIV knew that he had achieved all he could hope for by 1693, but his adversaries were inclined to keep up the fight. The end came, at last, in the fall of 1697 in the Treaty of Ryswick. The European monarchs traded a few possessions, but each belligerent knew that the war had settled nothing; Ryswick brought a temporary end to the conquests of Louis XIV, but the statesman in Europe looked upon that accord more as a truce than as a definitive peace settlement. For America, there was no pretense that this war had been conclusive. The European powers decreed that all territory was to revert to its prewar status

No one living in 1697 could have been so deluded as to have believed that King William's War had ended the struggle for supremacy in North America. After eight years of war, during which perhaps one thousand English, three hundred Canadians, and countless numbers of Indians had perished, nothing had been resolved. But that is not to suggest that this inconclusive war was insignificant. To the frontier residents who lived in gut-wrenching fear of an Indian attack, this conflict must have seemed the same as earlier struggles with the natives. But it differed in significant ways. For the first time the English colonists fought a war in America that was directly linked to a war waged by the parent state thousands of miles away. In addition, this war was the first in which Europeans and Indians fought side by side against other Europeans. What made this war truly significant, however, were the lessons learned from the conflict, although the provincials did not always act on their new knowledge. The futility of disunity among the provinces had been amply demonstrated. By the end of the decade New Englanders generally understood that their aims could be realized only by the removal of the French from Canada. What is more, some colonists understood that their hope of driving the French from Canada could come only with the assistance of the Iroquois, whose friendship they feared had been lost as a result of the provinces' pusillanimous military display. Finally, virtually all articulate colonists now knew that the destruction of New France could be achieved only through the assistance of English imperial forces, naval and military.

Queen Anne's War: Phase One, 1701–1708

The peace brought about by Ryswick was short-lived. War erupted again in 1701, a conflict that each of the major powers appears to have postponed until it recovered from the previous round of bloodletting. The war grew from a squabble over whether a Bourbon, a Hapsburg, or some third party would succeed to the throne in Spain following the death of Charles II in 1700. After much diplomatic maneuvering, Philip of Anjou, the grandson of Louis XIV, assumed the throne. Soon, the resulting Franco-Spanish union became intolerable for several great powers, especially after the Sun King annexed parts of the Spanish Netherlands and assumed control of the Spanish slave trade and much of its commerce in cloth, hardware, leather, and staples. The results were intolerable to the English and Dutch. Together with Hapsburg Austria, they formed the Grand Alliance in 1701 against Bourbon France and Spain. This alignment of power soon resulted in what Europe called the War of the Spanish Succession. In Anglo-America the war came to be known as Queen Anne's War, even though that English monarch did not assume power until six months after the anti-Bourbon alliance had formed.

The conflagration in Europe had an impact in America like that of hurling gasoline on a smoldering fire. The greed, ambition, bigotry, and hatred that had spawned previous conflicts in the New World were reignited. Indeed, during the brief interlude between the wars, aggressive French behavior in America had renewed the same fears that had troubled many English officials for a generation. In the year after Ryswick, a French expedition under Pierre Le Moyne, Sieur d'Iberville, established a settlement at Biloxi on the Gulf of Mexico. The settlement later moved to Mobile Bay, barely fifty miles from Spain's outpost at Pensacola. Meanwhile, Antoine de la Mothe Cadillac, a visionary and disciple of the expansionist Frontenac, erected a French fortification at the strait—the *detroit*—that links Lake Huron and Lake Erie. Fort Detroit not only was meant to assure French hegemony in the western fur trade, but it was to be a crucial lifeline for French missions and posts ranging from the Mississippi Valley to the Gulf. Anglo-American colonists interpreted the French actions differently. To some it appeared that their colonies faced the menace of

Franco-Spanish encirclement; to others, such as the inhabitants of the Carolinas, it seemed certain that their lucrative trade with the western Indians was jeopardized.

Fighting in America erupted first in the South. In 1698 the mere rumor of French designs along the Gulf coast had prompted the Commons House of Assembly in South Carolina to direct the governor to extirpate any French settlement in the region. The reason for South Carolina's alarm is apparent. In addition to the prospect of losing its deerskin trade with the natives of the interior region, South Carolina feared being surrounded by French-allied Creek Indians to the west and by the Spanish, together with their native allies, to the south in Florida. Nothing came of the assembly's resolution, but when word arrived in the fall of 1702 that England was at war with France and Spain, Gov. James Moore hurriedly prepared an expedition against Spanish Florida, a more inviting target than Iberville's distant outpost on Mobile Bay.

Moore's objective was Saint Augustine, the Spanish settlement on Florida's Atlantic coast, a site that European powers had first fought over nearly 150 years earlier. Fruit orchards aside, there was not much in Saint Augustine. An Englishman who visited the town shortly before Governor Moore's arrival described it as small and dilapidated, although well-kept groves of orange, lemon, lime, pomegranate, and peach trees added beauty and color. Moore's expeditionary force—five hundred Carolinians, three hundred Indians, and an armada of fourteen small vessels—arrived in October and began a siege. It was doomed from the start. A siege operation required time and was best conducted by a well-disciplined body of regular troops; in addition, Moore's siege was ineffectual because he failed to bring along explosive artillery shells that might have been lobbed into the enclosed *castillo*. Two balmy autumn months slowly passed. By mid-December the Spaniards not only had not been starved into submission, but Moore's men had grown anxious to return home. Moore persisted, however, until shortly before Christmas. Early one morning, when sentries glimpsed two Spanish men-of-war standing off the coast,

Moore hurriedly abandoned his siege. The warships, dispatched by Havana to save the Florida outpost, had brought to a conclusion an operation that had been flawed from the outset.

Thirteen months later, Moore returned to Florida with an army of fifty Carolinians and one thousand Indians. He struck on the Apalache frontier, a fertile stretch along the Apalache and Ocilla rivers that extended to the northeastern corner of the Gulf of Mexico. His objective was to terrorize the Indians and stanch the flow of goods from this region to both French and Spanish coastal posts. He succeeded on both counts, killing numerous natives, enslaving over three hundred others, and removing four times that number from the region.

As a result of Moore's campaign of terror, South Carolina soon allied with the Creeks and forced the Alabamas to defect from the French. But neither the Spanish nor the French presence ended. What ended was South Carolina's hope of making "her Majesty Absolute and [the] Sovereign Lady of all . . . as far as the Mississippi River." Aside from pacifying a few tribes, the principal result of Moore's expeditions was to invite reprisal. In 1706, thirty months after Moore's foray into Apalache country, a joint Franco-Spanish force attacked Charleston. Poorly led and confronted by a stout, well-prepared defense, the invaders failed miserably, losing more than 250 men and one of their five vessels.

Only a handful of southern colonists were directly touched by the fighting in the early years of Queen Anne's War, but this conflict, as had so often been the case in the past, brutally affected the lives of New England's frontier settlers. A year of peace followed the news that France and England were again at war. But on August 10, 1703, the world of Maine's frontier inhabitants suddenly changed. In the early morning, Indians and a few Frenchmen struck at Wells and Spurwick, and at Cape Porpoise and Perpooduck, tiny English farming and fishing villages. Twenty-two members of one family were killed or captured at one outpost; elsewhere, more than one hundred English residents were slain or carried into captivity on that single day. Isolated raids followed throughout the summer and into the autumn, but in February 1704 the heaviest French and Indian blow in this war fell at Deerfield, the northwesternmost settlement within Massachusetts, a small village of 270 inhabitants.

The first English immigrants to reach this portion of Massachusetts had been exultant at what they observed. First entering the area about the time of the Pequot War, the English had been enthralled by the miles of rich green meadows, the fertile soil, and the tall elm and buttonwood trees. Nearly forty years passed after Boston's founding, however, before Puritan frontiersmen established an outpost, which they had called Pocumtack. The settlement grew rapidly until the frontier was embroiled in King Philip's War. Pocumtack did not survive that conflict. After one-third of the adult male residents had perished in an Indian ambush, the settlers abandoned the village; the Indians quickly razed the empty houses and barns left behind.

Only a few years after Philip's demise a second English settlement was planted on the ashes of Pocumtack. This village was called Deerfield. It was barely a decade old when war once again came to the Connecticut Valley. In 1689, when King William's War broke out, Deerfield was still rebuilding, though it now was a bit larger than Pocumtack had been when it was destroyed in 1675. The residents understood their vulnerability, and they immediately took precautions. The militia drilled regularly, and a town meeting ordered that "a good sufficient fortification" be constructed near the meetinghouse. Every adult male was compelled to work on the construction project. During the next four years Deerfield remained out of harm's way, although other nearby frontier communities suffered attacks. In 1693 and again the following year, however, Indian warriors raided the village. While the town survived, farmers working alone in their fields or tending their livestock in isolated pastures were taken by surprise; some men were killed, some were taken captive. Casualties were light, although, as the residents told the government of Massachusetts, the war resulted in the "great impoverishment" of the villagers' property and emotional well-being.

The news of the Indian attacks along the Maine frontier in 1703 quickly reached Deerfield, spreading the all too familiar fear spawned by uncertainty and danger. A town meeting convened immediately. It ordered the defenses from the previous war to "be righted up," that is, repaired and improved. Work proceeded rapidly, especially after the governor of New York reported that Deerfield had once again been targeted for attack. Throughout the summer and the warm, dry autumn that followed, Deerfield braced for a blow that never came. It also requested and received help from Massachusetts. The province waived the taxes owed that year by the village so that the money could be used for local defense preparations; in addition, Massachusetts garrisoned twenty soldiers in Deerfield.

In October two residents were captured by Indians as they took the town's animals out to pasture, but no further incidents occurred that fall. As in the previous war, blows fell elsewhere, including Haverhill and Exeter, closer to Boston and presumed to be much safer than Deerfield. When the short, cold days of winter came, the residents of Deerfield breathed a sigh of relief. They and many others among the English believed, as one put it, that "the approaching winter gives hope of some respite and allowance of some Ease . . . for it seems reasonable that no attempt can be [made] from Canada now at this season."

They were wrong. Early in February a war party of two to three hundred French and Indians had set out from Canada on the three-hundred-mile trek for Deerfield. The leader was the son of a French soldier who had been a member of the army that had attacked Salmon Falls, New Hampshire, fourteen years before. This army came south on snowshoes, cumbersomely marching across the white landscape, easily traversing frozen rivers and lakes. The attackers arrived in the last pale light of day on February 28. From nearby woods they watched as Deerfield's residents, their day's work completed, converged on the village from their scattered farms. The villagers were acting as Mary Rowlandson and her friends in Lancaster had acted in another war more than a quarter-century before. They entered twelve freshly built, cramped strong houses within a ten- to twelve-foot-high wall at the center of the village; as night descended, a militia watch was posted. One sentry stood guard.

The attackers waited patiently, watching and planning. They noticed that high drifts of snow against the palisade would enable them to surmount that wall easily. In the wee hours of the morning they also noticed that the sentry was no longer to be seen; he probably had fallen asleep. The time to strike had arrived.

The blow against Deerfield fell at about four o'clock in the morning. Moving as silently as a cat stalking its prey, the French and Indians penetrated the palisade. When all were inside the signal was given—a shot was fired. With "horrid shouting and yelling," said one survivor, the attack commenced. The assailants were everywhere, "like a flood upon us," that same inhabitant added. All who resisted—and some who did not—were killed. Forty-four residents died, including nine women and twenty-five children; among them were the John Hawks family, for it was during this raid that this family suffered its tragic fate in the cellar of their burning house. Five of the garrison soldiers also perished. The attackers took 109 prisoners, about 40 percent of Deerfield's population. Seventeen houses, nearly half of those in the town, were destroyed. Miraculously, 133 residents survived. One was the pastor, John Williams, who later described the attack:

They came to my house . . . and by their violent endeavors to break open doors and windows, with axes and hatchets, awakened me out of sleep. . . . I called to awaken two soldiers in the chamber, and returned to my bedside for my arms; the enemy immediately broke into the room, I judge the number to be about twenty, with painted faces and hideous exclamations. . . . Taking down my pistol, I cocked it, and put it to the breast of the first Indian that came up; but my pistol misfired. I was seized by three Indians who disarmed me, and bound me, leaving me standing only in my nightshirt for nearly an hour.

Later, near sunrise, Williams watched as Indians killed two of his children and his two black servants. As Williams was led off to captivity, he saw his house burst into flames.

The attack and pillaging ended an hour or so after sunrise. The captives—frightened, confused, wretchedly cold, and nearly paralyzed by the shocking scenes they had witnessed—were ordered to march north to Canada. Two hours later, around nine o'clock, a fifty-one member rescue party, composed of surviving inhabitants, the remaining garrison soldiers, and a score or so of militiamen summoned from two neighboring villages, sought to liberate the prisoners. Not only did they fail, but the pursuit party stumbled into an ambush; nine of the would-be liberators died.

Lacking numbers, devoid of snowshoes, and somewhat fearful that another rescue attempt might prove fatal to the captives, no further military action was taken to free the captives. Reverend Williams and 108 others started the long trek toward Canada that bitterly cold morning. Only fifty-nine of the captives ever returned home. Twenty-one of the Deerfield prisoners perished before the march to the north was completed; others died during a long captivity. The earliest repatriations did not occur for fifteen months. Williams, whose wife and son were among those who died during the march to Canada, was not released until thirty months had passed. Some faced an even longer captivity. Williams's daughter Eunice, seven years old at the time of the attack, was not offered freedom until the war was almost over, seven years later. By then she had forgotten the English language; after living with the Indians she had rejected her English upbringing. She refused to return to Deerfield, and in 1713, at age sixteen, she married a Caughnawaga Indian. Twenty-eight other captives, almost all young children at the time of the raid, also refused to return to English society.

In Deerfield and along the Maine frontier, Abnaki and Caughnawaga warriors had done most of the fighting, but New France lay behind the attacks. The Abnaki sought to stop the steady encroachment of New England upon their traditional

lands. Philippe de Rigaud, Chevalier de Vaudreuil, the governor-general at Quebec, had his own agenda. Vaudreuil, an
officer in the French army, had been posted in New France in
1687 as commander of an eight-hundred-man force of French
regulars. He had served in Denonville's and Frontenac's frontier campaigns; he became governor of Montreal and, in 1703,
the chief executive of New France. Vaudreuil was friendly with
the Abnaki because he knew that these natives were crucial to
France's retention of Acadia. The Abnaki also were important
trading partners. Vaudreuil additionally hoped that the Abnaki
raids would force New England into a defensive posture, fore-
stalling an English invasion of Canada, such as the one Phips
attempted in 1690.

New England responded in this crisis as it had in King
Philip's War. Frontier inhabitants gathered into garrison
houses within each settlement. Frequently, these arrangements
provided a fair measure of protection. A few weeks after the
Deerfield raid, a French and Indian force struck Lancaster,
Massachusetts—Mary Rowlandson's village, decimated in
1676—but the assault was repulsed with a loss of only three
inhabitants. Massachusetts also rushed conscripted militiamen
to the war zone. These soldiers provided defense and conducted forays against the Indians, missions that were often
carried out with considerable zeal—though with precious little
skill—once Massachusetts agreed to pay forty pounds for each
native scalp. By midyear, Massachusetts had taken still another step. Benjamin Church, now obese and sixty-five-years
old, emerged from retirement to lead still another expedition;
he agreed to take 550 volunteers up the rugged Maine coast
and into Acadia. Enticed as usual by the prospect of booty
(including an offer of one hundred pounds per scalp), these
soldiers chased down a few Indians and looted and burned the
French villages of Minas and Chignecto, both far into the Bay
of Fundy. Strictly interpreted, Church's orders did not au-
thorize an attack on Port Royal, and although he briefly considered such an enterprise, he and his commanders decided
against the assault. Nevertheless, Church's six-week campaign

succeeded in throwing the Abnaki on the defensive. Gradually, the guns fell silent across the northern frontier, perhaps because all parties were sated by a year of killing, perhaps from disillusionment because neither France nor England was willing to make a major commitment in the American theater.

Tranquillity prevailed for approximately twenty months before French and Indian frontier raids and privateering resumed. The renewal of hostilities culminated in a second campaign by Massachusetts to take Port Royal. As with the Phips expedition in 1690, Massachusetts did not act in 1707 simply in response to French and Indian depredations. Powerful economic interests—principally the fishermen, fur traders, and merchants—had long believed that the capture of Port Royal would open to them a cornucopia of financial opportunities. Despite a resolution by the House of Representatives at the outset of the war "for the taking of Port Royal," Gov. Joseph Dudley demurred, evidently unwilling to act without some assistance from London.

Four years later, Dudley changed his mind and authorized an expedition unaccompanied by the British navy. In May 1707, 24 vessels, over 1,100 soldiers (140 of whom were from New Hampshire and Rhode Island), and 250 sailors—a huge force by contemporary standards—sailed from Boston, but their campaign soon proved a fiasco. Despite a manpower superiority of three to one, the New Englanders landed, looked about, concluded that the tumbledown fort at Port Royal was too heavily garrisoned to attack or besiege, and departed seven days later. An outraged public greeted the soldiers on their return to Boston. Women constituted most of the crowd at Scarlet's Wharf as the army disembarked. Waving wooden swords, the women shouted derisively, "Welcome soldiers." Cries of "Fie, for shame," were heard, and others shouted "So-ho, strike you cowards." The disgusted governor sent the fleet back to Acadia in July under new leadership, a triumvirate of officers. But this expedition fared no better than its predecessor. Only the most modest attempt at a siege was made before these soldiers also headed home. These failures once again made apparent the unpredictability of warfare when waged by unpracticed leaders in command of inexperienced troops, and they demonstrated that Massachusetts, with its still-primitive economic infrastructure, insufficient capital, inadequate revenue-raising capabilities, meager naval capacity, and want of surplus manpower, was unable to wage war satisfactorily over a vast territorial expanse. This last muddled initiative had cost Massachusetts twenty-two thousand pounds and seventeen lives, and it had accomplished nothing. By the time the armada returned to Boston at summer's end, men in America had been fighting for five years and had achieved little beyond untold suffering.

One Success, One Failure: The End of Queen Anne's War

Joseph Dudley had never been a popular governor in Massachusetts. He was the son of the second governor of the colony and a graduate of Harvard College, but as a convert to Anglicanism he was looked upon by most residents as an apostate. Moreover, as the one-time president of the council in the hated Dominion of New England—the Lord of Trade's attempt in the 1680s to consolidate several northern provinces—he was thought by some to have been a traitor to his colony. When the king sent him back to Massachusetts in 1702 as the royal governor, the inhabitants were displeased. They thought him a man whose "God is Mammon," as one contemporary remarked, and as a royal servant who "had as many virtues as can coexist with so great a thirst for honor and power," as another judged. His popularity plummeted even further following the military failures of 1707. The armada that retreated from Port Royal was barely glimpsed in the choppy waters of Boston Harbor before an outraged public began to heap abuse upon the chief executive. Dudley and the great merchants whom he represented were unfairly accused of having traded illegally with the French in Canada. They were alleged to have traded arms to the Abnakis, and the charge was aired that they had not desired the defeat of Port Royal, with which they supposedly carried on a lucrative, though traitorous, commerce. The General Court even fined some merchants.

In part, these charges shaped Massachusetts's conduct in this war. Fighting for his political life, Dudley immediately dispatched a memorial to London that pleaded for a British commitment of regulars and frigates to join a provincial force in an invasion of Canada to expel the French from North America. But politics alone can not adequately explain New England's sudden appeal to London. The two failed attempts to take Acadia, as well as Phips's unsuccessful campaign against Quebec in 1690, demonstrated the colonists' need for British military and naval assistance.

Dudley's entreaty was not the only supplication dispatched to the home government. About the same time that his communiqué started across the Atlantic, Samuel Vetch, one of the merchants who had been fined, sailed for London on another vessel. He, too, planned to beseech the imperial government for military aid. Dudley and Vetch acted independently. Nor did either have any connection with New Hampshire's request—also carried to London about this time—that the "nests" of the French in Canada and Nova Scotia "be rooted out" by an Anglo-America expeditionary force. The three appeals reached London simultaneously.

The British government seldom made hasty decisions. Two years passed after Vetch arrived in London before the Board of Trade made a recommendation to the Crown. The wait must have seemed interminable to Vetch, a vigorous, restless, enterprising man of action. The son of an Edinburgh clergyman, Vetch had studied at Utrecht and soldiered for Scotland in the last war against Louis XIV. Afterwards he immigrated to New York, where he quickly married a rather plain-featured young lady from one of the province's most prominent families. Her family provided him with the financial assistance he needed to succeed in business, and soon he and his wife lived in what a contemporary described as a "palatial residence with . . . [a] high roof and two stacks of chimneys." Vetch would today be called a "doer,"—a hustler, an opportunist. Driven by a lust for wealth and power, Vetch's every step appears to have been dictated by a cool calculation of the profit to be gained. Queen Anne's War simply opened new vistas for him. He hoped to profit from supplying armies and trading with Indian allies. If Great Britain succeeded militarily, Vetch hoped to gain a royal office in the British province that supplanted New France.

Vetch formally presented his proposal early that year, although he had previously circulated an earlier draft to well-placed friends in England. He played on several themes: France and its Indian allies had committed repeated atrocities against English frontier inhabitants; the enlargement of New France along the "back side" of Virginia, Pennsylvania, and New York must be stopped or those English colonies would be hemmed in and unable to expand; Acadia must be seized to prevent its use by France as a haven for privateers who preyed on English shipping; with its fertile land and salubrious climate, a Canada controlled by England would attract immigrants from northern Europe, settlers who would add to the empire's wealth and power; the Royal Navy would benefit from the acquisition of Nova Scotia, a region rich in naval stores and blessed with excellent harbors; finally, New England would grow and flourish if Canada was conquered, not an inconsequential matter to London, for those northern provinces provided England and its West Indian colonies with fish, flour, lumber, and above all, a favorable balance of trade.

Officials in London had heard these arguments and more previously. Soon after England gained New York from the Dutch, concerns had been expressed that France coveted London's new possession; for New York, with its close association with the Iroquois Confederacy, could obstruct France's continued expansion in America. Almost every governor of New York after 1670 had issued such a warning, and most had urged England to consider the conquest of Canada. While contemplating Vetch's proposal, the Board of Trade received a letter from New York's governor Edward Cornbury that urged England to send military forces to America for the purpose of "expelling the French out of Canada." Similar entreaties also arrived from two other governors and from the board's agent in Philadelphia, who cautioned that if New France was not immediately destroyed "it will be too late afterwards" to gain such a prize. Vetch and the other proponents of the conquest of Canada promised a substantial commitment of colonial arms in any such endeavor, and most contended that a British victory would be easy. Canada was weakly defended, they insisted. Vetch even asserted that he was "almost morally sure" that the governor of New France could never muster an army above five thousand men, a pittance of what Anglo-America could raise.

These numerous appeals—but especially that of Vetch, who was well-prepared and a man with military experience—carried the day. At the end of 1708 the Board of Trade recommended a "vigorous attempt" by Anglo-American forces to drive France from North America. Two ends might be accomplished "should the French be driven out of the Northern Continent." First, the "ease and security of your subjects" in America would be enhanced, it declared. Second, an "increase of the trade so beneficial to Great Britain" would occur. The Privy Council, acting for the monarch, endorsed the proposal early in 1709. Great Britain would send an army of four thousand men and a fleet of six men-of-war; the northern colonies were to raise twenty-seven hundred men, one-third of whom would be recruited in Massachusetts. Once Canada was taken, Vetch was to be named its first British governor.

Preparation proceeded quickly, if not easily, in the provinces. Connecticut, New Jersey, Pennsylvania, and New York were to raise a force of fifteen hundred men that was to assemble at Albany and invade Canada through the Champlain Valley, the route that Fitz-John Winthrop's army had sought to travel nearly twenty years earlier. Enthusiasm for the Canada project was modest at best in these colonies, but by mid-summer the ranks of the western army swelled above its quota. Meanwhile, recruiting continued for the second army of twelve hundred men. It was to join the British armada that was at that moment presumably en route to America, whereupon the combined Anglo-American units would sail for Quebec. Nearly 10 percent of those raised for this New England army were Indians. They were to act as spies, scouts, and warriors, and they were recruited because—as one colonial leader acknowledged—"We have found none like Indians to hunt down Indians." Employing Indians in the army was attractive for other reasons as well. Not only were they paid less than Anglo-American volunteers, but their absence from civilian pursuits had no impact on the provincial economy. By late August recruiting had been completed for the eastern army. Training began in Boston under the watchful eye of British professionals. The army would move north as soon as the British armada arrived.

London, however, failed to fulfill its part of the bargain, dashing the hopes of the northern provinces that Canada might be taken. In October America learned that Great Britain had cancelled the project, convinced that peace in Europe was at hand. Fifty companies in Boston and the equally large frontier army, which had progressed as far north as Wood Creek, were disbanded.

New England's leaders did not rest, however. Following this bitter disappointment, they simply scaled back their objectives. During the winter of 1709–10, some New England merchants, together with fishermen, loggers, and entrepreneurs who wished to mine Acadian coal now that the supply of wood had dwindled in the vicinity of Boston, took the lead in petitioning London for assistance. Their pleas did not fall on deaf ears. Great Britain's imperial leaders sent over a small armada of six warships.

With some difficulty New England enlisted an army of nearly thirty-five hundred men. Both Massachusetts and Connecticut were compelled to raise the pay of its soldiers above that of the previous year; both now offered their recruits a remuneration roughly equivalent to the annual income of a common laborer, as well as a good coat and a musket. Connecticut even waived the payment of taxes for those who enlisted. Nevertheless, both failed to meet the quotas set for them in London, and each resorted to conscription to fill out their armies.

In September the Anglo-American armada set sail for Port Royal, defended by barely three hundred French soldiers and militiamen. What followed was the only real success for the English in Queen Anne's War. Inadequately fortified and meagerly defended, Port Royal fell quickly to the English force that stood at its gates. On October 2, 1710, Annapolis Royal, as the English renamed it, and for all practical purposes all of Nova Scotia—what the French had called Acadia—became part of the British empire.

News of the easy conquest inspired officials in London to resurrect plans to invade Canada. By February 1711 planning was well under way. Officials selected Rear Adm. Sir Hovenden Walker to command the expedition. He was not a good choice. A twenty-year veteran, Walker was a man with an unexceptional record, an officer devoid of dash or daring. Moreover, Walker brought to this assignment an all-consuming fear of the Canadian winter. He expressed nightmarish concerns over its "adamantine frosts, and . . . high mountains of snow," of spending a winter in this "barren and uncultivated region," of commanding "great numbers of brave men famishing with hunger and drawing lots [to determine] who should die first to feed the rest." In April this diffident admiral sailed for America from Plymouth, England. He commanded a fleet of sixty-four sailing ships, including eleven men-of-war, and an army of forty-three hundred under Brig. Gen. John Hill. His army included seven veteran regiments, including the very best of the Duke of Marlborough's Flanders army, reassigned to America.

As Walker's armada crossed the Atlantic, the northern provinces once again struggled to field large armies. A western force of twenty-three hundred raised in Connecticut, New York, and New Jersey formed at Albany. Commanded by Col. Francis Nicholson, once governor of Virginia and later of

Maryland, this army was to advance on Canada through the Champlain Valley. Meanwhile Rhode Island, New Hampshire, and Massachusetts recruited thirteen hundred men for an eastern army that would be linked to Walker's armada. Massachusetts exceeded its quota; one-fifth of its able-bodied men were under arms. The twin forces would envelop New France in a pincer movement, Nicholson driving on Montreal from the south, Admiral Walker on Quebec from the east. Since Quebec was defended by only twenty-three hundred men, the prospects for British success appeared to be good.

But ominous problems faced the expedition. Walker's fleet arrived in Boston on June 25, then lay at anchor in Boston Harbor for more than a month while the admiral floundered in a sea of difficulties. With his men encamped on barren, cheerless Noodles Island in Boston Bay, Walker first sought to fill his pantry in preparation for a lengthy operation, one that might extend through the coming winter. Nearly a month elapsed before he could buy the first loaf of bread from Massachusetts. The provincials refused to sell until a favorable rate of exchange between English and colonial currency had been established. Walker was also detained by his search for pilots who were familiar with navigation on the treacherous Saint Lawrence River and by the necessity to recruit additional seamen, a chore brought on because of the alarmingly high rate of desertion among his sailors. This "Canada expedition proceeding very heavily," Walker sighed after fifteen days in Boston; four weeks later he noted in his journal: "I went ashore to finish everything at Boston, with respect to the victualling and stores." A week later, on July 30, he sailed.

Because of the maddening obstacles the Anglo-American force faced in Boston, they did not enter the Saint Lawrence until mid-August, which was late in the season for the commencement of a siege. Quebec's usually bitter winter was barely two months away. In addition, Walker's cupboard was not as well stocked as he would have liked. He sailed with only three months' supply of bread, pork, beef, and cheese, the most he could obtain from the merchants of Boston. Yet

Walker's force totaled seventy-five hundred soldiers and marines, vastly more men than his adversary at Quebec commanded. A protracted siege might be unnecessary.

Disaster struck on the twentieth day after the fleet began its ascent of the Saint Lawrence. Proceeding at night up the fog-bound river, eight transports and two supply ships ran aground on the rocky northern shore at Île aux Oeufs, where the Saint Lawrence is nearly seventy miles wide. Approximately nine hundred persons—about 10 percent of those on the expedition—perished.

This tragedy was the final straw for Walker. Atop his increasing doubts about the likelihood of success, Walker now was convinced that his pilots could not even deliver him safely to Quebec, still 160 miles away. He summoned a council of war on August 25, at which his officers unanimously voted to abandon the operation. Word of the decision reached Colonel Nicholson as he arrived at Lake George after several days of difficult marching from Albany.

Bitterness swept over the North at word of Walker's retreat. Instead of a victory that would have resulted in an "unspeakable advantage unto us," as the New Hampshire assembly put it, nothing had been gained. The colonists' anger only increased when Walker and other British officials later attempted to shift the blame for the failure to the provincials. The admiral carped at Massachusetts's reluctance to raise a larger army and its unwillingness to supply his fleet. Walker's charges were especially galling to a Massachusetts citizenry that in five separate years—1704, 1707, 1709, 1710, and again in 1711—had expended vast sums to seize Nova Scotia or Canada. Nor did it set well in Boston when some Tory ministers in London alleged that some American merchants had deliberately sabotaged the expedition to prevent the destruction of their profitable trade with the French in Canada.

Walker had barely commenced his return voyage to England before word arrived in America that peace talks between Great Britain, France, and Spain had begun in Holland. As is their custom, the diplomats proceeded languorously. The battlefields fell silent, and the only reminder that the nations remained at war came in isolated encounters on the high seas. Finally, in April 1713, the Peace of Utrecht was signed.

In reality, the accord consisted of a series of treaties designed to reaffirm the European balance of power. Great Britain received Gibraltar, Minorca, and the West Indian island of Saint Kitts, as well as Hudson Bay, Newfoundland, and Nova Scotia from France. The French recognized British suzerainty over the Iroquois Confederacy. From Spain, which had floundered throughout this war, Britain secured the *asiento,* a monopoly on the annual importation of forty-eight hundred slaves into Spanish America. The failure of Walker's expedition, however, left Canada in French hands, while Governor Moore's inability eleven years earlier to take Florida or Louisiana meant that those possessions remained under the Spanish and French flags.

For the inhabitants of British America, Utrecht ended hostilities that had continued sporadically since Frontenac's savage blow against Schenectady twenty-three years earlier. Yet few real benefits for the provinces were discernible. The greatest advantages, presumably, were derived by merchants and the fishing industry as a result of Britain's seizure of Newfoundland and Nova Scotia; these acquisitions, it was hoped, would also pacify the northern frontier and permit the rapid expansion of New England settlements deeper into the hinterland. Otherwise, Anglo-America, with a population roughly fifteen times the size of New France, had not accomplished much.

Why had the English colonies not been more successful? Disunity among the colonies was a formidable obstacle to military success, as was Britain's habitual lack of interest in the American theater, with the exception of the last stages of Queen Anne's War. Moreover, success was impeded by the colonists' habit of raising large armies composed of inexperienced men commanded by untested leaders, a virtually unavoidable practice, for—as Samuel Vetch told the authorities in London—the provincial soldiers would serve only under provincial officers. Still another difficulty arose because these wars were fought over a vast geographic expanse and on a continent that remained largely a primeval wilderness. To surmount the logistical and transportation problems that resulted, a strong naval arm was essential, an appendage that simply did not exist within the provinces before 1713. Finally, whatever the point of view of their leaders, most inhabitants of Anglo-America looked upon these wars as a defensive response to the frontier raids of the French and Indians. Viewed from that standpoint, New England did not fare too badly, for the destitution and despair wrought by their adversaries between the attack on Salmon Falls in 1690 and Utrecht in 1713 paled by comparison to the suffering inflicted during King Philip's War a generation earlier.

The wars had a substantive impact on some colonies, especially those in New England. More than 10 percent of New Hampshire's population had perished or been captured during King William's War; within that province, population growth slowed, and the expansion of settlements onto new frontiers stopped altogether for a full generation. One can only guess at the emotional burdens borne by those living on the exposed frontier during these conflicts, for in addition to the danger, many appear to have struggled with the conception that God had provoked these terrible wars as a "scourge for the punishment of our sins." Nor were the frontier regions the only victims. By 1705 French privateers had captured one hundredforty naval craft off the New England coast. Five years later nearly four hundred Anglo-American vessels were seized in these waters. By the end of Queen Anne's War, the coastal trade in New England had ceased to exist.

Massachusetts especially reeled under the impact of these wars. Nearly one in four of those who soldiered for the province between 1690 and 1713 died in service. In 1712, moreover, the General Court informed Queen Anne of the province's heavy debt, a legacy of the war named in her honor. Four-fifths of the Massachusetts budget in 1704–5 went to military expenditures. In 1709 Massachusetts spent more than thirty thousand pounds, the equivalent of its customary peace-time budget, on the Canada enterprise that collapsed when London failed to send the promised ships and men. The public debt in Massachusetts had risen to £120,000 even before Walker sailed for Quebec, compelling it to raise taxes to unprecedented levels. Local taxes skyrocketed as well. In some counties taxes increased by 20 percent or more after 1706; in some towns assessments rose by as much as one-third between 1707 and 1712. A Boston homeowner paid 42 percent more taxes in 1713 than in 1700, and he paid those duties in the midst of a galloping inflation brought about by the war. Virtually everyone in Boston suffered at times from food shortages that resulted from victualing large armies, and many faced far worse; before the end of King Williams's War, Cotton Mather, Boston's most esteemed clergyman, noted that the conflict had greatly increased the number of beggars within the city.

Other changes that were due in part to the wars occurred throughout New England, but especially in Massachusetts. As the realization dawned that their frontiers could best be secured by destroying the French presence to the north, provinces such as Massachusetts and Connecticut, traditionally aloof from London since the Puritan migration early in the seventeenth century, sought military assistance from the parent state. As a result, New England colonies became more fully integrated within Britain's empire. These provinces had not actively sought closer ties to England; while they wanted aid from London, they sought it on their terms. Only gradually, after 1707, did they realize that subtly, steadily, they had been dragged into closer and more costly cooperation with the parent state. Only by degrees did New England understand that it had been drawn within the Crown's American patronage network and that, as Samuel Sewall lamented during Queen Anne's War, "a considerable part of the executive authority is now gone out of the hands of New England men." The royal governors of Massachusetts now possessed greater patronage powers and exercised more authority over fiscal matters than ever before; Governor Dudley, for instance, expanded his jurisdiction by regularly intruding in militia appointments and even by seeking to negotiate with the French in Canada. In addition, King William's War and Queen Anne's War were partially responsible for an increased centralization of authority within the provinces and a burgeoning of executive power. By 1713 Massachusetts residents not only paid more taxes to their provincial government than to their towns, but they found that the decisions made by their colony's government increasingly affected their lives. Massachusetts substituted volunteer regiments for its militia units, built permanent garrison houses in frontier towns, and even refused to permit some frontier inhabitants to leave their homes during time of war.

But in the long run, the most dramatic result of this epoch of warfare was the legacy of bitterness that resulted from Walker's failed campaign to wrest Canada from France. The resentment within England toward refractory New England only added to the lingering doubts about the loyalty of the Puritan colonies. New England was just as unhappy with London. Britain appeared to be indifferent to the military woes of the provinces. If there had been no more intercolonial wars, or if the tension that had sprung up by 1713 had not been reinforced by subsequent occurrences, what happened in King William's War and in Queen Anne's War would have been of little significance to America's eventual relationship with the parent state. But future wars kept alive the distrust and produced fresh recriminations.

CHAPTER THREE

The Struggle for America Resumes

Bloody Frontiers: New England

The Peace of Utrecht and a series of lesser treaties brought peace to Europe for a generation, but for the inhabitants of the beleaguered American frontier, bloody warfare remained a way of life. Soon after the signing of the peace accord in a faraway European village, the New England frontier once again was ablaze, and in 1722 the governor of Massachusetts issued a proclamation that was tantamount to a declaration of war against the Eastern Indians, chiefly the Abnakis.

The cause of the war was clear. Peace in 1713 obliterated the constraints on expansion that had existed as long as the frontier was a killing ground. Immediately after Utrecht settlers from eastern Massachusetts and southern New Hampshire, often the younger sons of large farm families and their new wives, began to push up the Connecticut Valley, out toward the Berkshires in western Massachusetts, and beyond the Kennebec River in Maine, a region claimed by the Massachusetts Bay colony. In Maine, on lands that Massachusetts claimed to have purchased seventy years earlier, the homesteaders sometimes reoccupied villages that had been abandoned during Queen Anne's War; at other times the settlers founded new settlements. Massachusetts granted several six-mile-square townships to proprietors, and soon a half-dozen or so of these New England pioneer villages were being laid out in Maine. The land that the English husbandmen surveyed and cleared was the region that the Indians believed had been left in their possession in 1713. As their hunting grounds and fishing retreats vanished, the embittered natives struck back against these intrusive yeomen. Quebec, which claimed modern New Brunswick and northern Maine, and which was anxious to forestall English expansion until it could populate the area, encouraged these attacks. Vandalism occurred first. Violent incidents soon followed, prompting Massachusetts governor Samuel Shute to declare war on the native inhabitants of Maine in July 1722. "[N]otwithstanding the kind and good Treatment they have received from the Government," Shute's proclamation of war began, the Indians had acted with the "utmost Injustice and Treachery to plunder, despoil, . . . assault, take, burn, and destroy" the property and lives of the English residents in that sector; consequently, he went on, "I do . . . hereby declare and proclaim the said Eastern Indians, with their confederates, to be Robbers, Traitors, and Enemies" of Massachusetts.

By 1723, almost ten years to the day since the news of Utrecht reached Boston, the people of Massachusetts once again had an army in the field. Hundreds of troops were sent into northern and eastern Maine, and a party of sixty was dispatched to Cape Sable in southern Nova Scotia—now a separate English colony—to regain fishing schooners seized by the Micmac Indians. The hostilities that ensued became known as Dummer's War, after William Dummer, who succeeded Shute as the governor of Massachusetts shortly after the war commenced.

The Indians struck at the isolated townships. (Later, some in Massachusetts whined that their government had created so many new settlements that none could be adequately populated.) The Indians shot down farmers as they worked their fields or drove their cattle to pasture; they also ambushed fishermen as they heaved their vessels ashore and seized solitary settlers. Massachusetts fought back. It waged a fierce war of attrition, winning the contest as it had triumphed in previous conflicts with the Indians. As in the Pequot War and King Philip's War, the turning point in these hostilities occurred when the provincials eradicated a large Indian village. In August 1724, a force under Capt. Johnson Harmon obliterated Norridgewock on the Kennebec. The attackers arrived in seventeen whale boats and launched a surprise attack against their unsuspecting foe. Numerous residents were killed, and the town was burned. The soldiers were paid one hundred pounds for each Indian scalp they carried back to Boston.

The war continued for three more years but not with the same intensity. Most of the tribes of Eastern Indians agreed to peace within fifteen months of the destruction of Norridgewock, confessing in the peace treaty their sensibility to the "Miseries and Troubles they have involved themselves in." In addition, the Indians surrendered eastern Maine to Massachusetts.

Bloody Frontiers: The South

Massachusetts was not alone in fighting frontier battles in this period. The southern back country erupted violently at the very end of Queen Anne's War. With the exception of Governor Moore's two campaigns into Spanish Florida, the South had largely been spared the bloodshed and despair that had tormented two generations of New England frontiersmen. Below the Chesapeake, in the Carolinas, this blessing occurred principally because the colonies remained sparsely settled. Thirty years after its establishment, South Carolina contained only five thousand settlers, most of whom lived within a few miles of Charles Town (later named Charleston); in 1700, North Carolina's population probably did not exceed four thousand and was confined to the region near the coast between Albermarle Sound and the Pamlico River. All was not harmonious in the Carolinas in the first half-century of their existence, but in contrast to Virginia's turbulent early years, the settlers in North and South Carolina enjoyed a long period of peace marked by a commodious trade with the natives. In North Carolina, however, the tranquility ended abruptly in 1711, two years before the Peace of Utrecht.

The cause of conflict in that colony is not difficult to discover. North Carolina expanded steadily after 1701. The town of Bath, situated up the Pamlico River, was founded in 1706. Soon thereafter settlers occupied lands along the Roanoke, Tar, and Neuse rivers as well, the domain of the Tuscarora Indians, kinsmen of the Iroquois. From the outset, the native peoples had been dismayed by the settlers' sharp trading practices and their unwitting spread of disease, prompting them to characterize the English as a "very wicked people." But it was the colonists' steady encroachment upon native lands that drove the Indians to the warpath. The final blow was the establishment of New Bern by four hundred Swiss and German immigrants. One year after the settlement was founded, in the cool, serene dawn of September 22, 1711, the Indians attacked isolated farms along the Neuse and Pamlico rivers, inaugurating what became known as the Tuscarora War.

About 150 settlers perished and up to 30 were taken captive in the first hours of the war. Atrocities all too familiar in frontier warfare were repeated. "Women were laid on their house-floors and great stakes run up through their bodies. Others big with child, the infants were ripped out hung upon trees," according to one eyewitness. In retaliation, inhabitants of New Bern seized a chief of the Bay River Indians and roasted him alive.

As a result of North Carolina's ineffectual response to the uprising, the Indians widened their assaults. By year's end, farms all along the frontier lay in ruins, and Bath County had been virtually abandoned. The colony was saved, however, by assistance from its neighbors. South Carolina answered the entreaties of North Carolina by raising a force of thirty-three white men and five hundred Indians, principally Yamassees. Early in 1712, in the space of a few days, the South Carolinians destroyed a Tuscarora fort and several towns, aided somewhat by Virginia militia units, dispatched to the border with North Carolina as a means of discouraging tributary tribes from joining the Tuscaroras. This success only stopped the Indians temporarily. The war resumed in the summer. Once again the assistance of the neighboring colonies proved crucial. Virginia supplied arms and other supplies while South Carolina rushed forward a force of thirty-three whites and nearly one thousand Indians under the son of former governor Moore. By the spring of 1713, the Tuscarora had suffered epochal destruction. In an eighteen-month war, over one thousand Indians had been killed or wounded, nearly four hundred had been sold into slavery. Native lands and towns had been razed. Some who survived fled to Iroquois settlements in New York, while others escaped into the Virginia mountains north of the Roanoke River, where, according to an eyewitness, they lived "like wild beasts on what the woods afforded."

Only two years later, on Good Friday in April 1715, South Carolina's frontier burst into flames when the Yamassees attacked white traders. In the seventeenth century and earlier, the Yamassee had lived along the coast of Georgia and in northern Florida; their dissatisfaction with the Spanish caused them to move north into the shadow of Charles Town, after that English settlement was founded in 1670. For a generation, relations were good between the natives and the English, for South Carolina saw the Yamassees as a buffer against Spanish Florida. Early in the eighteenth century, however, white settlers pushed into the region that the province had set aside for the natives. Tensions built; friction was exacerbated by the irresponsible behavior of the Carolina traders. Indians were cheated, illegally enslaved, plundered, beaten, and raped by these bully-boy merchants. Even the Carolinians spoke of these traders as being "infamous for their wicked and evil actions."

Contemporaries in South Carolina believed that still another factor caused the sudden attack in 1715. They were certain that the Spanish and French had incited the Yamassees. Each imperial power had good reason to be overjoyed by news of any difficulty that befell South Carolina. With the memory of Governor Moore's investment of Saint Augustine fresh on its mind, Spain looked upon South Carolina as a feared and troublesome rival; France, on the other hand, was anxious to prevent the establishment of English trade with the interior Indians, especially the Choctaws, who lived between the Tombigbee and Pearl rivers in present-day Alabama and Mississippi. While the suspicions of the contemporaries appear plausible, however, there is little evidence to substantiate the charge of French or Spanish complicity. In all likelihood the Yamassees, frustrated and embittered by the English practices, acted on their own, although they may have secured a prior commitment of aid from the Catawbas, a Siouan people who lived in northern South Carolina, and the Creeks, a large nation whose suzerainty extended over a vast stretch of present-day Georgia and Alabama below the Appalachians.

As with the blow inflicted by Opechancanough in 1622, the strike by the Yamassees in 1715 inaugurated an extended war. The Indians, as in almost every previous Anglo-Indian struggle, initially scored impressive gains. With the Catawbas and Creeks in the war by the arrival of the first warm days of spring, the conflagration spread rapidly across the vast frontier. Port Royal was decimated. At Pocotaligo Town only two or three inhabitants escaped. Small backcountry farms and large plantations alike were burned, and English trading posts deep in the interior—including one as far west as modern-day Macon, Georgia—were wasted. In the fall Indian warriors had struck within twelve miles of Charles Town; by the end of the year the English had abandoned 20 percent of the territory they had occupied in April.

South Carolina's response was similar to that of other English colonies who struggled with the natives. It was a "War with the Wolfs and Bears," the chief justice of the colony said at the outset, suggesting that English attitudes toward the native peoples and their way of fighting had not changed substantively during the past century. South Carolina immediately summoned its militia, although in this thinly populated colony the use of militiamen on a distant frontier would leave no one at home to defend property and loved ones. As in New England, therefore, the South Carolina militia units served largely in a defensive manner. The province augmented this force with a standing army of twelve hundred, nearly one-half of whom were African-Americans, conscripted and armed by a desperate, frightened white population. South Carolina dispatched urgent appeals for help. England sent arms and ammunition. North Carolina marched troops to South Carolina. Massachusetts shipped some surplus weaponry from their abortive invasion of Canada a few years before. Virginia sent a few troops and some arms and powder, but if South Carolina's later charges are to be believed, the Old Dominion's traders also vended weapons to the Indians; some in Carolina eventually concluded that Virginia was more interested in cultivating commercial relations with the western Indians than with assuring the survival of their fellow Englishmen. South Carolina approached Maryland, New York, and Pennsylvania without success.

South Carolina quickly knocked the Catawbas out of the war by defeating them in an engagement north of Charlestown in June, a battle waged by the Goose Creek militia. During the winter of 1715–16, South Carolina persuaded the Cherokees, inhabitants of present-day Tennessee, to enter the war against their traditional rivals, the Creeks, their neighbors to the south. The Cherokee decision came after a South Carolina force of three hundred men, many of whom were experienced Indian fighters, marched into the very heart of Cherokee country. The show of force awed the Cherokees and led them to conclude that South Carolina would defeat the Yamassees.

That diplomatic victory isolated the Yamassee and brought an end to the worst of the crisis.

The war did not conclude with a formal peace accord. For a time it seemed as though hostilities would never cease. After 1716 the Yamassees fled to Florida, where they passed under Spanish hegemony. Eviscerated to the point that their domain now consisted of only three villages near Saint Augustine, the Yamassees nevertheless still possessed sufficient power to cause problems. Together with the Lower Creeks, and often assisted by runaway slaves who had sought refuge in Florida, the Yamassees launched periodic forays over a period of several years into the South Carolina backcountry, liberating slaves and plundering isolated farms.

After 1716 South Carolina's survival was no longer imperiled, but its victory in the Yamassee War came at a heavy cost. Much of its farmland had been abandoned, some of it not to be resettled for a generation. Indebtedness and taxes rose. The most arresting result of the war, however, was the loss of life. About four hundred South Carolinians perished in the twelve months after the Yamassees first struck, proportionately a larger death rate than that inflicted on Massachusetts in King Philip's War.

For a time South Carolina appeared doomed, and it might have been destroyed had the Cherokees allied with other Indian belligerents. South Carolina survived; but the province's recent difficulties, as well as both the numerous appeals for assistance from American officials and Britain's nearly incessant warfare of the past quarter-century, provoked the Board of Trade in London to formally assess what imperial officials had only informally considered for a generation or more: how to safeguard and augment Great Britain's holdings in North America. Apprehensive that France had plotted the encirclement of its colonies, and fearing that a French-incited Indian uprising in the South might result in the extirpation of the Carolinas, the board proposed sweeping changes in the fall of 1721. Two goals were at the heart of its plan. It sought to build up British rule "at the two Heads of their Colonies, North and

South." New York and Nova Scotia were to be strengthened against the French in the North, and the southern borderlands were to be protected against France's design to erect "a Universal Empire in America." Nor was the West forgotten. The board envisioned the day when British colonists would cross the Appalachian Mountains and settle the sprawling prairies as far west as the Mississippi River. To achieve these ends, the board proposed constructing a series of frontier posts; transferring eight regiments of British regulars—about sixty-five hundred men—to garrison these installations; creating a captaincy-general, a royal official posted in America with authority to coordinate the various British military commands in the colonies; and creating a new barrier colony below South Carolina.

Little came of the board's ambitious scheme. The economic depression that wracked England in the 1720s and the general European peace that followed Utrecht eroded support for the board's recommendations. Only the construction of a fort at Oswego emerged from the plan for strengthening British defenses in New York and Nova Scotia, and that installation was built in 1721 by New York on its own initiative. The economically valuable South was another matter, however. Here Great Britain made a more concerted attempt to implement the board's designs, although in the end only a fraction of the board's audacious scheme was realized. In 1721 the Crown dispatched a company of royal infantry to South Carolina and ordered the construction of a British fort—it would be called Fort King George—at the mouth of the Altamaha River near present-day Darien, Georgia. Erected in an area that was claimed by both Spain and Great Britain—Spain insisted that London had recognized the mouth of the Altamaha as Spanish in the Treaty of Madrid of 1670—Fort King George was meant to be a barrier against French penetration of the region as well as a means of protecting South Carolina's southern frontier from attacks by the Yamassee Indians and the Spanish.

Fort King George failed to pacify South Carolina's frontier. Within five years of its construction repeated Yamassee raids forced the province to mobilize for war once again. The British Independent Company of Foot, the royal infantry company that had garrisoned Fort King George, was withdrawn to Beaufort Fort, about forty miles closer to Charlestown. The frontier militia was called out repeatedly, cavalry units patrolled the no-man's-land between the Edisto River and the Savannah River, and parties of scouts warily watched the region below Beaufort.

In 1728, its defensive network in place, South Carolina took the offensive. A large raiding party under Col. John Palmer, an experienced militia officer, crossed into Florida and destroyed several Yamassee towns in the vicinity of Saint Augustine. The frontier warfare abated for a few years thereafter. Indeed, in 1730 the Board of Trade ordered the establishment of eleven townships on South Carolina's frontier, including a settlement on the Edisto, three on the Savannah River, and two on the Altamaha; these towns were to be settled by English, Scotch-Irish, or German Protestant families induced to risk the hazards of frontier life by handsome proffers of free land and other subsidies.

These frontier townships never materialized, but in a curious twist of fate other settlements soon appeared in their place in a new colony—Georgia. The founding of Georgia grew from a campaign launched in England in 1729 to reform the treatment of debtors, unfortunates who in that age ordinarily were sentenced to jail for having fallen into indebtedness. James Oglethorpe, a former army officer and a member of the House of Commons, was the primary figure in the reform movement. Initially, Oglethorpe simply sought to bring an end to imprisonment for debt; America held little interest for him. Gradually, however, he came to believe that America held the key for improving the blighted lives of debtors; the secret to success, he concluded, was to combine his interest in debtors with the interest of the empire builders who wished to settle the region on and below the Savannah River. Thus, Oglethorpe and his philanthropic-minded associates applied for a charter to found a colony in this region. The Privy Council issued the charter in 1732. Georgia, therefore, grew out of a fusion of disparate movements. Some proponents of Georgia were inspired by altruism, the desire to create a refuge for debtors who otherwise would face incarceration in one of England's loathsome jails; others, however, supported Georgia's creation more because of the cold, hard interests of the imperial state.

The creation of Georgia was yet another indication of London's readiness to battle France and Spain for hegemony in the region to the south and west of South Carolina. France and Spain immediately divined Great Britain's intention. They understood that Georgia's creation posed an immediate threat to their commerce with the Indians. More important, both understood that in the long run the existence of Georgia threatened their survival in this part of North America.

The War of Jenkins' Ear

War between Great Britain and Spain broke out in 1719 and again in 1727, but in both instances the conflicts remained within Europe and ended before the other major powers on the continent or the belligerents' colonies in America entered the frays. That was not the case after 1739, however, when Britain and Spain once again went to war.

The Anglo-Spanish War grew out of incidents on the Spanish Main, where about 1730 the Spanish had begun to stop and search British ships that it suspected of illegal trade with its colonies. Outraged English merchants denounced Spain's conduct and orchestrated a campaign in the press for the "freedom of the seas." Opposition within the British Parliament seized the issue and rallied the nation to a bellicose frenzy that culminated in England's declaration of war. Many in England called the conflict the War of Jenkins' Ear because one of the incidents that helped fuel the war hysteria occurred when Capt. Robert Jenkins, a smuggler, displayed his severed ear to a parliamentary committee, explaining that he had suffered the mutilation at the hands of seamen on Spanish patrol vessels, the *guarda-costas,* in the Caribbean.

Once Britain went to war, its aims were clear. It sought to decimate Spain's shipping, paralyze its trade, and seize territory within the Spanish empire, including the disputed land below South Carolina. As result, the southern backcountry—and especially tiny Georgia—experienced the full fury of this war.

Georgia had been planned with martial considerations in mind. From the outset it was viewed as a military buffer state. Forts were quickly established at strategic locations, and sites for settlement were judiciously selected with an eye on security. In addition, the earliest residents were looked upon as citizen-soldiers, a system was devised to ensure that all land grants be contiguous to make defense easier, and the trustees prohibited slavery, lest the bondsmen aid the colony's enemies. Even the principal leader in early Georgia, Colonel Oglethorpe, was an adventurer who, like Capt. John Smith, had fought the Turks in eastern Europe. Single and pressing middle age, Oglethorpe saw in fledgling Georgia an opportunity—likely his last—to fulfill his yearning both for beneficence and action.

Oglethorpe soon had all the excitement that he could ever desire. For several generations, Spain had been alarmed by Britain's expansion below the Chesapeake. It no longer dreamed of settling the region itself, but it was apprehensive for the safety of Florida, a crucial jewel in its imperial crown. Florida was of vital importance for the protection of Spanish shipping in the Gulf of Mexico and the Bahama Channel; it additionally served as a buffer between Anglo-America and Spanish Cuba. The establishment of Georgia outraged the Spanish. The province's rapid growth exacerbated Spain's alarm. Within four years of Georgia's founding large numbers of English, Salzburg Lutheran, and Highland Scot immigrants had pushed the limits of the new colony from a fortified frontier post on the Saint Johns River about twenty miles north of Saint Augustine in Spanish Florida to present-day Augusta, well north of Savannah. Georgia's rapid push to the periphery of Spain's settlement at Saint Augustine could only be interpreted in Madrid as a mortal threat to the safety of Florida. When every attempt to negotiate a boundary between the two provinces failed, both sides prepared for war. Spain sent supplies from Havana to assist in an invasion of Georgia. In 1738, London dispatched to Georgia a regiment of seven hundred men, about one-quarter of whom were seasoned soldiers reassigned from Gibraltar; Oglethorpe was named commander of this British force. Three weeks after England had declared war on Spain—and several months before the news of war crossed the Atlantic—the first bloodshed in the mainland colonies occurred when the Yamassees ("Spanish Indians," groused Oglethorpe) killed and decapitated two Scotsmen garrisoned at Georgia's post on Amelia Island.

Friendly Yamacraws immediately struck a retaliatory blow. Oglethorpe soon followed suit. On New Year's Day, 1740, having pledged to London that his province would "die hard and will not lose one inch of ground without fighting," Oglethorpe moved out from Saint Simons Island with a force of two hundred men. The next day he reached the Saint Johns River and captured two Spanish forts about twenty miles behind Saint Augustine. Spain's link to the (Apalache) area to the west was severed. While the governor of Florida cried to Havana that the losses constituted "a foul stain on [our] catholic arms," Oglethorpe hurried to Charlestown to seek South Carolina's assistance for an attack on Saint Augustine.

Cognizant of the problems that Moore had encountered at Saint Augustine nearly forty years before, Oglethorpe concluded that he required about four thousand men to take the Spanish garrison. He asked South Carolina to contribute nearly one-half the manpower. Georgia's neighbor did not respond quickly. The operation likely would cost South Carolina up to one hundred thousand pounds; moreover, as South Carolina had only recently experienced a frightening slave insurrection—the Stono Rebellion, in which scores had died—many were reluctant to part with soldiers who might soon be required again at home. Finally, in the spring of 1740, several months after Oglethorpe made his appeal, South Carolina voted to contribute a regiment of 490 men, augmented by about 400 pioneers, or laborers. Altogether, Oglethorpe would have about 1,200 men under his command.

But on the same day the legislators in Charles Town acted, six naval vessels arrived at Saint Augustine from Cuba. This small flotilla frustrated Oglethorp's plans for taking the Spanish town by a direct assault; instead, he was compelled to institute a siege operation, even though he probably knew from the outset that it could not succeed. His own naval arm—a Royal Navy squadron of four twenty-gun ships—was scheduled to depart within a few days. The futility of his campaign soon became apparent. He could not move close enough to launch a truly effective bombardment; and disease broke out among his men after weeks of exposure to Florida's relentless summer sun, humidity, rain, insects, and vermin. On the final day of June, after fruitlessly cannonading the Spanish fort for nearly three weeks, Oglethorpe, ill himself, complained to the governor of South Carolina about his lack of troops. His missive was tantamount to an admission that the operation had failed and that he sought to fix the blame elsewhere.

Oglethorpe's complaint had merit, however. Had South Carolina provided more troops and had the army been raised promptly so that it could have reached Florida before the arrival both of the Florida summer and of the Spanish squadron, Saint Augustine surely would have fallen. But South Carolina alone was not to blame. A more experienced and imaginative leader might have overcome the considerable obstacles that confronted the British. Instead, Oglethorpe demonstrated his unfamiliarity with command, often appearing to be irresolute or confused. His limitations were exacerbated by the poor showing of the British fleet, which failed to institute an ironclad blockade; during the siege, three small vessels laden with stores from Havana reached Saint Augustine and relieved the beleaguered Spanish inhabitants. The British troops started home on July 4, taking a last look at the Spanish flag that still fluttered over Florida as they marched away.

Word of Saint Augustine's escape touched off jubilant demonstrations in Spain and prompted Philip V to order an invasion of Georgia and South Carolina. Madrid never imagined that it could expel the British from the valuable rice lowlands in South Carolina, but it was confident that if it defeated Oglethorpe's regiment at Saint Simon's Island and caused sufficient destruction near Charles Town, London would pull back to defend South Carolina, jettisoning Georgia and guaranteeing the security of Florida.

Spain's blow fell in 1742, almost two years to the day since the lifting of the siege at Saint Augustine. Curiously, the history of Spain's foray into Georgia closely resembled Britain's experience in Florida. Manuel de Montiano, the governor of Florida and commander of the invading force, sought a three-thousand-man army; he got barely half that number. In addition, following his landing on marshy, sultry Saint Simon's early in July, Montiano often appeared indecisive, despite the luxury of superior numbers. Finally, Montiano's plans were wrecked by the excellent performance of Oglethorpe, who fought well, and used his knowledge of the terrain to his full benefit. The Spanish terminated their operation after only three weeks, convinced that a British squadron was approaching. Their retreat to Florida ended two years of inconclusive warfare on the southern frontier.

While London's dreams of expelling Spain from Florida evaporated, British forces were also on the march elsewhere. Even before Britain declared war in 1739, it had dispatched Vice-Adm. Edward Vernon to the West Indies with orders to plunder Spanish shipping. His crowning achievement occurred at the end of 1739, after war had been declared; he conquered Porto Bello on the Isthmus of Panama, a major entrepôt of Spanish shipping. Soon thereafter word reached America that a British army under Brig. Gen. Thomas Wentworth would join with Vernon in Jamaica. In addition, the British government decreed that each colony, save for beleaguered South Carolina and Georgia, was to contribute men to a provincial force that would be shipped to the Caribbean to fight alongside their brethren from the parent state; the provincials were to be under the command of William Gooch, the chief executive of Virginia.

By the autumn of 1740 colonial troop transports were plowing through the Atlantic. Aboard were more than thirty-six hundred men, members of Gooch's American Regiment of Foot. Each man had volunteered for this service, enticed by the prospect of adventure or—more likely—of sharing in the plunder that would accompany the conquest of Spanish territory. They departed full of boyish enthusiasm and naiveté. Reality began to set in upon their arrival in Jamaica.

At Kingston and Port Royal on this emerald-green island, the provincials encountered shortages of almost everything save for daily rainstorms and blistering sunshine. Without adequate tents or fresh vegetables, many men fell ill, and some died.

Conditions did not improve substantially when the British expeditionary force pushed off for Cartagena, a fortified Spanish seaport on the rocky west coast of South America. Two out of every three colonials in the army were assigned duty as deckhands in the fleet during the 550-mile voyage, hardly the valiant enterprise these enlistees had imagined; nor is it likely that they had envisioned living for weeks with scant supplies on a malaria-infested plain while the force assembled and the assault was planned with painstaking deliberation.

By the time the British attacked in April 1741, disease had swept through the army, killing many who had survived the horrors of Jamaica. Nevertheless, about one thousand colonials saw action in the British offensive, an unsuccessful onslaught against the Spanish garrison. After that attempt, the British command decided that Cartagena was impregnable. It also began to search for scapegoats for its failure; the Americans received a large measure of the blame. The colonials, it was said, sometimes unfairly, were untrained and inexperienced rubes, the rank and file mostly consisting of ne'er-do-wells, the officers primarily of callow artisans and farmers.

Such criticism was a bitter pill for the provincials to swallow. Appalling numbers of their comrades had perished due to what they considered to have been Britain's bungling of logistical matters. To make matters worse, the Americans were kept on duty for sixteen months after the retreat from Cartagena, for the most part assigned hated naval duty. Finally, late in 1742, the survivors were discharged. Most came home penniless and harboring only contempt for British officialdom, but at least they got home. Approximately three thousand of the thirty-six hundred colonial soldiers who had enlisted with such high hopes two years before never returned.

CHAPTER FOUR

War in Eighteenth-Century America

Changing Views of War

The fortunate few survivors who trickled back to the colonies were heralded by their Anglo-American countrymen as heroes, especially in New England, where it was becoming customary to lionize those who soldiered. That had not always been the case. In the seventeenth century, when the colonists had relied exclusively on their militia units during the Indian wars, soldiering had been seen merely as a part of a man's responsibility as a citizen. In the Puritan colonies, it was an axiom that God, not the men who bore arms, determined the fate of armies and the outcome of battles; assuredly, the Puritan ministers taught that God helped those who helped themselves, but they also counseled that no "means or helps will make us successful Souldiers if *God* deny His Smiles."

As volunteer armies supplanted armies of militiamen and conscriptees toward the end of the century, new attitudes emerged. Men who bore arms—men whose services were not solicited by the state—soon were treated as heroes. During the eighteenth century, large demonstrative crowds, usually filled with "many pretty girls" who wept and waved farewell, gathered to usher the local enlistees off to war. Victories were celebrated by cannonades, fireworks, bonfires, and the pealing of bells. Officers, who had usually held command positions before they entered the volunteer armies, enjoyed an exalted status after their return home, and for the remainder of their lives they carried the title of the rank they had held and were respectfully addressed by their neighbors as "Captain" or as "Colonel." In some instances, newly founded villages were named for military heroes.

Soldiers such as Sir William Phips and Benjamin Church were lionized within their provinces, and the realization that martial exploits could be a rapid route to fame caused many young boys to dream of bearing arms. John Adams, in fact, once confessed that as a youth he had "longed more ardently to be a soldier" than to be recognized as a talented attorney.

Hand in hand with the lionization of soldiers came renewed interest in the training of warriors. A burgeoning literature in the eighteenth century, at least in New England, sought to catalogue those virtues that would shape the "True Hero." Above all, rigorous training, resolute courage, and iron discipline were the ingredients for molding "valient Heroes," although exemplary officers were necessary as well. Officers were exhorted to be neither petty nor capricious and to manifest serenity and courage. The officer who could command both the love and fear of his men, it was said, would be a successful leader.

Other changes in the colonial outlook occurred as well. Although religion remained a useful tool for arousing New Englanders against the Catholic French, hostilities no longer were as likely to be attributed to God's wrath. Geopolitical interpretations grew more fashionable, such as the explanation that war was necessary to extricate Anglo-America from foreign encirclement. Some leaders even spoke candidly of fighting to secure coal from Cape Breton or to seize fertile lands to the north. If France was driven from North America, it was said, Spain's American empire would be at the mercy of Great Britain, compelling Madrid to throw open its colonial ports to English commerce. Nor was it unthinkable to suggest that warfare was beneficial. Writers in the eighteenth century sometimes lauded conflict as a stimulant for new inventions and discoveries, and some even suggested that struggle improved the species by strengthening human beings' intelligence, courage, magnanimity, even self-control. The most common themes for the justification of war, however, played on the anti-French biases of the colonists, especially those who dwelled in the northern provinces. France was portrayed as an absolutist and decadent nation, bent upon spreading both its Roman Catholicism and its allegedly seductive and debauched manners.

Finally, many articulate Americans began to champion military tactics that had been denigrated by earlier generations. From the Chesapeake to New England, the earliest settlers had branded the Indian way of war as cowardly and treacherous. Occasionally an imaginative officer, such as Colonel Church, understood the need to modify European tactics in the American wilderness, but it was not until after Queen Anne's War that articulate provincials openly defended an "Irregular manner of Fighting," what they sometimes alluded to as the "American way of war." To borrow from the customary practices of the Indians only made good sense, some now said. Wilderness warfare required abandoning the "Hyde Park tactics" of the continent, as Charles Lee later remarked.

The Technology of War

The technology of war changed somewhat in the 150 years that elapsed between the English beginnings at Roanoke and the fever-ridden campaigns in Georgia, Florida, and South America in the 1740s. The first English soldiers in America had been equipped with armor and shields, and they had carried long spikes, swords, and matchlock muskets or wheellock muskets, some of which were so heavy that they could be fired only by resting the gun on a forked pole. Neither the heavy, restrictive armor nor the pikes were serviceable in America's dense forests; before the end of the seventeenth century, the flintlock musket had emerged as the infantry weapon of choice.

A smooth bore gun that weighed ten pounds or more, the flintlock was fired when sparks caused by the collision of flint and steel ignited the granulated black powder in the pan and barrel; the resulting explosion discharged the bullet, a lead ball that could travel well over one hundred yards, although its accurate range was only about fifty yards. A highly trained soldier—a British professional rather than a colonial volunteer—might get off five shots in a minute. If he hit something, the bullet could be expected to inflict extensive damage, for the ball began to spread upon impact, often tearing great, gaping, catastrophic wounds in its victim. The soldier who used a flintlock also carried several ancillary pieces of equipment. Attached to his belt was a cartouche box filled with cartridges, each consisting of a ball and powder securely wrapped inside a wad of brown paper; some men also bore a horn filled with additional powder, and all musketeers possessed a tool variously called a ramrod or rammer, an instrument used for tightly packing the projectile and powder in the gun barrel. The soldier also carried about a dozen pieces of flint, which, together with his powder, he was compelled to keep dry or face the disconcerting possibility that his weapon would be rendered inoperable. Finally, infantrymen in regular units were customarily equipped with bayonets and at times with swords, but the provincial soldiers usually carried only a light knife or hatchet, if they were furnished with any arms beyond their musket.

Precious space was reserved for artillery on the transports that brought the first English colonists across the Atlantic. Cannon had many uses in the warfare of early seventeenth-century Europe, including an obvious role in sieges. Siege warfare was as old as warfare itself. In antiquity, the inhabitants of cities—sometimes even entire regions—enclosed themselves within ramparts for protection against attackers. More often than not they had chosen a sound defense, for siege armies seldom possessed the means of reducing masonry and stone fortifications. The appearance of guns altered siege warfare. Thereafter, attackers possessed a weapon that could blast apart simple walls. By the fifteenth century Europeans had begun to construct new cannon-proof defenses, installations that looked upon moats and bare glacis, and which were designed to accentuate enfilade fire.

Because the Native Americans did not wage war in the European manner, siege operations were not part of the warfare of the earliest English colonists. During the intercolonial wars, however, the settlers discovered a use for the cannon they had transported across the Atlantic.

Until the mid-eighteenth century, when the science of fortifications caught up with that of the gun, the advantage in siege operations usually lay with the besieger. Indeed, while Oglethorpe demonstrated in miasmic Florida that an attacker still could fail, Europe rarely witnessed an unsuccessful siege in the eighteenth century. Largely because of the systematic methodology devised by Sebastien le Prestre, Marquis de Vauban, who served Louis XIV and who influenced generations of soldiers, siege armies had come to eschew risky frontal assaults. Attackers were to fight their way through the defender's outworks, laying their own trenches and traverses in the ground they had taken. These parallels, as the excavations were called, were so situated as to provide the best angles of fire for the mortars, howitzers, and heavy battering artillery that they contained. Methodically, the besiegers were to move closer and closer toward the fort under attack until the defender, realizing the folly of continued resistance, capitulated. A frontal assault came only if the defenders refused to surrender. Logic often discouraged die-hard resistance, however, and so did the conventions of European warfare, which permitted the wholesale massacre of the besieged who had been so misguided as to invite an assault by refusing to surrender.

Cannon were not limited to siege operations. They accompanied advancing armies, usually borne to the war zone by naval craft, thence to the front lines by sweaty, straining teams of horses or oxen. The largest cannon had an effective range of about one-half mile, and some could fire missiles that weighed in excess of two hundred pounds. Cannon could fire grapeshot (in this capacity they served as immense shotguns) or heavy balls, projectiles that would tear through the ranks of the adversary, causing appalling devastation and considerable fear among those who witnessed the carnage.

American Soldiers and Armies

In England's wars with France and Spain after 1689, the widespread military service that had been common in the colonies in the seventeenth century disappeared. The militia had been the primary arm for fighting the Indians in Virginia during the earliest period of settlement; from the beginning in New England, however, these units had served mostly for home defense, while active service companies, composed largely of conscripted militiamen (usually young bachelors drafted by the local community to meet the manpower quota assigned it by the colonial government), were sent into the field on offensive campaigns against the Indians. After 1689 warfare receded to more distant frontiers, and operations were conducted over vast distances. Whereas during the Pequot War Captain Mason's army had traveled only about fifty miles to assault the Mystic River fort, during the intercolonial wars New England armies might be dispatched to New York or faraway Canada, and the soldiers of Virginia or Maryland might march into Pennsylvania or be transported to the West Indies. Because each colony had enacted legislation that forbade sending militiamen beyond its borders, a source of manpower other than militia units was required for this warfare. New England's militia tradition continued into the eighteenth century, but the units mustered less frequently than before, and drill days were often more a social occasion than a day of martial preparation.

The militia remained more functional in the South, but, even so, in the eighteenth century it existed more for the purpose of controlling slaves than for defending against a foreign foe.

The new volunteer armies differed noticeably from their predecessors. While the new armies appear to have been composed mostly of young bachelor farmers and apprentices, men from sectors of society that had been excluded from militia duty now enlisted, often drawn to take up arms by cash bonuses and by the prospect of sharing in the plunder of victory. White indentured servants and apprentices, the transient poor (free but landless whites), friendly Indians, and free African Americans joined these armies. To these men who faced no prospect of upward economic or social mobility, military service was the only means by which to acquire liquid capital. South Carolina armed two hundred black soldiers during the Yamassee uprising in 1715; roughly 6 to 10 percent of Connecticut's troops at Louisbourg in 1745 were African Americans or Indians, and during the French and Indian War several provinces enlisted African-American soldiers. When a government was unable to raise a sufficient number of volunteer troops, it usually resorted to conscription; in 1740, for instance, Virginia met its quota for Gooch's American Foot by drafting vagabonds. But most colonial soldiers appear to have been voluntary enlistees. Only 2 percent of the membership of Massachusetts's army in 1756 consisted of men who had been impressed into service. When wars dragged on for long periods, however, the percentage of conscripts may have increased; fewer than 20 percent of those in Virginia's army of 1756 had been drafted, but the following year, the fourth consecutive year during which the province had sought to raise an army, 40 percent of its soldiers were draftees.

During the final colonial wars in the 1740s and 1750s recruitment of provincial soldiers normally began during the winter or early spring. Some colonies offered land bounties to enlistees, but cash bounties were more commonly used as enticement. Frequently the bounty equalled a month's wages of an unskilled laborer, but it varied from colony to colony. In a long war it often rose from year to year; Connecticut, for instance, offered a cash bounty in 1759 that was seven-and-a-half times greater than it had extended five years earlier. For some, of course, a quest for adventure or the opportunity to fight the hated French was as important as the economic incentives. Once the recruit passed a physical examination—seldom more demanding than the need to meet a minimal height standard and to display no discernible signs of infirmity—he was issued a few supplies, which often included a hat, coat, blanket, shoes, two or three shirts, a musket, and ammunition. Then he marched off to an embarkation point. Marching soon grew to be part of the daily routine for many soldiers, as they frequently trekked eighteen or twenty miles each day, sometimes for days on end. Formal training was scant, seldom exceeding a week or ten days of drill and practice with firearms. The troops lived under martial law, but in most colonies these rules were patterned on civilian judicial codes. The punishments in the provincial armies were less severe than those inflicted upon British regulars. Nevertheless, men were flogged, and those convicted of extremely serious offenses—sleeping while on guard duty, for instance—as well as habitual offenders sometimes received Draconian sentences, including hundreds of lashes. Some soldiers were executed, usually for repeatedly deserting, although capital punishment was rare in the colonial armies.

The men normally resided in camps, usually living in tents that could be unbearably cold, wet, and drafty in the spring and fall, but which turned to ovens in the summer. Fatigue duty (digging trenches, cutting wood, gathering hay, hauling supplies, cleaning the grounds) or guard duty was part of most men's daily routine. More civilians than soldiers, the men complained endlessly of their lot. Demoniacal officers, the unrelieved boredom and unfamiliar regimentation of camp, as well as the weather, inspired numerous grievances. But in each war the supply system provoked the most bickering. Under English and provincial laws, soldiers were to receive generous weekly allotments of beef or pork, bread, peas, beans or rice, butter, rum and/or beer, and, when available, fresh vegetables. Rations were often in short supply, however, usually because of the nightmarish complexities involved in procuring huge amounts of comestibles, then coordinating their transport to a distant military front.

Army life could be extremely dangerous, even when the enemy was not nearby. Virtually every eighteenth-century army encountered serious problems with disease. "The itch" usually came first, induced by vermin and poor sanitation. More serious ailments, such as dysentery, pneumonia, measles, smallpox, and the ubiquitous "camp distemper," followed, often seeming to peak in late summer or early fall. Men wrote in their diaries of the terrible stench of disease and death that hovered in the air, and worried that they might suffer an inglorious demise at the hands of a rampant fever. Many did meet such an end. Indeed, the death rate from disease suffered by New England troops in the French and Indian War appears to have been four times as great as that experienced by civilians living at that time in rural America. Far more soldiers died of camp diseases than of battlefield wounds.

Although combat usually produced fewer casualties than disease, eighteenth-century engagement could be cruelly destructive. Raw soldiers often eagerly awaited their first battle, anxious for the adventure, hopeful of performing gloriously. When battle came at last, some men seemed to relish the danger and excitement. George Washington wrote ecstatically of his first engagement: "I heard the bullets whistle, and, believe me, there is something charming in the sound." Most men reacted differently. The confusion and terror of battle overwhelmed many men, and the awful sight of wounded comrades, the pitiful screams of the injured and dying, and the spectacle of mangled bodies was often too much to bear. "We went over . . . in high spirits," remarked a veteran of a 1758 battle, "but returned back melancholy and still, as from a funeral." After the first experience of the macabre features of the battlefield, survival usually became more important than victory or defeat. Few came away from combat unscarred. Many men were disoriented by what they had witnessed. Some men experienced psychoneurotic disorders and a few, displaying symptoms of hysteria and anxiety neurosis (what would be called "shell shock" in World War II, a condition that might include stupor, inability to speak, amnesia, choking sensations, speech defects, depression, and loss of sight and hearing) were ruined as soldiers and had to be sent home.

Field-grade officers in the new volunteer armies were usually appointed by provincial officials. In New England, colonial assemblies appointed and commissioned junior officers through the rank of captain. These officers learned the art of command in a variety of ways. Some gained hands-on experience at occasional trainband drills and regimental musters. In addition, by the late seventeenth century several military manuals were in print, texts that discoursed upon the proper character of an officer, provided instruction in organizational matters, served as a guide to the intricacies of martial exercises, and often included a compendium of Great Britain's articles of war, the laws that governed the conduct of those who served in the military. In the eighteenth century, especially during the last colonial war in the 1750s, still another means emerged by which Americans could learn how to command men. American officers often could observe the British regulars with whom they served.

It was late in the colonial era before many colonists ever laid eyes on a British solider. Charles II dispatched over one thousand men to quash Bacon's Rebellion in 1676, and ten years later James II posted small garrisons in Boston and New York to discourage opposition to the Dominion of New England, but it was not until Queen Anne's War that London made its first wartime commitment of arms to the colonies. Thereafter, the imperial government stationed a handful of regulars on its vulnerable southern frontier in peacetime, and it dispatched modest numbers of redcoats to the American theater in King George's War.

Colonial officers accompanied Admiral Walker's ill-fated armada in 1709, and others served under experienced English soldiers such as Francis Nicholson and James Oglethorpe. Young George Washington is the best-known American officer who learned of armies and war through his association with the British. Washington and many other American soldiers spoke of the redcoats as exemplary soldiers and were awed by their discipline and courage under fire. In 1755 and again three years later, Washington, a green, fledgling Virginia colonel, accompanied British armies into western Pennsylvania. He carefully studied the organization of the British army and the administrative habits of its commanders; some young officers with whom he developed a cordial relationship even lent him copies of their military manuals, likely the first such tracts he had read. The lessons that Washington learned remained with him, first as he commanded the Virginia Regiment in the 1750s, and later as he led the Continental army during the War of Independence. Washington's greatest discovery was the maxim that "discipline is the soul of an army." But he also learned that to be effective an officer must devote attention to detail. He soon understood that it was his "duty to study merit and reward the brave and deserving," and that he must treat his subordinates fairly and equally. He also found that the most effective officer led by example; the officer who lived simply, worked diligently, and displayed courage under fire won the respect of his men. Finally, Washington learned that an officer should remain somewhat aloof from his men. Sociability and intimacy, he once said, eroded one's ability to control others. This principle did not mean that the officer was to be haughty or arrogant. Washington thought a mixture of "a commanding countenance"—the famous "stately bearing" and air of "mild gravity" that witnesses noted in his persona, what Washington simply referred to as a "demeanor at all times composed and dignified"—with an "easy, polite" manner would set the proper tone for a military commander.

But New Englanders discovered other traits of the British soldier, some not so pleasant. In particular, they were appalled at what they deemed the wretchedly low moral standards of the English soldiery. Colonial troops seemed to believe that every English soldier's speech was laced with profanity and that nearly all the redcoats consorted with miscreant women. More troubling to some was the brutal manner in which officers treated the British soldiers. Men were frequently sentenced to death for mutiny, sedition, and desertion, and a wide range of offenses were punishable by flogging. Similar punishments were administered in the colonial armies, but capital sentences were rarely imposed, and flogging seldom exceeded thirty-nine lashes, whereas a redcoat offender could be given hundreds of lashes, a barbarous punishment that often proved fatal. The demeanor of the British officers surprised and angered some provincials. Drawn almost exclusively from among the younger sons of elite families, many British officers appeared to be arrogant, haughty, and overbearing toward their colonial counterparts, making little attempt to hide their feelings that the provincials were their social and cultural inferiors. The ill will that resulted was sometimes exacerbated by clashes over rank; by law even junior regular officers outranked the loftiest provincial colonel. The colonists' greatest shock and outrage, however, resulted from their own treatment at the hands of the British officers. Colonists who served with the British quickly learned that they were thought of as the world's worst soldiers, as disinterested, undisciplined, and cowardly men who were prone toward either desertion or mutiny. British officers often refused to consult with their colonial counterparts, kept the provincials out of combat, and frequently assigned them to the least desirable details. Moreover, when campaigns ended in failure, as at Cartagena, British officers frequently attributed defeat to the alleged inadequacies of the colonials.

Was this nearly universal attitude of the British officers justified? The leaders of the British army were professionals who were accustomed to commanding men who had been reduced to utter subordination through incredibly harsh discipline and training. The colonials, by contrast, lacked training and combat experience. The American soldier was a citizen-soldier; a civilian when he entered the service, he remained a civilian at the completion of his tour of duty. Thus, devoid of a military ethos that Britain's soldiers had come to expect, American soldiers were judged by British officers to be unreliable and incompetent, an impression that was not entirely accurate.

American armies were plagued by desertion, but so were Britain's armies. The desertion rate within Connecticut's armies in the 1750s—roughly 4 to 6 percent—was only slightly greater than that among British regulars. In addition, what the British viewed as desertion was often something else. New England units in particular sometimes simply quit the field and returned home upon the expiration of their enlistment; in such instances the soldiery was convinced that it had fulfilled its obligations. In a society in which contractual relationships were pivotal, the New England soldiers looked upon their enlistment agreement as a contract that spelled out the terms of their service. Any attempt by the authorities to alter what had been previously agreed upon was resisted, if necessary by simply leaving the army.

Within the limits of their training and experience, colonial soldiers did not perform too badly. Unpracticed and inadequately prepared, and almost always led by amateur officers, the American soldiers could not be expected to perform as professionals. In many instances provincial soldiers performed bravely, however, and they excelled in the indispensable areas of garrison service—that is when they were posted in a vulnerable town or on a remote frontier—and in construction service. If the American armies were not always successful, it often was due less to the inability of the soldiery than to the incapacity of small, poor, disunited colonies to provide the resources that could have achieved victory.

Societies and governments, like the men who soldiered, likewise were affected by these wars. Hostilities opened new forms of business enterprise, including smuggling, piracy, and supplying armies; sometimes war stimulated the mainstays of the economy as well, such as shipbuilding. Some entrepreneurs flourished. For instance, Thomas Hancock, uncle of John Hancock, secured war contracts in the 1740s that increased his modest prewar income by over 1,000 percent. Wars also often meant full employment and steady incomes for urban artisans. But other citizens frequently fared poorly. Wars produced widows and orphans, disabled veterans, and higher taxes. Anxious periods of depression and heavy unemployment often followed in the aftermath of conflict.

The long period of war that began in 1689 and the renewal of hostilities in 1739 impacted on government and administration. Warfare increased the power of the executive in Great Britain. In some ways, however, these wars weakened royal authority in the colonies. In England, year after year of war generated gainful contracts and huge state appropriations, which in turn fostered the growth of ministries and bureaucracies, until, ultimately, the machinery of the state had been widened and strengthened. In America, the lower house of the colonial assemblies often refused to appropriate military funds until it had a voice in—or at least prior knowledge of—how the monies would be spent. At times, the assemblies discovered ways to influence military policy, usually the prerogative of the executive. For example, the Virginia House of Burgesses created units of rangers in 1691 to scour the frontier for signs of hostile intentions among the Indians, while South Carolina's assembly in 1718 explicitly told the governor how many men he could raise in the Yamassee War; many provinces adopted militia laws that strictly limited the chief executive's powers, such as the law prohibiting the militia from serving outside the colony.

America had been changed by its early wars. But its largest and most significant wars were yet to come. The first of these, King George's War, erupted in 1745.

King George's War

For the lucky survivors of Cartagena, as well as for those who had safely endured the heat and muck of the troubled Georgia-Florida frontier, the War of Jenkins' Ear ended by the close of 1742. For other colonists, the war was only about to begin. France concluded a treaty of alliance with Spain late in 1743, and early the following year France and England declared war upon one another, thus becoming belligerents in the War of the Austrian Succession, a conflict that had involved other nations for the past four years. Britain's belligerency with France immediately set Anglo-America's northern frontier ablaze, inaugurating the struggle that would be known in the colonies as King George's War.

New France learned of the European war before the news reached New England, and it struck first. From Louisbourg on Cape Breton Island, France's great, fortified outpost that guarded the entrance to the Saint Lawrence River, the French dispatched privateers to seize British fishing vessels and sent an expedition to take Canso in northern Nova Scotia. Both enterprises succeeded. A French and Indian siege of Annapolis Royal failed, however.

Word of the French assaults galvanized William Shirley, the governor of Massachusetts. Since before the outbreak of war, Shirley had warned that Massachusetts must protect Nova Scotia. Its loss would adversely affect the Massachusetts economy, he cautioned; more important, he added, if Britain lost Annapolis Royal, the Indians on the Bay colony's frontier would immediately renew their old ties with France. As soon as he learned of the French provocations to the north, Shirley urged that a force be sent to rescue beleaguered Annapolis Royal. The Massachusetts assembly voted to raise 180 soldiers; it offered a handsome enlistment bounty of twenty-five pounds. In July, 70 men were sent north. More followed in September, together with a force of Eastern Abnaki friendly to the English. It was their arrival that broke the French siege.

Shirley knew, of course, that the French would be back, and he importuned the British government to provide naval protection for Nova Scotia; London agreed. Next, Shirley urged a naval blockade of Louisbourg, confident that the stronghold would fall quickly and that France's capacity for mischief off the North American coast would be eliminated.

Before early 1745, however, he did not envision any role for Massachusetts in the taking of the French fortress. But he changed his mind when he discovered considerable support for such an undertaking within the fishing and commercial communities; moreover, based on the tales of released prisoners and New England traders, he concluded that Louisbourg was crumbling and that its defenders were demoralized. Furthermore, Shirley was swayed by the plans of several wealthy and influential advocates of a New England expedition. In January 1745, he told a secret session of the assembly that two thousand men could take Louisbourg and "bring an irreparable loss to the enemy."

The General Court was interested, but not in a unilateral campaign by Massachusetts. By a margin of one vote, it agreed to provide its quota to a large force recruited from several colonies. Preparation began immediately.

Ignoring several men who desired to command the expeditionary force, Shirley beseeched William Pepperrell to take the job. Pepperrell, a popular man despite his somewhat grave and dour manner, was a wealthy merchant and legislator; he was also the colonel of the Maine militia, although he had never commanded in battle. Pepperrell did not require much arm-twisting by Shirley. Not only did he crave action and adventure, but he was more than ready to take on the hated French. Pepperrell may have had still another motive. A timberman, Pepperrell coveted access to the forests of northern Maine, home of the Abnaki tribes, native peoples who were linked to New France and who would be substantively weakened if stripped of French assistance.

Recruitment soon began in earnest. In countless sermons and newspaper essays the message was broadcast that Louisbourg was ripe for the plucking, that the victorious soldiery would share in a rich plunder, and that this was to be a Protestant crusade against the Catholic French anti-Christ. "And how sweet and pleasant it will be ... to pull ... down that stronghold of Satan," one Calvinist told his flock. Another urged New England men to "destroy proud Antichrist ... and

quite consume the [French] whore." In Massachusetts, enlistment proceeded smoothly; the ranks of its army were filled
within only sixty days. All the men were volunteers. Most were
young laborers or artisans. Aside from a few men who enlisted
out of religious fervor, most appear to have been residents of
the economically distressed older settlements of overcrowded
eastern Massachusetts; economic gain inspired them to soldier.
Enthusiasm lagged outside Massachusetts, however. Connecticut and New Hampshire barely met their quotas; no colony
south of New England committed men to the enterprise, although New York furnished ten cannon. When the various
contingents rendezvoused in Canso early in the spring, the
force exceeded three thousand men, 80 percent of whom were
from Massachusetts.

While Pepperrell waited for the ice to melt near Louisbourg, he commenced training his men. It was such a raw army
that even today the odds against its success seem formidable.
The American officers were "People totally Ignorant" of military skills, according to one British witness, and they were
compelled to teach their callow troops such rudimentary arts
as how to fire their muskets. Not surprisingly, the American
camp was a "scene of confusion and frolic," a place of undisciplined revelry for young men away from home for the first
time and eager to enjoy the great adventure of their lives. The
American army had one advantage, however. While the men
trained and romped, Commodore Peter Warren, commander
of the British squadron in the Leeward Islands, arrived with
four warships. He had responded to Shirley's entreaties. Warren and Pepperrell conferred briefly, then the fleet moved off
to begin the blockade of Louisbourg. Pepperrell's army was
not far behind.

The New England soldiers were ensconced in several troop
transports convoyed by an armed snow and two sloops. Although the weather remained unseasonably mild, the vessels
"rolled and pitched malevolently . . . and stank abominably,"
according to one soldier. By daybreak on the second day the
great Anglo-American armada—four warships, nine smaller

armed vessels, fifty-one transports, and thirty or more assorted vessels, mostly supply ships—reached Gabarus Bay, four miles from the ramparts of Louisbourg. The French sighted the fleet as the spring sun, red and enormous, rose to illumine the seemingly endless forest of resplendent white sails. Cannon and church bells were sounded immediately to warn the outlying residents; strangely, however, the French commander failed to reinforce the small detachments guarding the most likely landing sites.

Pepperrell wasted little time. By late morning his rangers—a company of Indian regulars whom Pepperrell selected to lead the first wave of invaders, for these men were his best troops, the ones most likely to hold the beachhead against a counterattack—had scrambled into whaleboats and, under a canopy of fire from Warren's warships, rode the heavy seas toward land. But they could not get ashore. Twenty French defenders repulsed the first landing party at Flat Point Cove. Pepperrell was resourceful, however. He ordered the second wave of rangers to beach at Kennington Cove. This time the Americans succeeded. Only scant resistance awaited the rangers on this sandy, sloping beach; the few French defenders once posted here had marched to Flat Point Cove to repulse additional landings that never came. With the beach secure, wave after wave of New England men landed throughout the long, sunny day. Before nightfall brought a starry darkness to this craggy beach, more than two thousand American soldiers had waded ashore. One of those soldiers, a New Englander, wrote that evening in his journal:

We lay this night in the open air, but we cut a few boughs to keep us off the ground. This was vastly the most comfortable night's lodging since I left Boston. We should be careful to rejoice in what the Lord has done for all of us. It was a very pleasant evening. It was the first time [we] heard any frogs peep or birds sing for several days.

In the pink-blue glaze of dawn the following morning the siege operation commenced. While some men in the rear of this motley provincial army spent their day "racing, wrestling, pitching quoits, [or] firing at marks or at birds," as one soldier described the scene, the less fortunate were ordered forward to begin the arduous and dangerous work of securing siege lines about the great fortress. First, teams of two hundred sweaty men, harnessed with straps and ropes, pulled the cannon through the soft, marshy terrain toward the French fortress. Next, with picks and shovels the men dug deep trenches, or parallels, from which the English batteries would endeavor to pummel the French into submission. The preparation was hard, physical labor; nor was it without peril, for the men were often within range of French fire. The men groped for courage and battled their fear of death and injuries. Some who kept journals made notations as their comrades lost arms and legs, were shot in the knee, had skulls crushed by shrapnel. Guilt haunted some men. Some worried about killing the French civilians inside Louisbourg (a rumor made the rounds that a pregnant woman had been cut in half by an English shell). Still others fretted over what was happening at home (another rumor swirled about that the French had unleashed the Indians on the New England frontier during the army's absence).

Work proceeded slowly, steadily. A month into the campaign five batteries were operating, "playing on the town" and "greatly distressing the inhabitants," according to Pepperrell. While these operations proceeded, Pepperrell turned his attention to another concern. He knew that the siege could succeed only if he took possession of two French batteries that commanded the harbor, for until that occurred Commodore Warren could be kept at bay and French reinforcements might slip in. One of Pepperrell's problems was solved when the French abandoned the Grand Battery, judging it to be indefensible. The Island Battery was a different matter. Pepperrell sent his inexperienced troops after this objective in early June. The result was a fiasco. Rowed out in whaleboats under cover of darkness, the men landed successfully just after midnight, but some zealous soldiers, given additional buoyancy by repeated nips at their rum bottles, bellowed drunken hurrahs upon disembarkation. Alerted at last, the French opened fire.

After a night-long engagement, the New Englanders retired, leaving behind 60 dead comrades and 116 men who had been taken captive. "Some of our men fought manfully till about sunrise," one of the New England officers wrote, although he admitted that the attack was hopeless from the outset, when the French cannon began "cutting boats and men to pieces as they were landing."

A few days later the Island Battery did fall, although not as the result of an assault. Pepperrell managed to put his artillery on Lighthouse Point, near enough to blast the post into submission. Thereafter the siege was tightened. Yet, as successful as this army was during the first weeks of the operation, the raw New England soldiers soon grew homesick and heartily tired of army life. One soldier wrote to his father that the New England troops "say they want to go home, home is all they cry, and if I was at home they should never find me such a fool again" as to reenlist. As in all these wars, diseases infested the camp. By the end of May more than five hundred men were reported ill; some men died a slow, inglorious death from ills such as dysentery or pneumonia. In late May three Massachusetts cannon exploded, killing some of the crew; as if the French were not a sufficient danger, some complained, now the allegedly defective Massachusetts cannon constituted an additional peril. Illness and accidents aside, it was the French who made life difficult for the attackers. "The bullets flew in whole showers," one soldier wrote after spending a full day crouching in a muddy entrenchment. The sight of wounded and dead comrades eroded morale. It "is an awful thing to see men wounded and wallowing in their own blood," one man noted; "I passed by a dead man; though an enemy, it showed me my frailty," another concerned volunteer observed. France's allies, the Micmacs, also spread terror. Early in the campaign they captured twenty New England stragglers, whom they "scalped and chopped and stabbed and prodigiously mangled," according to one soldier. As the soldiers' enthusiasm for war waned, some fell into a state of dark depression, and

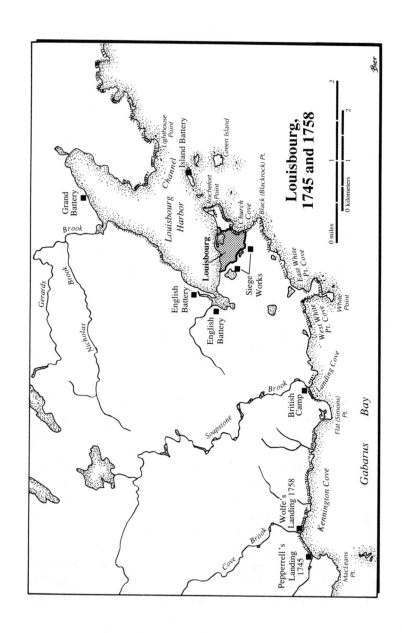

Louisbourg, 1745 and 1758

others resorted to alcohol for solace. Chaplains searched diligently for uplifting sermons.

What likely uplifted the provincials' spirits more than anything was the arrival of additional British vessels, ships that appeared on the misty horizon one day in mid-June. Thereafter, the blockade was impenetrable. With the sea-lanes closed to the French, and with New England artillerymen bombarding Louisbourg mercilessly, it was only a matter of time before the French capitulated. No one understood the folly of continued resistance better than the French. To be battered by nine thousand cannonballs within forty days was disconcerting; to realize that aid from home would not be coming was decisive. The French commander surrendered Louisbourg on June 17, but not until he had negotiated generous terms, including a proviso against British plundering, a stipulation he sought to protect his men. Pepperrell and Warren also sought to limit plundering so that the quarters would remain intact for the Anglo-American occupation that would follow. The American soldiers were exultant at the surrender. "The General went in and took possession of the city of Louisbourg! The greatest conquest that ever was gained by New England," a volunteer rejoiced in his journal when the French citadel fell.

New England had scored a great victory, and at a cost of only 101 lives. The Americans had fought surprisingly well, the French defense had been amazingly inept, and Warren's squadron, as expected, had performed expertly. When the news reached New England, spontaneous celebrations spread from village to village. London was no less ecstatic. Shirley was immediately rewarded with a colonelcy in the British army, Warren with a rear admiralship, and Pepperrell became the first colonial to be granted a baronetcy.

The midsummer exuberance soon vanished, however. Massachusetts resorted to conscription to keep an occupation army at Louisbourg through the cold, foggy winter that followed. About one-third of those men—nearly one thousand soldiers—perished within the walls of Louisbourg during that awful winter, victims, one participant wrote, of "putrid fevers and dysenteries" that caused men to die "like rotten sheep." Stephen Williams, a chaplain from Longmeadow, Massachusetts, who visited the sick and dying men daily, recorded the names of each dead soldier, except when the person was African American; then he listed the dead man simply as "a free Negro of Captain Heuston's company" or as "Glover's negro, peter." Reverend Williams often found "the smell [in the army hospital] was so nauseous that I did not tarry." On other days he lingered and "prayed and sang" with the patients, or pleaded with the Lord "please to pity and spare" the ill; there were times, however, when he prayed that God would show an incurably ill soldier how to die honorably.

The New England army brought much of the problem upon itself. Not expecting to stay past early autumn, the men had built inadequate housing for a Cape Breton winter. But there were other causes. The New England colonies failed to adequately supply their armies, leaving the men with insufficient food and fuel. Admiral Warren's successor, who arrived early in 1746, spoke of the garrison as "confused, dirty, beastly," the "most miserable ruinous place I ever beheld." He thought the New Englanders solely responsible. The New England men, already vexed at having been denied their plunder, privately attributed the logistical nightmare to British indifference and incompetence.

Continual problems and disappointments soon combined to make the glorious victory of June 1745 a distant memory. When France tried unsuccessfully to retake Louisbourg in 1745 and 1746, New England was compelled to raise still other armies. In addition, Shirley and Warren secured a British commitment in 1746 for a campaign against Quebec. Eight colonies raised armies. Massachusetts fielded three thousand men, the largest provincial force, while Virginia's army of one hundred men was the smallest. But, as in 1709, London ultimately scratched the expedition, preferring to concentrate on the war in Europe. Great Britain's action once again demonstrated to the provincials that London regarded the colonial theater as of little consequence in comparison to the campaigning in Europe.

By the time that news reached Boston, the financial realities of this war had become quite clear. Taxes rose yet again in Massachusetts; inflation was rampant. By 1747, two shillings were required for what one shilling would have purchased in 1745; two years later, prices had increased again, now by fivefold. Massachusetts was near bankruptcy.

The news only worsened. Late in 1748 the colonists learned that the war was over, and they discovered the terms to which Great Britain had consented. In the Treaty of Aix-la-Chapelle, negotiated in the Rhineland city of the same name, Britain agreed to return Louisbourg and Cape Breton Island to France in exchange for compensation in Europe and India.

The realization that the leaders of the British empire, without consulting the American officials and with apparent indifference to the welfare of the colonists, had relinquished Louisbourg, secured in part by New England through an enormous expenditure of treasure and the death of a great many of its sons, rocked many colonists. John Adams later recalled the raging fury of his father and other men in Braintree, Massachusetts, at Britain's coldhearted insensitivity toward the provinces; a contemporary writing in the *Boston News-Letter* (1749) spoke of the "insult" of having to "yield the Conquest that was ours." New England, the essayist added, had been "Vanquished by Peace."

Aix-la-Chapelle closed a long, indecisive war, a conflict in which the Americans developed scorn toward the British military establishment after the suffering in the Cartagena campaign and an enhanced wariness of the designs of the empire's leaders after the abandonment of Louisbourg. For all these efforts, neither provincial security nor American ambitions had been advanced in the slightest. These failures had not been caused by New England's armies. The ragged survivors of Louisbourg returned to a New England that lauded them as "fearless" warriors and "Characters of Praise." Indeed, some even said they were superior to England's soldiers. After all, America's citizen-soldiers had taken Louisbourg, whereas the British regulars had failed ignominiously at Cartagena.

CHAPTER FIVE

The Anglo-American Triumph

Origins of the French and Indian War

The exhaustion of the belligerents brought the War of the Austrian Succession to an end. The killing had failed to resolve Europe's most troubling problems. No one expected a permanent peace or even a lengthy respite from hostilities.

Indeed, peace had hardly broken out before Europe's diplomats were busily searching out new alliances. Each nation hoped to strengthen itself before war resumed. In America, as well, the statesmen were engaged. England built a naval base at Halifax and shipped over twenty-five hundred Protestant colonists to reside alongside the suspect, French-speaking Acadians in Nova Scotia; France and England, moreover, built fortifications on the isthmus of Chignecto, the narrow strip of land that connected Nova Scotia to the mainland above Maine. France also was active further west. With the arrival of peace France strengthened Fort Niagara, on the portage between Lake Ontario and Lake Erie.

On several previous occasions, Nova Scotia and the Great Lakes region had proven to be tinderboxes. In the 1750s, however, the spark that ignited a world war—a conflict, for a change, that began in America, then engulfed Europe—flashed first in the Ohio Country.

Both France and Great Britain found this region enticing. Each coveted the potentially lucrative Indian trade, while the English colonists, beset by an extraordinary natural increase in population as well as by a considerable European immigration, also found the seemingly endless expanse of land too inviting to ignore. In addition, the possibility that France might someday control this trans-Appalachian vista reawakened in England the old fear that France, together with its ally, Spain, would encircle Britain's mainland colonies. "They have driven us, as it were into a corner and blocked us up," wrote a London pamphleteer in 1754. France, on the other hand, understood that if Britain gained hegemony over the Ohio Country, French Canada and the colony of Louisiana could never be linked.

The imperial rivals had largely ignored the Ohio Country before King George's War. Shortly thereafter, however, both Virginia and France stirred. Virginia moved first. In 1748 several planters, including Lawrence Washington, George's older half-brother, joined to form the Ohio Company and applied to the Crown for title to a portion of western real estate. George II obliged, but only if certain conditions were met. After seven years the company would receive five hundred thousand acres along the Ohio River if it had settled one hundred inhabitants and erected and maintained a fort at the headwaters of the Ohio. The Virginians quickly set to work, and the French just as quickly responded. New France strengthened its garrisons in the Great Lakes area and in the Illinois Country, built a new fort at Kaskaskia, and in 1753 sent two thousand men south to construct a road and forts between Lake Erie and the head of the Ohio River. These men also were ordered to remove every English trader from the region. How should Virginia respond? That was the very question that Gov. Robert Dinwiddie asked the imperial officials in London.

London promptly instructed Dinwiddie to send an emissary to the French commander in the disputed region bearing the message that the territory belonged to Great Britain. George Washington was among those who volunteered to carry Britain's notice. Only twenty-one years old, Washington was the product of a good family; in addition, he was healthy (he stood 6' 4" and weighed about two hundred pounds), vigorous, and hearty, having worked as a surveyor on Virginia's rugged, mountainous frontier for the past five years. Washington got the job. In the fall of 1753 he led a small party to French headquarters at Fort Le Boeuf just below Lake Erie. The French received him amicably, but it was clear that English words would not drive France out of the West.

By the following spring, Washington was in the West again, this time as the second in command of the Virginia Regiment, a little army raised by Dinwiddie and the House of Burgesses to drive the French from the Ohio Country. Although he knew that a larger French army was near the Ohio River, Washington impetuously took his 134 ill-trained, "loose, Idle" men and a few Indian allies deep into western Pennsylvania. There, in the black wilderness about twenty-five miles south of the Ohio River, his scouts discovered a party of French troops. Washington appears to have acted without hesitation. Young, rash, eager for glory, and evidently indifferent to the inevitable response of the vastly superior French army just up the road, he ordered a surprise attack. Caught off guard, the small band of Frenchmen was easily overwhelmed. Ten French soldiers were killed. On that May 28, 1754, in a dense, sunless forest in a corner of the world that could hardly have been more remote from the luxurious palace at Versailles or the elegant paneled drawing rooms at Whitehall, the first shot had been fired in what soon would become a world war, a shot ordered by an obscure young provincial.

An Undeclared War

Soon after his successful frontier engagement, Washington learned that he had been named commander of the Virginia Regiment, his predecessor having perished in a fall from a horse. Had Colonel Washington been wise, he would have ordered his little army back to Virginia. Instead, he waited for the French army to come after him. They found him on July 3 at the Great Meadows, where he had built a circular stockade that he named Fort Necessity. Outnumbered three to one, Washington fought for only a few hours before surrendering. By then, one-third of his army was dead or wounded. Miraculously, given his treacherous ambush of French soldiers in a time of peace, Washington was permitted to surrender with honor and return home; he might have been compelled to endure a long, lonely, perhaps fatal, incarceration in a cold, insalubrious Canadian prison.

Washington's performance had not pleased Governor Dinwiddie, however. He reorganized the Virginia Regiment and offered Washington a lesser rank, an affront that the proud young man could not accept. Washington resigned from the provincial army and returned to civilian pursuits, his days as a soldier presumably behind him forever.

Yet the conflict that he had helped to start was just heating up. News of Washington's defeat at Fort Necessity reached London in September 1754. The English government also was informed that the French had constructed a fort—Fort Duquesne—at the head of the Ohio River. British officials gathered hurriedly at Whitehall to consider their response; they discovered immediately that deep divisions separated them. The monarch, George II, expressed his "utter aversion" to sending a British army to America to contest the French; Great Britain and France were at peace, a state of affairs he did not wish to disturb. Influential men urged a military response, however. The Earl of Halifax, the president of the Board of Trade, proposed joint Anglo-American operations to seize Fort Niagara, situated on the Niagara River, which linked Lake

Ontario and Lake Erie, and Fort Saint Frédéric at Crown Point, near the south end of Lake Champlain. Halifax reasoned that it would be far easier to mount campaigns in these sectors than through western Pennsylvania's wild mountainous approaches to the Ohio; moreover, once forts Niagara and Saint Frédéric were taken, he argued, Fort Duquesne, isolated and without hope of assistance from New France, could easily be taken by a relatively small provincial force. The Duke of Cumberland, the son of the monarch, expressed another view. The captain general of the British army and a tough, veteran soldier, Cumberland wished to send British regulars to the Ohio while, simultaneously, armies raised in the northern provinces attacked the French both in the Lake Champlain region and in Nova Scotia.

The ministry considered its options and reached a decision before the end of the month. After first inducing the king to change his mind, the government adopted a grand strategy, a plan that involved a little of Halifax's proposal and most of what Cumberland had recommended. The ministry agreed to commit two regiments to America to move against the French on the Ohio River; this force was to be augmented by provincial troops. Meanwhile, an army was to be raised in the northern colonies to strike at Fort Niagara, Fort Saint Frédéric, and the French installation on the isthmus of Chignecto.

Anglo-American forces would total nearly nine thousand men, quite large by contrast to the number of men committed to America in the previous intercolonial wars, but small when compared with the armies that Great Britain and its colonies would raise before peace ultimately was restored. Three factors caused the English to limit their commitment to the colonies in 1754. First, the ministers of state listened to Governor Dinwiddie, who had written that two regiments of British regulars could easily seize Fort Duquesne. Second, the government did not wish to push France into a declaration of war, a likely occurrence if Britain committed an army of sufficient size to imperil the existence of New France. Third, at this juncture Great Britain's goal was not the destruction of New France, but the more limited objective of forcing France to withdraw from territory that London believed to be part of Virginia, New York, and Nova Scotia.

The ministry selected Gen. Edward Braddock to command the two regiments it dispatched to the colonies. Braddock's thinning gray hair and the lines that crisscrossed his face bore mute testimony to the sixty years he had lived, almost forty-five of which he had spent as a soldier. Aside from limited combat experience in the warfare of the 1740s, Braddock had spent most of his career in peacetime army camps, training recruits and engaged in nothing more dangerous than drafting memoranda. He had never served in America, but he was thought to possess the qualifications necessary for the assignment. He had campaigned in the wilds of northern Scotland, thought to be good training for soldiering in the rugged hills of Virginia and Pennsylvania; moreover, Braddock, a gruff and ascerbic individual, had long been thought of as a stern disciplinarian, the very sort needed, it was said in London, to fashion an army from the rabble in the provinces. Not everyone agreed that Braddock was the best choice, however. Governor Shirley's son thought Braddock brave and honest, but unprepared to fight in the American wilderness. Benjamin Franklin, who had met Braddock, agreed; Braddock was too narrow-minded to succeed in America, he said, for the general had "too high an opinion of the validity of regular troops; too mean a one of both Americans and Indians."

Braddock, with his two regiments of infantry and a train of artillery, arrived in Virginia early in 1755. Prior to his disembarkation the colonists had been directed by London to assist by raising their own armies and by furnishing supplies, especially food, wagons, horses, medicines, and bandages. Braddock, in turn, had been ordered to consult with the provincials, although his task was rather clearly spelled out. He was to move against the French in the Ohio Country. Afterward he was to construct "a good and sufficient Fort" at the head of the Ohio River, then take Fort Niagara, unless a newly recruited provincial army had already succeeded in seizing that installation. In addition, Braddock was instructed to see that the colonies were sufficiently unified to repel any Canadian offensive.

Six weeks after his arrival in Virginia Braddock summoned five colonial governors to Alexandria to plan operations. Some debate likely occurred. Governor Shirley of Massachusetts wanted the British general to concentrate against either Fort Niagara or Fort Frontenac. His logic was impeccable; once either Lake Ontario or the head of the Saint Lawrence was in English hands, Fort Duquesne, the bastion that the French had erected at the head of the Ohio River, inevitably would wither on the vine. On the other hand, Dinwiddie and a multitude of Virginians urged Braddock to march directly to the Ohio. Ultimately, the conference agreed upon four British campaigns for 1755.

Braddock would take Fort Duquesne. Simultaneously, British regulars in Nova Scotia would unite with a New England army to strike against Fort Beauséjour and Fort Gaspereau, the forts that France had erected recently at Chignecto. William Johnson, just appointed the British Superintendent of the Five Nations, would command an army of northern provincials and Native Americans in a campaign to take Fort Saint Frédéric at Crown Point, the facility the French had maintained for almost twenty-five years near the south end of Lake Champlain. Finally, Governor Shirley of Massachusetts, in command of still another colonial army, would drive against Fort Niagara.

It was an audacious scheme. If the British succeeded, by year's end the flag of France would vanish from Nova Scotia to northern New England, from upper New York westward to the potentially bountiful prairies deep in the interior heartland. But the British failed, and they failed miserably. Braddock's problems commenced long before he took his army to the frontier. In June 1754, before his arrival in America, commissioners from seven colonies had met in Albany to discuss intercolonial cooperation in defense. The conclave sought to create a more unified front against the French by combining the colonies under a chief executive appointed in London and an elected American congress; this new provincial government would possess the authority to levy taxes throughout the colonies, raise a continental army, construct western forts, and conduct relations with the natives. The scheme, soon known as the Albany Plan of Union, got nowhere. The idea of colonial unity struck terror in the hearts of many in London, lest it might be the first step toward American independence; moreover, fearing the loss of provincial autonomy, no colonial assembly ratified the plan. Braddock would get some help from the colonies, but not what he might have obtained under the Albany Plan.

The British commander had not been in the provinces long before he denounced the "Supineness, and unseasonable economy" of the colonists. He discovered that he could procure the horses and wagons that his army needed only with great difficulty, and he paid an outlandish price for what he got. Nor did he have the funds he desired. London had encouraged the thirteen colonies to raise a common fund from which Braddock could draw; it never came into being. It seemed to Braddock that the colonies were largely indifferent to what London regarded as the French problem. Only a few colonies—those near Canada or those with an immediate stake in the West—seemed eager to help. As a result, only Virginia, Maryland, and North Carolina contributed troops to his army, about six hundred men altogether.

Braddock was ready to move by midspring. He ordered his army into western Maryland. From there he proceeded toward the Ohio River, following the road cut by Washington's Virginia Regiment during the previous year. Washington had emerged from his early retirement to join Braddock's staff and to assist in getting the army over the mountains. Washington ran errands and kept the orderly book; if his later reminiscences are to be believed, he grew close to Braddock, and in the evenings, over wine and late-night snacks, brazenly advised the veteran general to abandon his European ways in the wilderness theater.

Progress was painfully slow. A month was consumed in reaching the Great Meadows, barely thirty miles from their embarkation point. Fearing that their interminable pace would permit the French to rush in reinforcements from Canada, Braddock, in mid-June, sent much of the baggage to the rear and divided his army; he ordered a force of about eight hundred men to proceed ahead. By the first days of July this advance force, or "flying column," as eighteenth-century armies called such units, had penetrated to within a few miles of Fort Duquesne; at the end of the first week of July Braddock and the main body of the army caught up with the flying column.

At three o'clock in the morning on July 9, members of the advance units, commanded by Lt. Col. Thomas Gage, were up and moving, confident that before sunset they would reach Fort Duquesne and take the first steps to assault the French installation. Lieutenant Colonel Gage, a veteran soldier, was the son of an Irish peer. Gage had been an officer in the British army since 1741 and had served with distinction in the last war. Still young—he was thirty-four years old in 1755—he would soldier for many more years, eventually commanding the British army in America during the fateful days of April 1775. On this humid morning, Gage and his men splashed across the Monongahela River, gentle and, at its summer ebb, easy to ford. British scouts spotted some Indian tracks, but Gage secured the area with his artillery, and the remainder of the army followed.

The British army was spread over a long distance, as armies on the move customarily were organized during a European campaign. Thirteen hundred men comprised Braddock's force, about 40 percent of whom were colonials; approximately fifty camp followers, wives and mistresses of some of the men, also were present. Guides and cavalry were in the vanguard, twenty men in all, including a few Indians; their leader was George Groghan, an Irish immigrant to America who had lived on the frontier for nearly fifteen years. Next came the vanguard of the flying column, a line of more than two hundred that extended for one-hundred yards or more. Gage, with about three hundred men, followed. On his heels came an independent company of grenadiers, the elite of Braddock's army, as well as a company of British regulars recruited in America. A working party—sawyers and the like—came next, after which came more light horse, American cavalry in this instance, commanded by a Virginian, Capt. Robert Stewart, wearing the buff and blue uniform that Colonel Washington had designed the previous year for the Virginia Regiment. "Pioneers," mostly Americans recruited to build the road through the Pennsylvania wilderness, followed closely behind. Finally, the main body of the army, more than five hundred regulars and provincial soldiers extending over one-third of a mile, followed the pioneers; Braddock and his staff, including Washington, still weak from a recent, serious bout with a camp disease, rode at the head of this part of the army. One hundred yards in the train of this contingent came the rear guard, about eighty men posted behind and vigilant against an attack, but just as watchful for deserters from the myriad columns that splayed out ahead. Adam Stephen, the Scottish physician and immigrant who soldiered for Virginia, commanded the rear.

The army moved slowly. The trek was up a steady grade; the incline, the heat, and the uncomfortable footing in the tangled woods tired the men. In addition, crossing a river (the Monongahela was forded twice that day) was deliberate work, and moving artillery and baggage wagons up the slope of the riverbanks required careful preparation. By noon, when the second river crossing began, the army had advanced about four miles. By one o'clock Gage and his men were well past the Monongahela; Braddock, meanwhile, was watching as the rear guard of his army, wet but cooled by the sparkling river, struggled ashore. Suddenly the general heard shots well ahead. He and his staff, including Washington, spurred their mounts and galloped toward the shooting. They heard more shots as they rode, as well as what Washington called the "whooping and hallowing of the enemy." When they reached the scene of action they found confusion in the British ranks.

The advance units under Gage had stumbled into a large unit of French, Canadians, and Indians. The men on both sides were startled, but the French forces recovered first. Seizing a hill on the right and a ravine on the left, the French poured a murderous fire upon the British. Cut to pieces and outnumbered, Gage's vanguard fell back, collapsing into Braddock and the main British army. Terror set in. Jammed together, pummeled from in front as well as on both flanks by an enemy that was often hidden deep in the enveloping green wilderness, panic coursed through the British ranks. One of the British officers later described what happened.

The British Troops were thunderstruck to feel the Effect of a heavy Fire and see no Enemy; they threw away their [return] Fire in a most indiscreet Manner, and shamefully turned their Backs on a few Savages and Canadians. . . . They kept in a mere huddle in spite of the most ardent Endeavors of many brave officers. . . . Shame unto the infamous Dogs!

In several letters written over the ensuing weeks, Colonel Washington described what occurred:

We have been scandalously beaten by a trifling body of men. . . . [Our] troops, chiefly regular soldiers . . . were struck with such a panic that they behaved with more cowardice than it is possible to conceive. The officers behaved gallantly in order to encourage their men, for which they suffered greatly. The Virginia troops showed a good deal of bravery and were nearly all killed. [T]he dastardly behavior of those they called regulars exposed all others that were inclined to do their duty to almost certain death. [T]hey broke and ran as sheep pursued by dogs; and it was impossible to rally them. . . . [However, the] Virginians behaved like men and died like soldiers.

The panic described by Washington was echoed by many other witnesses. One of Braddock's aides later wrote that the Indians began to scalp fallen British soldiers in the first moments of the engagement; such a scene, he thought, undoubtedly spread the sense of panic. Several British officers perished in the first volley of French and Indian fire; a British officer subsequently said he believed their loss so soon after the start of the battle added to the confusion. Discipline broke down. Men fired wildly, quickly expending their ammunition; some men grabbed the arms of their fallen comrades and continued to fight, but others ran for the rear as soon as they fired their last shot. Still another problem arose. Bunched together and firing recklessly, many British soldiers accidently killed and wounded their comrades. Horror was added to the terror. Gripped by fright—by the fear of pain, of death, and most of all, perhaps, of falling captive to an enemy renowned for the ghastly tortures it inflicted upon its prisoners—some men fled the battlefield soon after the first shots were fired. One British officer told how he almost died in this panic:

We were suddenly attacked from the Woods. Every Man was alert, did all he could, but Men dropped like Leaves in Autumn. All was confusion, and in spite of what Officers and the bravest Men could do, many ran away. . . . I was wounded in one Leg, and in the other Heel, so could not go, but sat down at the foot of a Tree, praying of everyone that ran by that they would help me escape; an American Virginian turned to me and said: "Yes, Countrymen, I will put you out of your Misery, these Dogs shall not burn you." He then levelled his gun at my Head, but I cried out and dodged him behind the Tree; the Piece went off and missed me, and he ran on. Soon after Lieutenant Grey, with a Party of Dumary's Company, came by; the firing was not Quite ceased . . . and he got me carried off.

General Braddock was not so fortunate. He fought bravely, continuing to command, vainly seeking to restore order, even as five horses were shot from under him. Eventually, however, a musket ball found him. The bullet passed through his right arm and into his lungs. Mortally wounded, the general swam into and out of consciousness. A total rout began the moment Braddock went down. A few brave men, including Washington, stayed to fashion a litter and carried Braddock to the rear. Most men ran away as quickly as their legs would carry them, not stopping until they had crossed the Monongahela.

The battle was over. The Indians "could not wait to plunder and drink," a French officer later charged; the French, however, were no less anxious to turn their attention to a captured hogshead of rum. That delay alone permitted the fleeing English soldiers to escape. In addition, both the French and Indians, understanding that they were still outnumbered even after all the redcoat losses, appear to have feared a British counterattack, however unlikely such an event.

The engagement had lasted about three hours. More than nine hundred of Braddock's men died or were wounded. Several of Virginia's officers and most of its enlisted men perished. Washington reported that barely 30 of approximately 150 Virginians survived; a Virginia cavalry officer later said that 25 of 29 of his men were cut down. It was here that young Lt. William Polson, the Scottish immigrant who had seen military service as a means of advancement, perished, and that Adam Stephen was wounded. Miraculously, young Washington emerged unscathed, though two horses were shot from beneath him and his "upper coat was entirely shot to tatters with musket bullets," according to an anonymous eyewitness. This defeat was the worst suffered by an army of British regulars in North America in the nearly two hundred years that stretched from Roanoke Island to the outbreak of the War of Independence.

The rout of Braddock's force on the Monongahela presaged other British failures. Of the four British campaigns in 1755, only the Anglo-American strike against the French installations at Chignecto succeeded. Financed by Nova Scotia and commanded by Col. Robert Monckton, a British regular, most of the manpower—1,900 of 2,150 men—for this expeditionary force was provided by New England. Beauséjour, defended by only 160 French, fell after a four-day siege. Gaspereau capitulated twenty-four hours later. But what followed is the best-remembered occurrence of the British operation in this sector. Fearing a French counteroffensive from Louisbourg, the British government in Nova Scotia ordered the removal of all Acadian inhabitants, most of whom steadfastly refused to take an oath of allegiance to Great Britain. The mass deportation commenced that autumn. While the authorities appropriated their livestock and New England soldiers burned their homes, up to fifteen thousand men, women, and children were herded into British transports and sent into exile throughout England's mainland colonies.

About the time the French flag was being lowered for the last time at Chignecto, Johnson and Shirley—Braddock's successor as the British commander in America—marched from their bases in the Albany-Schenectady area. Johnson's men ultimately saw the most action. A jovial, gregarious, forty-year-old Irishman who was as comfortable smoking the pipe in a sachem's hut as he was sharing tea in a well-appointed drawing room, Johnson led his army of three thousand—nearly four-fifths of whom were New England men—up the Hudson River valley toward Lake George, a laborious journey. The army literally constructed a road through the solid forest; in addition, it paused about fifty miles above Albany to build Fort Edward, then it stopped again farther north to construct Fort William Henry at the southern end of Lake George. As the men toiled in the thick, airless forest, Mohawk scouts brought word that a French army of eight thousand was moving south to defend Crown Point. The Indians overestimated the size of their enemy, but a three-thousand-man force of French under Jean-Armand, Baron de Dieskau, recently dispatched from Brest as the French counterpart of Braddock, was indeed moving into Fort Saint Frédéric, Johnson's target, an installation about forty miles north of Fort William Henry. Dieskau had with him some fifteen hundred French regulars sent from home that year; approximately one thousand men who were either members of the Canadian militia or of provincial units; the *compagnies franches de la marine*, outfits that consisted of men recruited in France but commanded by inhabitants of New France; and about six hundred Indian allies.

Dieskau's force had found Johnson's army divided between Fort Edward and a rude encampment at the site that had been selected for Fort William Henry. Dieskau also discovered that the defenses at Fort Edward were inadequate; the English possessed few mounted guns and but fragmentary entrenchments. Dieskau decided to strike Fort Edward immediately. His plan was to destroy that installation, sever the supply lines to Johnson's men to the north, and ultimately wipe out the outnumbered and undersupplied—and hence doomed—English provincials at Lake George.

Dieskau transported his three thousand men from Fort Saint Frédéric to Fort Carillon farther south. From there on September 6 Dieskau led a raiding party of fifteen hundred men—about equally divided between Canadians and Indians—toward Fort Edward. But the planned attack never occurred. Dieskau's Indian allies balked at assailing the unfinished, albeit well-defended, fort. Forced to improvise, Dieskau opted instead to attack Johnson's camp at the Fort William Henry site. On September 8 his army set off to the north, back toward the crystal blue waters of Lake George. At about this same moment Johnson once again learned through his Mohawk scouts that a large French army was on the move, this time from Fort Saint Frédéric toward Fort Edward. He ordered twelve hundred men, mostly colonial soldiers, back to reinforce Fort Edward. Thus, Dieskau's army and the English relief force, neither suspecting the intentions of the other, were marching toward one another. Dieskau was first to discover what was happening, and he prepared an ambush, hoping to trap the British in a ravine about four miles south of Lake George.

The unsuspecting English colonials walked into the trap. The opening round of fire by the French and Indians was devastating. Caught in a crossfire, nearly 8 percent of the men in the provincial force were killed or wounded instantly. The English offered little organized resistance; fewer than one in ten of the surviving English soldiery even fired a round in self-defense. Panic set in, and the men—with "Marks of Horror and Fear in their Countenances," according to a witness—raced for Johnson's nearby camp. This brief encounter, which came to be called the Bloody Morning Scout, once again demonstrated the limitations of the British colonists when fighting in the wilderness.

Colonel Johnson was fortunate to have lost so few men in the ambush (the carnage would have been greater had not some of Dieskau's Indian allies revealed themselves too soon), but he still faced a perilous situation. While most of his army toiled to complete Fort Edward well to the south, he still had to defend Fort William Henry, which was far from completed. Indeed, the fort consisted of nothing but a breastwork constructed of logs, wagons, and even boats that Johnson's men hastily muscled up from the lake. Johnson, however, had more men than Dieskau, and he also possessed some cannon.

Dieskau struck at Johnson's camp in the heat of the late afternoon on September 8, just a few hours after the Bloody Morning Scout. The French fire was as thick as "hailstones from Heaven," according to one soldier, and it resulted in heavy casualties. Johnson lost 15 percent of his men. Nevertheless, the attack was repulsed, and the French were forced to retreat to Fort Saint Frédéric. The colonial soldiery had held firm inside the rude fort, although it was Johnson's murderous use of his heavy cannon against the French assaults that proved decisive. French losses were frightful, totaling nearly one-third of their army. Dieskau was among the wounded. He suffered three wounds and was captured near the end of the engagement. The English, Dieskau later said, had at first fought like boys, then like men, and, as the battle wore on, like devils; he believed, he went on, that the British might have scored a truly crushing victory had they pursued their retreating adversary. But Johnson demurred. His men were too exhausted to face an immediate fight. In the days that followed, other problems arose that inhibited Johnson from taking additional action. Not only did his Indian allies melt away soon after the battle at Fort William Henry, but his intelligence service reported that both Fort Saint Frédéric and Fort Carillon were well built and heavily defended. Moreover, Johnson could not locate sufficient wagons to supply his army. Finally, Johnson's inactivity also may have resulted from his incapacity, for he, too, had been wounded at Fort William Henry, having taken a ball in the thigh.

The Battle of Lake George, as these September engagements soon were called, concluded Johnson's campaign. Even though reinforcements arrived through the autumn, he proceeded no further, pleading a lack of supplies, an army depleted by camp fevers, and the breakdown of morale and discipline within his cold, hungry ranks. Eschewing an offensive, Johnson had his men complete the two fortifications they had begun, while the French erected Fort Carillon at Ticonderoga, twelve miles south of Crown Point.

Shirley, meanwhile, accomplished even less than Johnson. His army of twenty-four hundred men moved from Albany to Fort Oswego on Lake Ontario, but it spent the remainder of the year repairing the old, crumbling post, a fortress that had deteriorated so badly in its twenty-seven years that Shirley feared its walls would quake and collapse when the English discharged their own artillery. Nothing came of his plan to attack Niagara, therefore. Later, Shirley's failure was attributed to his lack of command experience, but he was compelled to abandon his original strategy by the condition of Oswego and by Braddock's misfortune. He knew that twelve hundred French were posted at Fort Frontenac, barely fifty miles from Oswego; in addition, he realized that the French could reinforce Niagara with the victors from Fort Duquesne. The best that Shirley could do was to maintain and strengthen that which he possessed and plan for 1756.

War Is Declared

While Shirley watched the foliage turn to lustrous reds and ochres, disappear, then return in the spring in its bright green splendor, he concocted a plan of action for the new year. Unfortunately for him, however, his carefully laid designs were obliterated by a series of crucial decisions in London. Late in the spring of 1756, Britain and France finally declared war on one another. The causes of the conflict were as much European in origin as American. Britain's King George II gave the French invasion of Minorca as the principal reason for hostilities in his declaration of war upon France; the other major powers on the continent, most of whom had no stake in America, soon found themselves to be belligerents in what would ultimately be known in Europe as the Seven Years' War.

England and France, of course, had a long-rooted interest in America. But in this conflict, as never before, their attention was riveted upon the New World. Both Great Britain and France understood that a part of this war involved a struggle for supremacy in North America, principally a contest for dominion in the vast area beyond the Appalachian Mountains, a clash that each country had gradually come to see as irrepressible. Both sides appointed new commanders in the American theater early in 1756: France to replace Dieskau, Britain to remove Shirley, an amateur militarist who had failed to accomplish the task that Braddock had set before him. The French appointed vain, impetuous Louis Joseph, Marquis de Montcalm. Forty-four years old, Montcalm was a well-educated man who for much of his life yearned to teach; he had joined the French army at age fifteen and fought with distinction in the War of the Austrian Succession, suffering two severe wounds and capture by his enemy. Montcalm arrived in America bearing the rank of *maréchal de camp*, equivalent to major-general in the British army.

Great Britain named John Campbell, Earl of Loudoun, a fifty-two-year-old Scottish peer, to command its armies. With no wrinkles and a full head of sandy hair, Loudoun at first glance appeared to be a very young man. He made an excellent first impression. An American officer described him as short and strong, a man with a pleasant countenance dominated by bright eyes that were "sprightly and good humored." Benjamin Franklin, usually a good judge of character, first met Loudoun in 1756 and was impressed by his mettle, pronouncing him "very well suited" for his command in America. Loudoun's appointment was greeted enthusiastically in the colonies. His high rank, years of experience, and distinguished record of service indicated to most provincials that Great Britain, after the failures of Braddock, a training camp general, and Shirley, an inexperienced soldier, had finally begun to take the war in America more seriously. Loudoun arrived in New York in July 1756 much as a potentate might have landed. He was accompanied by sixteen servants and his mistress; his personal belongings were so considerable that one entire royal vessel had been required to bring them to America. Montcalm and Lord Loudoun would square off in a war that various generations of Americans would know as the French War, the French and Indian War, and, more recently, The Great War for the Empire.

Loudoun was feted enthusiastically upon his arrival in New York, but grim reality soon set in. Only days after he alighted in America on his mission to secure a reversal in Britain's fortunes, news arrived that Fort Oswego, and with it Lake Ontario, had been lost to the French. The British should never have suffered such a debacle. Weeks before, British intelligence indicated that the French were moving against Oswego; the report was discounted, even though in March a French light infantry force had succeeded in blowing up a huge British supply depot near Oswego. The fort, meanwhile, remained uncompleted. The repair work that Shirley had ordered proceeded during the first half of 1756, but the endeavor was inadequately funded and the installation remained unfinished by midsummer, nearly a full year after the British had discovered the fort's tumbledown condition. The English failed even to secure the supply route that linked Fort Oswego to Albany. The supply route was interdicted repeatedly by the French from March onward, resulting in great suffering among the men posted at Oswego. Scurvy swept through the garrison that winter and spring. The men who died were not all replaced, in part because some colonies refused to raise more men to serve under Shirley, whom they regarded as a military incompetent. A paralysis seemed to grip the British, from Governor Shirley, who knew by April that he was to be replaced by Loudoun, on down through the command structure.

In spring of 1756, the governor-general of New France, Pierre de Rigaud de Vaudreuil, was convinced that Britain could be contained. The key, he believed, was Fort Oswego. If Oswego fell, he reasoned, he would control Lake Ontario, and if he controlled Lake Ontario he would control the Iroquois Confederacy and, with it, much of the transmontane West. "I shall take care to crush in the bud" the "hopes of his Britannic Majesty," Vaudreuil boasted. Montcalm, who feared that there were too many obstacles to be overcome, resisted a campaign on Lake Ontario. Vaudreuil won the dispute. By the second week of August, Montcalm's men confronted the English garrison. The French possessed a three-to-one manpower advantage; the siege ended in just three days with an English capitulation. More than sixteen hundred English were taken prisoner; about fifty of them were butchered when Montcalm briefly lost control of his Indian allies following the seizure of the British store of liquor. Another twenty or so captives were given to the Indians for adoption in place of their warriors lost in the engagement.

Montcalm remained inactive following his victory at Oswego. He briefly toyed with the thought of a foray against Albany and, later, he contemplated a campaign from Fort Carillon to win control of the Champlain Valley. He rejected both considerations, the first because he knew that it exceeded his grasp and the latter because the early onset of winter made all such thoughts impractical. Loudoun also scotched all thought of an immediate major campaign and put his men in winter quarters, but in the process his actions provoked almost as much alarm as an advancing enemy force. Loudoun understood the terribly ambiguous English laws and judicial rulings with regard to quartering an army to mean that he was allowed to take private dwellings and public buildings for the use of his men. The colonials believed otherwise, and they contended that English custom and legislation, especially the English Bill of Rights, parliamentary enactments in 1689 that included a provision that declared that the keeping of a standing army in time of peace was illegal, protected them from arbitrary quartering. The conflicting views reached crisis proportions that winter in Albany when Loudoun used force to compel homeowners to provide lodging for British officers and men until barracks could be constructed. His actions sent tremors of anger and concern through several provinces, provoking legislation from some and prompting others to allocate funds for the construction of facilities so as to forestall the army's seizure of quarters.

Although the redcoats took up winter quarters, Loudoun was not inactive. During these months he made extensive use of British ranger units. Indeed, in these years the British made a substantial commitment to the tactics of irregular warfare, what in Europe was called partisan war or *la petite guerre*.

During the previous spring, Governor Shirley had created five companies of rangers, one consisting of Stockbridge Indians. They were to be intelligence-gathering units, but they were also to engage in guerrilla operations with the intent of keeping the enemy "under a continual Alarm." Robert Rogers, a rough-hewn New Hampshireman who had fought the Indians since he was fourteen, commanded one of the companies and eventually became the most renowned American ranger, but others, such as John Stark and Israel Putnam, who fought with distinction in the War of Independence, earned their spurs in such service. Loudoun was so impressed with the manner in which the rangers had "roughly handled" their foe that he created five additional companies. Because of his service in the Scottish Highlands, Loudoun attached great importance to what he called the "bush fight," the use of mobile bands of backwoodsmen to create confusion in the army command. It was not a suitable task for a conventional army, he thought. Instead, he assigned the duty to the rangers, but never completely trusting the American frontiersmen, he posted among them numerous volunteer regulars, hoping they might maintain some semblance of discipline and, while they were at it, perhaps also learn "the ranging of the wood-service," as he quaintly put it.

The rangers pursued sundry objectives. They sought to disrupt the French supply system, to capture prisoners for interrogation, to ambush the enemy's advance units, to lead diversionary raids, and to conduct reconnaissance missions. Ranger service was difficult duty, often involving numerous privations. Rogers spoke of one mission when he spent days slogging over "wet sunken ground, the water most of the way near a foot deep." On other forays he spent protracted periods living in the wilderness during the coldest spells of winter, often without benefit of a comforting fire, lest the enemy learn of the rangers' presence; Rogers often traveled on snowshoes with nearly one hundred pounds of food and equipment strapped to his back, and on many occasions he slept on a bed of spruce boughs and dined on dried beef and cornmeal, if he had any food at all (on a mission in 1759 against the Saint Francis Indians he endured three days without victuals). This duty was hazardous as well, for the most part carried out deep in enemy territory, where a wrong turn or a slight miscalculation could result in instant death or, worse, capture by a terrifying adversary. Rogers was shot in the wrist during an engagement with the French near Fort Carillon in 1757. One of his men, captured with seven others during another battle, was stripped naked and compelled by his captors to march for nine days, all the while subsisting on mushrooms and beech leaves. He was finally liberated by friendly Indians. Israel Putnam, who would serve as a general just beneath George Washington throughout the War of Independence, had an equally harrowing experience. Captured in a battle near Fort Anne—in which Rogers saw forty-nine of his men killed—Putnam, while burdened with heavy packs strapped to his back and stripped of his shoes, was made to march a considerable distance. He eventually was brought to Fort Carillon where he was questioned by Montcalm, then taken to Montreal and captivity.

Loudoun was convinced of the necessity of such work, but he eventually grew to doubt the capability of undisciplined frontiersmen to do the job. After eighteen months in the colonies, he created the Royal Americans, a corps of lightly armed, mobile men who were commanded by British regulars who had learned the art of the bush fight from the likes of Robert Rogers.

During 1756, Loudoun's headquarters were in New York, and his focus appeared to be trained on the North, but the war continued to rage elsewhere. Buoyed by the success of the French, the Indians had taken to the warpath in the backcountry of Virginia, Maryland, and Pennsylvania. By early 1756, seven hundred frontier settlers in these colonies had been killed or captured. The commander of the Virginia Regiment acknowledged that the Shenandoah Valley had been lost to settlement. That commander was Col. George Washington, whose valorous conduct alongside Braddock had made him a hero to many Virginians and had compelled Governor Dinwiddie to ask him to once again lead the provincial army. Washington directed a long, lonely, often desperate struggle. One in three men who served under him died in 1756; conditions hardly improved the next year. It was a war of ambush and dangerous raids, and as the casualty rate increased with no apparent end to the bloodletting in sight, Washington's leadership was criticized in private by Dinwiddie as well as in public by an anonymous newspaper essayist. Only twenty-three when he resumed command of his province's army, Washington's youthful inexperience often caused him to act unwisely, although his lack of success flowed directly from the failure of the British armed forces in other theaters. So long as the natives in Virginia were armed and assisted by the French, Washington's little army could not hope to pacify the frontier.

Virginia fought alone in this grim war. To be sure, it received no assistance from Pennsylvania, its neighbor, whose own frontier was being ravished. At the outset of hostilities in 1754, Benjamin Franklin had sought to rally support for intercolonial cooperation. He had urged the adoption of the Albany Plan of Union, and in the spring of that year he had printed in the *Pennsylvania Gazette* a cartoon of a snake cut into eight sections, each identified as a colony or a part of Anglo-America, with the caption, "Join or Die." Like the other colonies, however, Pennsylvania had not joined with its neighbors in a military alliance. Indeed, the Quaker leadership in the assembly resisted the use of force against the Indians, a position that grew untenable when the Indians unleashed attacks as far east as the Blue Mountains, striking near Reading and at Gnadenhutten, only seventy-five miles from Philadelphia. Angry frontiersmen wanted protection. London wanted action. There was talk in the Privy council of disqualifying the Quakers from government service. To forestall such a step, every Quaker in the Pennsylvania assembly resigned his seat during the course of 1756.

Franklin's credo, that "we shall [never] have a firm peace with the Indians till we have well drubbed them," was adopted by Pennsylvania following the departure of the Quakers, but the province's largest military operation achieved only partial success. In 1756 the province sent a three-hundred-man force under Col. John Armstrong to destroy a string of Indian villages at Kittanning, about fifty miles above Fort Duquesne. The Pennsylvanians struck early in September, only three weeks after the British surrender at Fort Oswego. The soldiery torched numerous dwellings and inflicted heavy losses, yet most of the inhabitants escaped. Even so, this demonstration that Pennsylvania was no longer defenseless and that the natives could anticipate retaliation if they took to the warpath, reduced frontier hostilities in 1757.

Meanwhile, through the long, bitter winter that followed the debacle at Oswego, Loudoun planned his campaign for 1757. Even before the spring thaw set in, however, events forced him to improvise. Governor Vaudreuil of New France struck first, compelling the British commander to react to his initiative.

In March, Vaudreuil dispatched his brother, Rigaud, a thirty-six-year-old career officer, with fifteen hundred men to attack Fort William Henry, the post that Johnson had constructed at the bottom of Lake George. If successful, Vaudreuil would, at a minimum, impose delays on the British, perhaps even prevent an Anglo-American campaign until 1758. His gamble succeeded. Rigaud arrived on snowshoes, silent and undetected, and in four days of fighting he inflicted heavy damage, demolishing several exterior buildings, three naval craft, and innumerable bateaux, although he hesitated to assault the main British garrison; that was work for regulars, he thought, and his men were mostly Canadians and Indians.

Nevertheless, Rigaud's despoilation induced Loudoun to shift gears. To campaign that summer in the Champlain Valley would require too much rebuilding, he concluded. He decided instead on a campaign against Louisbourg, the installation that Great Britain so myopically had returned to France nine years before, a post that the British ministry now wished to reclaim. To capture Louisbourg, Great Britain and its commander in America believed, would mortally weaken New France, for its lifeline to the parent state would be imperiled.

While winter yielded to spring and spring vanished before the sultry days of summer, Loudoun remained at his headquarters in New York absorbed in the myriad complexities of assembling his attack force. Meanwhile, the French were on the move. In July, Montcalm came south to "sing the warsong," as he told his wife, fetching eight thousand regulars, Canadian militia, and Indians, as well as 250 bateaux and 200 canoes. His objective was to complete what Rigaud Vaudreuil had begun at Fort William Henry in March, and if he succeeded at that, to destroy Fort Edward and to threaten Albany.

Montcalm lost the element of surprise that Rigaud Vaudreuil had enjoyed, but he had four times the number of troops that defended Fort William Henry. The French commander positioned his forces and commenced a classic European siege operation. Col. George Munro, a British regular in command of the post, was fully aware of his adversary's strength, but he held out as long as he could, hoping in vain for reinforcements from the New York militia and nearby Fort Edward. By August 9, however, all of Munro's heavy artillery was gone, either split or burst. To continue to resist, Munro realized, was to face an unavoidably successful grand assault by angry French and vengeful Indians who likely would spare no survivors. Mont-

calm called upon the British to surrender while "I have it yet
in my power to restrain the Savages." Munro thus capitulated,
but not until he negotiated a parole of honor. The men could
keep their arms and baggage, they could not serve again for
eighteen months, and the twenty-three hundred captives were
to be escorted to safety by their French captors. Munro signed
the surrender document and ordered the destruction of all
liquor within his fort to prevent it from falling into the hands
of the natives. Then he threw open the great doors to Fort
William Henry.

What followed was not pretty. As at Oswego, Montcalm
was unable to control his Indian allies. Bursting into the fort
in search of the loot they had been promised when they were
recruited, the Indians massacred most of the sick and wounded
and seized the African-Americans as slaves. The captured soldiers, too, were attacked by the Indians, who engaged in an
uninhibited orgy of stealing, kidnapping, and killing. Montcalm attempted without success to stop the murdering. One
captured New Englander later recollected that his French pro-
tectors advised the English to "take to the woods and shift for
themselves." Most survived by following this advice, but many
were butchered, some were boiled and eaten, and others were
taken into a protracted, in some cases permanent, captivity.
Most of the captives were eventually liberated, but the best
available figures suggest that nearly 270 English—11 percent
of Munro's garrison—were killed or never heard from again.

Montcalm, meanwhile, abandoned his earlier scheme of
assaulting Fort Edward. Soon after his victory, he learned that
the fifteen hundred English defenders of that fort had been
reinforced by New York militiamen. In addition, many of his
own militiamen were anxious to return home for the pending
autumn harvest, and Montcalm feared that his undisciplined
Indian allies would be unreliable in a long campaign. A gam-
bler might have seized the moment and inflicted a crushing
blow upon the already demoralized northern colonies. But

Montcalm was not that daring. It was his style to react to the enemy, not to make his adversary dance to his tune.

While Montcalm might have gained more during 1757, the year nevertheless ended sweetly for France. Loudoun's attempted siege of Louisbourg, begun while the French army was still en route to Fort William Henry, ended in yet another failure for the British. Placing a battalion of regulars in Pennsylvania and twenty-three hundred additional regulars in New York to hold the line, Loudoun turned his energies toward Louisbourg during the summer, working so hard that his aides feared for his health. By mid-May he had gathered six thousand troops, about one-third of them English regulars posted in the colonies; the bulk of the others were culled from New England. He could do nothing, however, before reinforcements and the royal fleet arrived from London. Sixty days passed. Finally, in mid-July, the armada, which had been delayed by adverse winds and provisioning nightmares, arrived at Halifax with five thousand troops. These reinforcements, together with several regiments of regulars stationed in Nova Scotia, brought Loudoun's strength to nearly fifteen thousand men and seventeen ships of the line, the largest, most powerful vessels in the eighteenth century. He possessed a force that was vastly superior to that which Pepperrell and Warren had commanded in 1745.

But France, anticipating an attack on Louisbourg, had hurried eighteen of its ships of the line to Cape Breton. They had arrived during the weeks when Loudoun sat awaiting help from England. France's action sealed Loudoun's fate. A British siege could not possibly succeed. On August 5, one day before Montcalm opened fire on Fort William Henry, Loudoun jettisoned his operation and scattered his army to winter quarters. If the royal fleet had arrived in spring, he told the ministry, he would "have been in Possession of Louisbourg very early in the Season, and with a very small loss of . . . Troops." Instead, Britain had nothing to show for its costly efforts in 1757, while Loudoun, after two summers in America, was unable to point to a single achievement.

New Leadership, Mixed Results

Loudoun's failure to take Louisbourg proved to be his un-doing, and like Shirley before him, he was called home. James Abercromby, Loudoun's second-in-command, succeeded him. Some thought of Abercromby as old, obese, and "infirm in body and mind." Others regarded him as "a very good Second Man." No one was especially satisfied with him, and, indeed, he was a compromise choice. The reservations with regard to Abercromby were manifold: he had never held an independent command; he was not an aggressive, hell-bent-for-action sort; rapid-fire decisions were not his forte; finally, although only fifty-two years old, he had aged prematurely. Against these real or imagined liabilities, he had nearly thirty years of military experience, including service in the War of the Austrian Succession; in addition, he would be surrounded by many bright, young officers, and by temperament Abercromby was likely to seek out and heed their counsel. London promoted Jeffery Amherst and John Forbes to positions immediately below Abercromby. The latter appointments reflected the in-fluence of William Pitt, who had recently emerged as the prime minister.

Pitt, the youngest child in a family of seven, the grandson of an important businessman, and the son of a member of Parliament, grew up on a fifty-acre estate near Enfield, close to London. Later regarded popularly as a common man who had risen from poverty, Pitt had grown up in quite comfort-able, if not opulent, circumstances. Men from his family had occupied positions of influence since the days of Queen Eliz-abeth, and his grandfather frequently enjoyed the company of Queen Anne and, later, George I. Young Pitt was trained to follow in their footsteps. He studied law and politics at Eton, Oxford, and the University of Utrecht, but he would have pursued an army career had his health permitted. In 1730, at age twenty-two, he entered the King's Own Regiment of Horse, but his service was cut short by chronic physical problems, perhaps the gout, perhaps some gastrointestinal malady. He turned to other endeavors, and was elected by Okehampton to the House of Commons in 1734. Ten years later he entered the cabinet or ministry. After another dozen years, in August 1756, he was made secretary of state and prime minister. A tall, thin man with a long nose and wide piercing eyes, Pitt manifested a grave and distinguished air. He tended to thunder and rattle when he spoke, causing many to fear him. But in private he was witty and charming, and his closest friends described him as "a most agreeable and lively companion."

Pitt brought a new outlook to his job. He believed the growth of the empire was as crucial—perhaps more so—to Great Britain's well-being as were gains in Europe. He did not plan to ignore Europe, but he fully understood the value of the colonies and the potential for greatness that would belong to the nation that gained hegemony in America. He knew, too, that a France that was weakened in America would be weaker in Europe. Unlike his predecessors, therefore, Pitt looked upon the course of events in America as more than a mere sideshow to the extravaganza playing on the European stage. In comparison with those who had gone before him, Pitt sent larger armies to America; indeed, Pitt's armies were the largest that Britain had ever committed to North America. In Pitt's scheme, English regulars would assume the principal role in the subjugation of New France. British armed forces would take charge of the war; the colonies would help with men and supplies, for which they would be reimbursed, an innovation that Parliament had introduced three years earlier. In 1758 Pitt implemented his plans.

Although innovative in many ways, Pitt's strategy was not entirely original. His strategic plans for 1758 hardly differed from those that Loudoun had proposed just before his recall. The British were to drive the French from the Champlain Valley, taking Fort Carillon and advancing to Montreal. Abercromby was assigned this task. Louisbourg must be taken. This job was for Amherst. Fort Duquesne on the Ohio River must also be seized. Forbes was given this duty. The final objective was Quebec, to be left to Abercromby and Amherst after they accomplished their initial assignments. Pitt did make some alterations in Loudoun's plans. Loudoun had planned to hammer Louisbourg with an Anglo-American siege army, but Pitt made British regulars responsible for this operation. In addition, Loudoun's plan to attack Fort Frontenac was abandoned.

France, meanwhile, had reacted quite differently to the military situation at the outset of 1758. Despite his victories during the previous year, Governor Vaudreuil knew that he had only delayed Britain's attacks on his country; to defend against his foe, moreover, he knew that he required assistance from the parent state. But the aid he sought was not forthcoming. Confronted by mounting odds in the European war, France had difficulty sparing more men for the American theater; in fact, faced with steady losses in its naval contest with Great Britain, the French probably could not have shipped sufficient supplies across the Atlantic to sustain a large force in America. Vaudreuil was ordered to assume a defensive posture. France gambled on winning the war in Europe while it preserved Quebec and as many other of its North American possessions as it could successfully defend. French strategy was simple: whatever it succeeded in holding militarily, it likely could retain at the postwar peace conference. As a result, France sent over only five hundred additional men, raising its troop strength in New France to six thousand. Pitt, however, dispatched sufficient reinforcements to bring the number of British regulars to more than twenty thousand.

Generals Abercromby and Forbes had served under Loudoun and were in America at the beginning of 1758, yet Amherst, who did not arrive until nearly June, was to launch the first operation to capture Louisbourg. Major General Amherst had been elevated suddenly from the rank of colonel and sent by Pitt from the German theater to America. He was a veteran of twenty-three years, although he was only forty-three years old in 1758. Much of Amherst's service had been as a supply officer, that graveyard of ambitious soldiers, and when he had fought—generally capably and steadily—he had never been granted an independent command. But powerful friends brought his name to the attention of Pitt and the king. Amherst was portrayed as capable, pragmatic, and obedient; George II and Pitt agreed that he should be given an opportunity to show what he could do.

Amherst was in far better shape for a siege of Louisbourg than Loudoun had been a year earlier. By early summer 1758 the French had succeeded in getting only five ships of the line to Louisbourg; Vice Adm. Edward Boscawen had more than twice that number of powerful English vessels, as well as several frigates. Boscawen could blockade Louisbourg and pound the citadel with the heavy guns of the men-of-war. Yet to succeed the British still had to put ashore an army and institute siege operations on land. Brig. Gen. James Wolfe was assigned responsibility for the landing.

Not handsome—his chin was too small, his forehead too long, his nose too upturned—Wolfe nevertheless was a striking man, the result largely of his piercing, expressive eyes. Thin and of fair complexion, sporting long red hair that he kept tied in a queue and mostly hidden beneath a black, tri-cornered hat, resplendent in his scarlet coat, white britches, and polished black boots, Wolfe looked every inch the soldier—and, in fact, he had soldiered for eighteen of his thirty-one years. Wolfe's father had been an officer, and from his boyhood he, too, had never yearned for anything but a career in the British army. His wish came true, and so did his desire to taste the harsh realities of combat. Indeed, he saw so much fighting in the War of the Austrian Succession that he feared what it was doing to him. Had he grown to be "a mere ruffian?" he wondered. Had he come to enjoy "imbibing the tyrannical principles of an absolute commander?" he asked. At age twenty-three he took a leave of absence from his regiment to enjoy the sensual pleasures of Paris. But he returned to the army and soon fought in Scotland and, in this war, on the continent. Just before he was transferred to America he wrote his mother that all he wished was to be a brave soldier, to "look steadily upon danger," to "meet that fate we cannot shun, and to die gracefully and properly when the hour comes."

At Louisbourg Wolfe was ordered by Amherst to land at Kennington Cove, the site of Pepperrell's successful amphibious assault in 1745. Wolfe, however, faced heavier odds than those that had confronted the New England rangers. The French had prepared for this day since the moment Louisbourg was restored to them by the Treaty of Aix-la-Chapelle. They had completed a chain of entrenchments, each secured by an abatis of fallen spruce and fir trees, at every possible landing cove on Gabarus Bay. Artillery protected most of the earthworks; so, too, did up to three thousand regulars, militia, and Indians posted throughout these works. Wolfe knew that resistance would be heavy. He also knew that the surf, often heavy and swirling in this region, had to cooperate, or his men would never get ashore.

Wolfe was ready to move as early as June 3, but either high seas, or gales, or heavy fog forced daily postponements. When the weather improved, sometime after midnight on June 8, the men were ordered into their landing craft. It was a slow, methodical procedure, not completed until nearly sunrise. Wolfe waited anxiously until the first sign of pink and gray appeared in the morning sky, then he signaled his flotilla to the beaches. Everything went wrong. Boats splintered on heavy rocks. Churning waves overturned craft. French muskets and cannon took their toll. In no time nearly a hundred men perished. A few minutes into the operation Wolfe gave up. He signaled for the men to return to their ships. But some of his men did not notice (or disregarded) their commander and pushed on to a cluster of jagged rock west of Flat Point, such a seemingly impossible landing area that the French had left it unprotected. These were Nova Scotia men. Somehow they reached the shore. Observing their success, others followed. Brigadier General Wolfe, armed only with a cane, was one of the first in line, and he scrambled up the rock and ashore.

The French offered only a brief resistance. Demoralized at the unexpected sight of the British on land and fearful of being taken captive, the French defenders hastily retreated the four miles to Louisbourg. Throughout the day the English poured ashore. That evening, safely on this inhospitable land, many supped on wine and bread left behind by the French. Day one of the siege of Louisbourg had ended successfully, as much because of luck as skill. Even Wolfe later remarked that the endeavor had been "rash and ill-advised," and that "by the greatest of good fortune imaginable we succeeded."

Once Wolfe's men landed ashore the outcome of the campaign to take Louisbourg was determined. The British gradually tightened the noose about the French fortress. Boscawen immediately instituted a naval blockade, and within ten days the artillery had begun to pound the French fortress, which brought a quick end to the siege. Louisbourg had been rebuilt since 1748. Its pantry was filled, and it was defended by over three thousand men. Yet the French garrison capitulated five weeks after the siege guns first erupted. The decision was made by the governor of Cape Breton Island, Chevalier de Drucour, one of the besieged. His was not a terribly valorous act, but it was humane. His position was hopeless. With about one hundred artillery shells per hour raining upon the garrison, it would have been criminal to have continued to risk the lives of the inhabitants, which included many civilians.

As Amherst completed the siege of Louisbourg, Abercromby and Forbes readied their forces, waiting for the arrival of the provincial soldiers. Some of the Americans who marched into their camps belonged to specially raised regular units, for Great Britain sought during this war to enlist colonists into the British army. This practice was not new. Since late in the seventeenth century the British army had recruited men into regular regiments in the colonies. While such recruitment was legal—and even welcomed if the enlistee was a criminal or unemployed, for that removed a burden from the shoulders of the provincial taxpayers—it often provoked resentment within the colonies when the recruit was an apprentice or an indentured servant. Masters were outraged at the prospect of losing their bound servants, laborers who represented a considerable financial investment. Crowds sometimes demonstrated against such practices, and riots occasionally erupted when the British actively recruited servants. In Connecticut during King George's War, colonists used violence to discourage others from enlisting in the British army. The colonists' ire was also raised when recruiting officers acted improperly, as when they plied a likely candidate for bearing arms with strong drink, then signed on the unfortunate inebriate. Despite the opposition, however, large numbers of colonials entered the British army. Approximately eleven thousand Americans served in the British regular forces in the French and Indian War (about one-third of Britain's manpower), although the willingness of Americans to enlist decreased as provincial opposition to service in the British army increased; in 1758 the British army recruited about half the number of Americans that it had procured two years before.

Most provincials who entered military service enlisted for one year in a colonial army. In 1758 Pitt directed the six northern colonies to raise twenty thousand men. Ultimately, they fielded over sixteen thousand men. Forbes also received considerable help from the southern provinces, finally drawing upon more than six thousand of the colonials for his campaign against Fort Duquesne. While the northern provinces fell somewhat short of London's expectations, America's manpower contribution was extraordinary; nor was 1758 an uncommon year. Connecticut raised twenty-five hundred men in 1756, the same number again the next year, and nearly five thousand in 1758. Virginia raised more than one thousand men each year; in fact, even the smallest colonies, such as Rhode Island, New Hampshire, and Maryland, often furnished between three hundred and five hundred men annually. Perhaps no colony provided more men than Massachusetts during this war. Massachusetts raised armies of seventy-two hundred (1755), thirty-five hundred (1756), eighteen hundred (1757), seven thousand (1758), sixty-five hundred (1759), five thousand (1760), three thousand (1761), and three thousand (1762). Even allowing for reenlistment by a large percentage of its soldiery, it is probable that at least twenty thousand men from Massachusetts out of a total population of about two hundred thousand soldiered in this war; in England, by contrast, fewer than one hundred thousand men out of a total population of seven million bore arms.

The colonies drew upon surplus manpower to fill the ranks of their armies, but the American soldiery did not represent only the marginal elements in society. At one time, historians believed that these armies drew heavily upon the displaced and disaffected, such as convicts, vagabonds, the unemployed, and social misfits. Recent studies have revealed a different picture, however. Almost all of Connecticut's soldiers were farmers and laborers, and most were young, single men of limited means. Likewise, nearly three of every four men who volunteered in Massachusetts in 1756 were farmers or skilled artisans. Many young farm boys in mid-eighteenth-century New England found themselves in limbo, waiting for the day they would inherit their father's farms and achieve the economic independence to marry and begin a family; many young journeymen earned only meager salaries. To these young men, military service conferred attractive financial benefits. Between an enlistment bounty and a substantial monthly salary, a soldier could earn up to about fifteen pounds for eight months' duty, roughly the cost of 150 acres of unimproved land on the frontier. As a consequence, the army in Massachusetts reflected the social structure of the province.

A somewhat similar pattern eventually was evident in the Virginia Regiment. Authorities in Virginia discovered in 1754 that they were waging a war that was bitterly unpopular in some quarters. Many Virginians looked upon the contest with France for the West as a war instigated for private gain by wealthy stockholders in the Ohio Company. When Governor Dinwiddie sought to raise the militia at the outset of the conflict, he not only learned that many trainbandsmen were unwilling to risk their lives for the economic enhancement of the "blades"—their derisive term for affluent planters—but that small farmers looked upon prolonged militia service as an economic liability. Virginia quickly turned to a volunteer army. Originally no one was compelled to serve, and few signed on in an army that paid enlisted men less than unskilled laborers earned in the civilian sector. In 1755, Virginia raised an army barely 40 percent the size it had hoped to field.

In desperation, the House of Burgesses offered postwar land bounties for those who would enlist. In addition, it resorted to conscription. All able-bodied, unmarried men of military age were subject to impressment. Hundreds were forced into the Virginia Regiment between 1756 and 1758, yet nearly two-thirds of those who served under Colonel Washington enlisted voluntarily, lured by the prospect of immediate pay and an eventual grant of frontier land. These were young men—the median age was twenty-four—and most came from the older Tidewater and Piedmont counties. Opportunity for a young man was limited in those parts of the province. Land was scarce in comparison with the more sparsely settled western counties, and the land that was available often was worn out. As was the case in Massachusetts, Virginia's army was representative of the colony's society, and it drew upon men who looked on military service as an avenue toward the acquisition of land and independence.

One striking difference did exist between the armies of these two provinces, however. Within the army of Massachusetts many lower-level officers and enlisted men came from the same stratum of society, whereas almost all of Washington's officers came from the upper class. No unskilled laborers became officers in Massachusetts, but almost one-half of the officers were men with manual occupations, chiefly farmers or tradesmen, as were the men they commanded.

Throughout the spring of 1758 these men were raised from the cities and tiny hamlets within the provinces until, in June, his army almost intact, Abercromby finally set out from Albany toward the Champlain Valley. Although he was unaware of Britain's fortunes at Louisbourg, his army began its ascent just as Amherst clamped his vicelike siege upon the doomed French fortress. Abercromby would not be as successful as his subordinate.

By early July his men had trekked past the decaying ruins of Fort William Henry, descended Lake George in hundreds of bateaux, whaleboats, and rafts, and reached the vicinity of Fort Carillon, or Ticonderoga as it was called by the British. The size of Abercromby's force demonstrated how the battle for America had changed since the days when the principal engagements had been fought between armies of sixty to seventy regulars and a few hundred Indians. Abercromby's army was only slightly smaller than the population of Boston, America's second-largest city in 1758. More than six thousand regulars served under him; about the same number of provincials were with him as well, although the general had expected more colonials—only about 40 percent of those promised by Massachusetts had arrived—and he had little confidence in the abilities of those who were present. Nor was Abercromby happy with the number of Indian warriors on hand. William Johnson had provided fewer than four hundred tribesmen, a bare fraction of what the general had anticipated. Pitt had envisioned an army of twenty-seven thousand pushing toward Montreal; instead Abercromby had some twelve thousand troops. Nevertheless, the British outnumbered the French by approximately five to one.

As the hour of battle approached, Montcalm anticipated only a holding action at Ticonderoga. His aim was to retard the English advance until reinforcements arrived at Crown Point. He would then fall back to Fort Saint Frédéric, a superior installation, and make a stand. The French commander judged Ticonderoga to be indefensible. A French engineer told Montcalm that the place was "little susceptible of defense," and he added: "Were I entrusted with the siege of it, I should require only six mortars and two cannon." Montcalm posted the bulk of his troops behind an abatis of felled trees (so arranged that their sharp, tangled branches were pointed toward the advancing enemy) in front of the fort. He dared the British to attack.

Abercromby failed to reconnoiter the French line before he ordered an assault. Nor did he order an artillery bombardment before the attack, an action that not only would have set fire to Montcalm's abatis, but would have blown down part of the Frenchman's great log wall. Believing that French reinforcements were imminent, Abercromby did not even take the time to bring up his artillery. In the heat of midday on July 8 he sent his men forward, rangers and regular infantry in the vanguard, followed by Connecticut, New York, and Massachusetts men, then more regulars. The British advanced slowly, interminably it must have seemed to those who became entangled in the thicket of Montcalm's tree limbs and who presented easy targets for the French. What followed on that warm summer afternoon, one day short of the third anniversary of Braddock's catastrophe, was a stunning, humiliating, and unnecessary defeat for British arms. Abercromby's losses were actually greater than those suffered by the British on the Monongahela, although the proportion of his army that went down was not as great as that lost by his predecessor. Abercromby lost over fifteen hundred men, nearly one-third of whom were killed; his casualties amounted to approximately 12 percent of his army, whereas Braddock had lost well over half his men. If one combines the losses of both armies at Ticonderoga, this engagement was the bloodiest fought on American soil before the War of Independence, a battle in which over two thousand men were killed or wounded.

Even after his defeat Abercromby possessed an army vastly superior in size to that of his adversary. He might have tried again to conquer the French post, this time using his artillery; he also might have sought to skirt Montcalm's right flank and establish himself between Ticonderoga and Crown Point, a position that would have compelled Montcalm to retreat. He did neither. Chastened and drained of his will to fight, Abercromby retreated. Meanwhile, like many a previous English commander, he immediately sought to shift the blame for his failure to the colonists. Perhaps they could do an adequate job as carpenters, he said, but otherwise

it is with Concern that I tell you that from what I have seen and what has happened no real Dependence is to be had upon the Bulk of the Provincials. How can it be otherwise? The Provinces scarcely began to raise a Man until the middle of April. Many of those that joined us were hired in place of others who should have served, and others were drafted or forced out their militias. Their officers with a very few exceptions are worse than their men. Nay, some of the officers have actually deserted and pretended sickness, and we are always much longer in getting them to do their Duty.

Montcalm, by contrast, saw the hand of God in his startling victory.

Whatever the rival generals fancied, the real reason for the French success was that Abercromby, presented with all the tools necessary to take Ticonderoga, had acted unimaginatively and incompetently. Indeed, one of the young British officers (Charles Lee, later a general in the Continental army during the War of Independence) thought Abercromby's performance had been "astonishingly absurd," and he went on to add that in his estimation the general was a "blockhead . . . so far sunk in Idiotism as to be obliged to wear a bib and bells." That charge was unfair, but the heat that generated such a sentiment grew from disappointment, as well as from the realization that because of Abercromby's unnecessary failure Britain's other commander, General Amherst, was obliged to discard his plans for a campaign that year against Quebec.

To the south, meanwhile, Abercromby's fellow Scot, General Forbes, was about to drive against Fort Duquesne. John Forbes, scion of a well-placed family, had studied for a medical career but abandoned that calling for what he believed would be the greater adventure of a military life. Now fifty years old, Forbes had spent all his adult life in the army, and he had fought and acquitted himself in the War of the Austrian Succession. But most of his career had been spent in peacetime, and when his army had been at war Forbes normally had been posted behind the lines, as a quartermaster (supply) officer.

Meticulous and efficient, he had performed well in a job that received neither attention nor glory, yet within the army he had earned a reputation as a patient, tireless, practical man, a soldier with a penchant for organization.

During the spring of 1758 Forbes's campaign to take Fort Duquesne had proceeded slowly. Although he gradually accumulated an army of seven thousand men, it was a smaller force than he had desired. Some colonies refused to heed his calls for manpower. For instance, the Maryland assembly, unwilling to force its men to fight beyond its borders, even resolved that "no person [within the province] is punishable for obstinately refusing to appear and serve in Arms" under the command of Forbes. The British commander faced a second difficulty. Like Washington and Braddock before him, he had to move his army through a dense wilderness; indeed, Colonel Washington advised Forbes of what lay ahead, explaining that the army somehow would have to penetrate "an immense forest of 240 miles extent, intersected by several ranges of mountains, impenetrable almost to anything human, save the Indians ... who have paths or tracks through these deserts." Daunted, Forbes spent several months piecing together an effective supply network. When he did move, he chose to cut a new road through the primeval forest, ignoring Braddock's (previously Washington's) highway; the new route was more direct, although hacking a roadway out of the almost impermeable timberland and hills was time-consuming and fatiguing. French and Indian parties added to Forbes's woes by harassing his road builders and raiding both his herds of livestock and the British baggage train.

Summer came and went, and by early November, when the first frost descended on Pennsylvania, some soldiers talked of abandoning the campaign until the following spring. Such talk ceased, however, when two English parties—one composed of Virginians under Colonel Washington—seized several French raiders, who revealed that Fort Duquesne was lightly defended. Forbes courageously decided to gamble on the veracity of his prisoners. He dispatched three brigades, each taking a different route to the Ohio River. Two were commanded by regular officers. Washington led the third, a force consisting of the Virginia Regiment and soldiers from three other colonies. The English moved quickly, covering six miles or more per day. By November 24 they were only a day's march from Fort Duquesne when, near sunset, a scout hurried breathlessly into camp with happy tidings. The French fort had been sighted—in flames. The French had abandoned Fort Duquesne and retreated, leaving behind only blackened chimneys. Colonel Washington quickly dispatched the happy news to the governor of Virginia. He wrote that the

enemy, after letting us get within a days march of the place, burned the fort, and ran away (by the light of it) at night, going down the Ohio River by water, to the number of about 500 men, from our best information. The possession of this fort has been a matter of great surprise to the whole army—and we can not attribute it to more probable causes than those of French weakness, want of provisions, and desertion of their Indians. This fortunate and indeed unexpected success of our arms will be attended with happy effects.

Ten years had passed since the Ohio Company had formed to gain the land that sprawled westward from the forks of the Ohio. It now was in the possession of Englishmen.

Word of Forbes's success reached London shortly after the arrival of good news from Abercromby. Although the British commander shrank from another attempt at Ticonderoga, he had sent an army of three thousand provincials under a crusty regular, Col. John Bradstreet, to take Fort Frontenac, the first French installation upriver from Montreal, the supply and communication post that linked New France to its forts in the transmontane West. Bradstreet was a Nova Scotian. An officer in the British army since 1735, he had served as William Pepperrell's special military advisor during the 1745 campaign to take Louisbourg, a fort in which he had once been held prisoner by the French following a raid on Canso at the outset of King George's War. Bradstreet rose to the rank of captain during that war and subsequently was named lieutenant governor of Nova Scotia. When the French and Indian War broke

out, General Braddock had placed Bradstreet in command of
Fort Oswego. Later, during the campaign to take Fort Niagara,
Governor Shirley made him responsible for keeping the supply
lines open between Schenectady and Oswego. Bradstreet had
done what was asked of him. Command of a company of Royal
Americans followed in 1757, and he served briefly as an aide-
de-camp to Loudoun. Early in 1758 Bradstreet served Loudoun's successor, Abercromby, by fighting capably during the
attempt to take Ticonderoga. By then Bradstreet was a lieutenant colonel and deputy quartermaster-general in America.
Thinking Bradstreet a determined, persistent, and brave officer—another British officer later called him an "extraordinary
man"—Abercromby assigned Bradstreet the task of taking Fort
Frontenac.

Montcalm soon knew what was happening, and he knew
that the post was too lightly held to save itself. He faced a
difficult choice. To go to the rescue of the beleaguered garrison
at the head of the Saint Lawrence was to abandon the Champlain Valley; to remain at Ticonderoga was to forfeit Fort
Frontenac. Whichever choice he made, the door to Montreal
would be ajar. He chose to hold on to the Champlain Valley.

Montcalm's decision virtually assured a victory for Bradstreet, although few things could be taken for granted in a
backwoods campaign. In mid-August Bradstreet set forth with
3,000 men, all but about 150 of whom were provincials. Con-
veyed in bateaux, his army crossed placid Oneida Lake and
proceeded down the Oswego River to Lake Ontario. It was
near the end of the month when Bradstreet's army arrived
before Fort Frontenac. Bradstreet wasted little time. He understood the logistical nightmare he would face if this became a
protracted operation, and he knew full well that amateur soldiers often were ill-suited for lengthy sieges. Shortly after wit-
nessing his first sunrise over this French installation, Bradstreet commenced his bombardment. By the second morning
he had moved his gun emplacements even closer to Fort Frontenac. Bradstreet's fire was quite effective. Only a few more

hours of shelling produced a French surrender. Bradstreet had won a great victory without the loss of a single man.

Why had Britain's fortunes undergone such a dramatic turn for the better in 1758? The answer, in part, is that Pitt poured English money and manpower into the war in America. The number of British regulars fighting in America had increased fifteenfold since the days of Braddock. In 1755, only 15 percent of those who fought in America under the British flag had been British regulars; in 1758, fully one-half of those who bore British arms were regulars. What enabled Pitt to commit larger armies to America? He was aided by a treaty that he signed with the king of Prussia who agreed, in return for British subsidies, to keep fifty-five thousand men under arms against the French in Europe, which permitted Pitt to transfer some units from Europe to America. Yet this agreement only partially explains his success. Pitt was extremely popular—writers often called him the "Darling of the Public"— and he capitalized on his popularity not only to pry huge appropriations from the Parliament, but also to quell dissent in the House of Commons when he exceeded his bloated budget. Pitt had more money to spend on the British army than his predecessors did, and he had more cash with which to hire more mercenaries for the European theater; indeed, British expenditures on the war in Europe were seven times greater in 1758 than in 1757.

Likewise, the role of the Royal Navy had been expanded, despite the wishes of many who preferred to channel almost all military funding into army operations in Germany. During 1758 raids were made on French seaports, and one town, Cherbourg, was destroyed. In addition, British vessels virtually sealed the Straits of Gibraltar, depriving France of commerce with North Africa, the Levant, and India, and a French fleet attempting to sail from Toulon to America was intercepted and confined to the Mediterranean. During this remarkable year, France lost five times more ships of war than the British did, six times as many privateers, and three times the number of commercial vessels. At the outset of 1757 France still be-

lieved that it could send a squadron to America to retake
Acadia; by the end of 1758, it knew that the British fleet was
paramount in American waters because it ruled Europe's
waters.

Britain's victories in 1758 had a salutary impact upon its
long-standing attempts to reclaim the friendship of the Iroquois. At the outset of the war, the Iroquois appeared bewil-
dered. Uncertainty about Britain's staying power; resentment
over aggressive Anglo-American speculative enterprises, such
as the Ohio Company; fear of French retaliation; and the effectiveness of Canadian missionaries who sought to win the
Five Nations to their side had left the British-Iroquois alliance
in tatters. The Albany Congress had been called in 1754 in
part to lure the Iroquois from their neutrality, but it had been
unsuccessful. The French victories that followed further weakened Britain's ties to its one-time ally. The success of British
arms in 1758, however, did not go unnoticed within Iroquois
councils. The fall of Louisbourg and Fort Frontenac that summer prompted William Johnson, the British Indian superintendent, to predict that the victories "will fix the 5 Nations
firmer to our side & tend to destroy what influence the French
had among them." He was correct. In the Treaty of Easton
negotiated that autumn, the Iroquois agreed to the pacification
of the frontier in Pennsylvania and assented to Britain's demand that no aid be given to the French; in return, Britain
repudiated an earlier land transaction to which the Indians
objected and recognized the Five Nations' land claims beyond
the Allegheny Mountains.

During the course of 1758, therefore, France's aspirations
for controlling the region below the Great Lakes had been
annihilated. Moreover, Quebec had been rendered vulnerable
as never before. Recognizing the peril, some in Canada wrote
to Versailles pleading for peace before all was lost in America.
Quebec clearly would be Britain's target in 1759, and the assignment would fall to Amherst, designated over the winter
as the successor to Abercromby, who was called home. The
northern provincials were not unhappy to see that tentative,

sometimes irresolute, general go. Since his retreat from Ticonderoga, many had called him "Mrs. Nabbycrombie."

Anglo-American Victory

From the warmth of his office in cold, damp London, Pitt devised Britain's military plans for 1759. Amherst, now headquartered on the south end of Lake George, was to sweep down the Champlain Valley, then advance down the Richelieu River to the Saint Lawrence, from whence he could assault Montreal or Quebec. In addition, he was authorized to consider other objectives, so long as the Montreal-Quebec enterprise was not jeopardized. General Wolfe was to proceed from Cape Breton Island to Quebec.

French intelligence quickly fathomed Britain's intentions and fashioned a plan of defense. Col. François de Bourlamaque was posted with three thousand men at Fort Carillon; his job was to delay Amherst's descent, preventing British forces from uniting before Quebec, defended by Montcalm.

France achieved its goal, although Amherst enjoyed considerable success. Amherst began his campaign by sending a detachment of twenty-five hundred provincials and six hundred Indians to attack Fort Niagara, which guarded the route between Lake Ontario and Lake Erie. Late in July the French surrendered that garrison after a brief siege. Meanwhile, Amherst's army materialized so slowly that he did not go into action until late July, six weeks or more later than had been planned. Finally, under a scorching summer sun, he transported his army of eleven thousand—more than half of whom were regulars—to Fort Carillon, where Bourlamaque planned only a token defense, a holding action to slow the British advance to a snail's pace. Amherst outnumbered the defenders by nearly four to one, but he did not wish to meet the fate that had befallen Abercromby the previous summer; the British commander painstakingly brought up his artillery and prepared for a siege. As soon as all was in place, Bourlamaque blew up Carillon and retreated. The English at last had possession of Ticonderoga, and with the loss of fewer than a hundred men; Bourlamaque, however, had staved off his adversary until the end of July. The French planned a similar holding operation at Fort Saint Frédéric, but when reinforcements failed to arrive Bourlamaque destroyed that installation and fell back once again without offering resistance. The English had taken both of France's Champlain Valley forts; even so, the path was not clear for Amherst to advance. The French commander had a schooner and three heavily armed xebecs on Lake Champlain, sufficient firepower to destroy Amherst's fleet of whaleboats and bateaux. Amherst, therefore, was compelled to pause, this time to build a fleet of his own. It was mid-October before Amherst's little navy—a brig and a sloop—overwhelmed Bourlamaque's smaller flotilla. By that time Wolfe's campaign for Quebec had ended. Amherst had failed to unite with the British army before Quebec. Nevertheless, he knew that the British flag now flew at the headwaters of the Ohio, over Ticonderoga and Crown Point as well, and above Niagara, which once had safeguarded New France's lifeline to Detroit, Michilimackinac, and the Illinois Country. With an autumn drive on Montreal no longer crucial, Amherst fell back to Crown Point for the winter. Amherst doubtless was disappointed that he had been unable to rendezvous with Wolfe's army in 1759, although he perhaps believed, as have some historians, that by drawing reinforcements away from Montcalm his endeavors had assisted Wolfe in his campaign to take Quebec.

Wolfe began his campaign at the same moment that Amherst was preparing to advance on Fort Carillon. The campaign did not begin well for this British officer. Despite its possession of Louisbourg, Britain had failed to establish an airtight naval blockade of the Saint Lawrence; France was able to ship supplies, albeit only meager amounts, to Quebec throughout the spring. In addition, French intelligence had detected Amherst's plans for 1759. Realizing that Quebec would face more immediate danger than Montreal, Vaudreuil shifted his defenses to prepare for Wolfe's arrival. Montcalm would have sixteen thousand men—regulars, militia, and Indians—under his command, nearly a two-to-one numerical advantage over his enemy.

Devoid of a naval arm, Vaudreuil and Montcalm were helpless to prevent Wolfe's arrival. Nor did the treacherous Saint Lawrence prove to be a fatal obstacle, as it had for Admiral Walker a half-century before. Wolfe, with nearly nine thousand men aboard 119 transports, safely reached Quebec late in June. His army was transported by a fleet of twenty-two warships under Adm. Charles Saunders. Wolfe immediately seized Pointe Lévis directly across from the city, from which he commenced an artillery bombardment. Considerable destruction resulted, including the gutting of the great cathedral church in the upper town, but Wolfe knew that the French garrison was not seriously threatened.

A month after landing, Wolfe had little to show for his efforts. By then he knew that Amherst would not reach Montreal for several weeks, if he arrived at all in 1759; he also knew that the fearsome Canadian winter was but ten to twelve weeks away. But what could he do? A frontal assault on Quebec was out of the question. The French citadel was situated on a plateau atop steep cliffs that rose 250 feet or more above the Saint Lawrence; Quebec appeared to be impregnable. In addition, Wolfe doubted that the British fleet could run past the French batteries and land the army on the upper river to the west, considered to be the weakest side of Quebec. In late July Wolfe tried the one course that he believed was available to him. He landed below the city, near Montmorency Falls, and struck at the French entrenchments on the Beauport flats, redoubts that guarded the Saint Charles River and the eastern approaches to Quebec. This spot was where Major Walley had sought without success to breach Frontenac's lines during Phips's assault on Quebec nearly seventy years before. Wolfe's idea was the same as his predecessor's. If he could pierce these defenses, he would accomplish one of two things. Either Montcalm might be lured from the city and into a European-style encounter that Wolfe believed he could win, or, once through

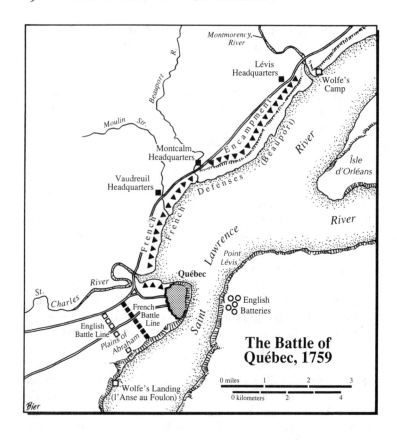

The Battle of
Québec, 1759

the Beauport lines, the British might swing around the town
to the Plains of Abraham on Montcalm's weaker western flank.
But Wolfe's plan failed; the French repulsed two attacks. The
British had sustained 450 casualties, the French barely one-
tenth that number.

In August Wolfe turned loose his rangers and light infantry
to lay waste the countryside as an act of retaliation against the
partisan attacks made upon his army. It recapitulated the systematic destruction that Britain had visited upon the Scottish
Highlanders following the defeat of the Jacobites, a vicious
endeavor in which Wolfe had participated. It was the manner
of war that he understood. But it was also still another ploy

by which he hoped to pull Montcalm out of his defenses, to force him to fight in order to stay the carnage. Within a few weeks, over fourteen hundred farms and some small villages had been destroyed. Montcalm did not emerge.

Soon despair set in at British headquarters. Winter was thirty days closer. Supplies were so short that some men ate horsemeat; camp diseases had begun to make their inevitable appearance. Some spoke of abandoning the campaign. Others talked of a desperation frontal assault against the city. In late August, however, a glimmer of hope surfaced. Six British ships successfully sailed up the river, past the artillery gauntlet at Quebec. A few days later more ships made the run into the upper river. These brave actions demonstrated that it might be possible to land an army on the north shore upriver from Quebec. Wolfe's three brigadier generals immediately urged such a course. Forget the seemingly impregnable Beauport defenses, they argued. If the British army landed above the city, Quebec's ties to both Montreal and Batiscon, Montcalm's principal supply depot more than sixty miles upriver, would be cut; Montcalm, already experiencing shortages, would face a logistical nightmare. He might have to emerge and fight. Wolfe agreed to the plan.

Montcalm knew of the British navy's success in eluding the guns of Quebec, but he took few steps to augment his upriver defenses. He persisted in his belief that the British assault would come at Beauport, which Wolfe's artillery continued to hammer. When the British withdrew from the Montmorency sector on September 3, Montcalm thought it a diversion. He readied his men in the Beauport lines. A week passed. The English continued to bombard the Beauport trenches all the while. No additional warships slipped upriver; indeed, every act of the navy suggested that the British blow would fall somewhere along the Charles River and the eastern approaches to the city. Two more days passed, days that brought nothing new.

But at one o'clock in the morning on September 12, as night's sooty darkness concealed the black waters of the Saint Lawrence, changes occurred. Wolfe ordered about eighteen hundred light infantry from the south shore across from Quebec to board ships. Their commander was Col. William Howe, scion of a powerful English family that had already lost one son in this war, George Augustus Lord Howe, who had died in Abercromby's campaign to take Ticonderoga. Thirty-year-old William Howe, a veteran soldier who had first experienced combat twelve years before, was viewed by his superiors—especially by Wolfe, who had praised his valor in the Louisbourg operation—as a brave and resolute young commander.

The first of the thirty flatboats carrying Howe's men moved out at two o'clock in the morning, about the same moment that several warships made yet another demonstration before the Beauport defenses, a feint designed to deceive and preoccupy Montcalm. Two breathless hours elapsed as Howe's redcoats were transported to their landing site a scant six miles upriver. The men were forbidden to speak or smoke; coughing had to be suppressed. The success of the operation hinged on surprise. If Montcalm learned of Wolfe's intent, he could easily prevent the British from scaling the steep banks that hugged the north shore of the river. The British were fortunate. The flatboats glided noiselessly up the cold river. They were blessed, too, to find only a modest French garrison posted at the site of their disembarkation, l'Anse au Foulon. The French knew nothing of Wolfe's intent until they heard noise on the beach. The sounds were unmistakable: the clatter of rocks and rubble dislodged and falling to the shore below, the rattle and bang of muskets and bayonets striking stone, the thumping of men struggling to climb the wooded precipice. The French defenders opened fire, but their resistance was brief. They were overpowered by a British force of vastly superior numbers. Howe's men rapidly secured the area so that more of their brethren could ascend the hill and assume positions on the Plains of Abraham. In the first pale glint of morning light, some two hours after Howe had landed, Montcalm discovered that approximately four thousand British were ashore and more were still coming. Montcalm had refused to consider this operation a possibility. "Only God . . .

can do the impossible," he had remarked when the governor asked whether Wolfe might attempt such a landing.

Once Montcalm knew what was happening, he did not hesitate. He emerged from the city to fight the British on the Plains of Abraham. Actually, the French general had three options. He might have attempted to withstand a siege or an assault on the city. Any British siege would have been of short duration, for the season was late and Wolfe's supplies were low; however, Montcalm evidently feared that the British could breach the walls about Quebec. A second alternative was to emerge and fight, but to have done so after a delay of several hours, even for a day or longer. Half of Montcalm's men were elsewhere; some were entrenched on the Beauport lines, while others, under Louis-Antoine de Bougainville, were stationed about two hours away, approximately eight miles upriver, to prevent the British from severing Quebec's ties to its supply depots in Trois-Rivières and Montreal. By delaying his action, Montcalm could have gathered sufficient troops to have gained manpower equity, perhaps superiority, and he might have trapped the British between his main army and the three-thou-sand-man force under Bougainville, a force that included an elite corps of French regulars. The problem with this course, the French commander must have thought, was that given additional time, Wolfe's army could put more artillery into play (he had only two small cannon) and prepare defenses. The third option, the one that Montcalm chose, was to engage the British immediately, that very morning, before more red-coats—and especially before additional British artillery—could be landed.

The battle was brief. It began about ten o'clock and lasted only fifteen minutes. It ended so quickly that the French troops posted upriver did not arrive to assist Montcalm. The en-counter commenced when Montcalm ordered his artillery to pummel the massed British lines; simultaneously, he moved his men forward in a classic European battle array. With loud cries (*"Vive le roi!"* and *"Vive notre general!"*), the French force hurried forward, stopping about 130 yards from the British line to fire their first volley. At this distance their fire was ineffectual. The English did not respond. The French reloaded, advanced thirty yards, and discharged a second volley. Still, the English held their fire. Once again the French reloaded and moved forward, until they were only about seventy yards from the scarlet line of English soldiers. Montcalm ordered a third volley. The clap of musketry rolled and echoed across the plain. From this range the musketeers were more efficient. English soldiers fell. Yet Wolfe, incredibly patient and firm, still refused to return the fire. One more time the French reloaded and dashed forward. Only forty yards now separated the two armies. At the moment the French advance ended Wolfe cried out his order: "Fire!" A great, thunderous explosion erupted. The English volley blew huge holes in Montcalm's lines. The French right wing immediately collapsed. The center and left panicked. In an instant the battle turned into a rout. The French army broke into a desperate flight. Men rushed for the supposed safety of the citadel, their British foes, brandishing bayonets, hard on their heels. Those who were overtaken were killed.

Casualty rates were high, although not excessive for an engagement of this sort. Approximately 15 percent of the men on each side were killed or wounded. Both commanders were casualties. Wolfe had experienced much fighting in his life. On the evening before the battle, perhaps feeling unlucky, he gave his will and papers, as well as a miniature portrait of the woman he planned to marry, to a friend who would remain behind the lines. Wolfe survived the three French volleys; but during the English charge he was fatally wounded. Standing exposed before his grenadiers, Wolfe was shot through the wrist, then again more superficially. He hastily dressed the initial wound and continued to lead. But moments later he took a third shot, this one in his chest. He went down immediately. In an instant he knew that he could not survive, and he refused medical attention. He sat in the field with some of his staff about him while the final chaotic scenes of his great conquest were played out. He gave a last order, then just before he lapsed into a final black unconsciousness, he said: "Now, God be praised, I will die in peace."

Montcalm, who presented an inviting target as he sat astride his favorite steed, also was fatally wounded during the final moments of the fray. A musket ball hit his midsection, producing enormous internal destruction. Two soldiers kept him on his horse until he was safely inside the walls of Quebec. Civilians wept upon seeing their stricken leader; a woman allegedly screamed, *"O mon Dieu! mon Dieu! le Marquis est tué!"* Montcalm, in shock and oblivious to the swirl all about him, was carried to the home of his surgeon. Nothing could be done for him. He survived through that long day, but on September 13, in the still blackness before dawn, about twenty-four hours after Howe's men had begun to move toward l'Anse au Foulon, Montcalm breathed his last.

Following the encounter, Vaudreuil pulled together the remnants of the French force and retreated behind the Jacques-Cartier River, thirty-two miles above Quebec. The token garrison left in the city formally surrendered six days after the battle. Six months later the French returned. Regrouped during the winter, a force under Brig. Gen. François-Gaston de Lévis struck at the English-occupied citadel in April. Lévis, possessing superior numbers, defeated the redcoat defenders outside the walls of the city, then imposed a siege on the garrison that remained within the city's walls. But this Second Battle of Quebec ended with the arrival of British relief ships in mid-May 1760.

Thereafter, New France could only hope that word would arrive that peace had been agreed to in Europe. Otherwise, said Bourlamaque that summer, "the last moment has come." But Europe was not yet ready for peace. Only one more objective remained for Britain's armed forces—Montreal. Pitt directed the colonies to raise as many troops as in the previous year, but he left the disposition of those men to General Amherst. The plan that ultimately evolved called for a three-pronged advance upon this last French outpost. Amherst would proceed from Oswego, Lt. Col. William Haviland from

Crown Point, and Wolfe's successor, Brig. Gen. James Murray (who subsequently would be appointed governor of the new English colony of Canada) would proceed upriver from Quebec.

Nature had not blessed Montreal with ready-made defenses as it had Quebec, but reaching this French city was not easy. Amherst's army had to travel 200 miles, surmounting enemy-held installations en route; Haviland, too, faced a gauntlet of outer defenses about Lake Champlain, and Murray's fleet anticipated danger from shore batteries along the Saint Lawrence, especially at Trois Rivières, about halfway into the 150-mile voyage. Nevertheless, the British campaign proceeded smoothly.

Murray reached the mouth of the Richelieu in mid-August. Col. Bougainville, in command of the French at Ile aux Noix on the Richelieu, immediately returned to Montreal, fearing that he would be trapped between the armies of Murray and Haviland. Bougainville's retreat left the way open for Haviland to advance. He arrived to find that Amherst had already reached Lachine. Amherst had come with an army of ten thousand, more than half of whom were provincials, mostly New Englanders. The French had offered only token resistance as he proceeded down the Saint Lawrence. Few Indians, once New France's greatest military asset, emerged to resist his advance; the unrelenting reversals suffered by France during the past two years had lessened the natives' willingness to fight for an old, dying friend. Amherst arrived at full strength. In fact, during his descent to Montreal he lost more men to the dark, swirling rapids on the Saint Lawrence than to his adversary.

By the end of the first week in September, fifteen thousand British troops were poised near Montreal. The French command, which watched in dismay as its militia melted away and fifteen hundred regulars deserted in the face of the assembling enemy, had but two thousand men. On September 7, Britain's forces began to maneuver in preparation for an assault. Wisely, Governor Vaudreuil immediately opened surrender talks. Discussions continued through the afternoon and the night, and on the morning of September 8, 1760, the French submitted. Not only did Vaudreuil surrender Montreal, but he agreed to suspend resistance throughout Canada and to cede all remaining French posts to the British. Although the French soldiery objected, they were made to lay down their arms and to pledge to fight no more in this war with Great Britain. General Amherst insisted upon this clause, he said, in retaliation

for the infamous part the troops of France had acted in exciting the savages to perpetrate the most horrid of barbarities in the whole progress of the war, and for other open treacheries, as well as flagrant breaches of faith, to manifest to all the world, by this capitulation, his [Amherst's] detestation of such ungenerous practices and disapprobation of their conduct.

With the signing of this scrap of paper the war was over in New France. Indeed, New France was no more.

Vaudreuil's capitulation terminated the long, bloody European struggle for North America before the American Revolution, but it did not end the Seven Years' War. The world war that had officially begun in 1756 continued on the seas, in Germany, in India, where the British East India Company and the Compagnie des Indies were old rivals, and in Africa, Southeast Asia, and the Caribbean. Fifteen months after the fall of Montreal, Spain entered the war in a futile attempt to preserve the balance of power that had endured since Utrecht in 1713, and the conflict widened; fighting soon raged in the Spanish colonies, including Cuba and the Philippines.

French defeats in several sectors prompted Louis XV to open peace talks in 1761, but the discussions collapsed within a few days. A year passed before the negotiations resumed. By then France had lost even more, and Spain was reeling as well, having recently surrendered Havana to a British force. Versailles's second stab at peace succeeded. The diplomats reached an accord, the Treaty of Paris of 1763.

The French military setbacks were reflected in the treaty, for France suffered losses in the Caribbean and in India, and it was stripped of some of its fishing rights in Newfoundland and in the Gulf of Saint Lawrence. For Britain's mainland colonies, however, the heart of the treaty was contained in France's formal surrender of Canada, Cape Breton Island, Nova Scotia, and all territory east of the Mississippi River, except New Orleans. France had already promised that prize to Spain. The Spanish did better at the peace table than they had a right to expect. Even though it was on the losing side, Spain escaped with nothing worse than the cession of Florida to Great Britain, in return for which London agreed to restore Cuba to its former owner; in addition, Spain received New Orleans and all territory west of the Mississippi River previously claimed by France. Clearly, this war had been decisive. As a result of Great Britain's stunning military successes, France, a colonial power whose influence in America appeared to be growing in 1753, was virtually removed from the continent ten years later, and Spain, whose threatening presence along the Atlantic coast had helped bring the English to Roanoke Island so many generations before, had been eliminated as a concern to Great Britain east of the Mississippi River.

Why had Great Britain and its colonies won this war? Six months before the fall of Quebec Montcalm had predicted the collapse of Canada, unless it was rescued by "some unforeseen good luck . . . or some gross blunders on the part of the enemy." Neither materialized in sufficient quantity to save New France. Montcalm had understood that his adversary held a significant edge in many areas, advantages that ultimately contributed to Britain's victory. A considerable numerical superiority was one British advantage. Manpower had much to do with its victory. At the outset of the conflict, approximately 1,250,000 people lived in the thirteen mainland colonies and Nova Scotia as compared to the barely 75,000 who dwelled in Canada and Louisiana. The British provinces raised large armies, and the colonial soldiers were joined by British regulars, who arrived in unprecedented numbers as the war wore on; during the crucial campaigns of 1758 and 1759, nearly thirty thousand men served under the British flag in America. By contrast, even in the European theater, France fought this war with smaller armies than Louis XIV had raised a half-century earlier, both because a national will never crystallized in France and because its antiquated taxation system inhibited proper financing. Pitt once remarked that he was "conquering America in Germany," by which he meant that France, hard-pressed on the continent, was unable to part with the troops that might have led to success in North America. The result was that French strength in America—even if one counts its Canadian militia and Indian allies—never exceeded sixteen thousand men.

Nor can the role of the Royal Navy be ignored. The Canadian climate, as well as the nature of settlement in New France, inhibited self-sufficiency in the production of food, clothing, and arms. New France depended on imports from home for food, clothing, weapons, and munitions, shipments that had to run the gauntlet laid down by Britain's navy. At the outset of the war Britain possessed better than a two-to-one advantage over France in ships of the line, although Britain's fleet was divided between American waters and those kept near home to defend against a possible French invasion. It took time, but the Royal Navy gradually gained control of the seas and slowly strangled the French empire. Before the war was even declared in 1756, France had already lost more than three hundred merchant vessels and over eight thousand sailors. Thereafter, France's maritime problems only worsened. By the beginning of 1759, the year Quebec was lost, French commercial shipping had been so crippled that Versailles was unable to revictual its colony, whose inhabitants were reduced to bare subsistence rations. The end of New France, as Montcalm had predicted, loomed.

William Pitt had presided over the successes in 1758 that brought New France to the precipice of extinction, and in subsequent years he brought the war to a glorious close for Great Britain and its colonies. Pitt had succeeded where his predecessors had failed. Much of his talent lay in his organizational and administrative skills, in his facility for arranging the financing and raising the necessary manpower to success-fully conduct the war. But there was more to Pitt. He excelled at finding ways to arouse the colonists, even to foster coop-erative endeavors among the colonies, though collaboration often came about grudgingly, and all too frequently the inter-action that occurred between the provinces was slight. Pitt additionally possessed a deft feel for grand strategy. He under-stood the interrelationship of the various military theaters, from the tangled wilderness frontier in the Ohio Country to vast, windswept Canada; from steamy Asian colonies to the more traditional battlefields in Europe; from the role of the great ships of the line on the inky high seas to that of small bomb-ketches along the sandy shores of France. Pitt's strategy for America was clear from the beginning. He ordered "offen-sive Operations against the Enemy . . . toward removing and repelling the Dangers that threaten the Frontiers of any of the Southern colonies," and he sought to find sufficient bodies of "The King's Forces for Invading Canada . . . and carrying War into the Heart of the Enemy's Possessions." Nor did Pitt merely advocate such enterprises. He possessed the popular-ity—and hence the power—to assume the prosecution of this war almost autonomously.

No one man can be said to have won this war single-handedly. But no other individual deserves as much credit for Britain's victory as does this extraordinary statesman. William Pitt, it can be said, was the architect and manager of Great Britain's triumph in the Great War for Empire.

It must be acknowledged, however, that London's triumph—its advantages and Pitt's skillful leadership notwith-standing—was not foreordained. Indeed, New France nearly survived. It had only to rebuff its adversary to win the conflict, and through the initial phase of the war France stymied every British advance. In 1758, Britain's manpower and naval ad-vantages became apparent. Yet had Britain not won the en-gagement at Quebec in 1759—and Wolfe might well have been repulsed or even suffered a humiliating defeat had Montcalm acted less precipitously—Pitt's government might have been compelled by a war-weary public to agree to peace. But the capture of Quebec, which had appeared so unlikely only a few hours before it was accomplished, assured Pitt that his American aims would be realized. By the next fall, General Amherst, in possession of Canada, could in truth inform the prime minister: "I can assure you, Sir, this country is as quiet and secure as any other province of his majesty's dominions."

The Significance of America's Early Wars

The outbreak of the French and Indian War had been greeted patriotically in the English colonies. "I am a Briton," Benjamin Franklin had exulted, expressing a commonly shared feeling. When word arrived of the Treaty of Paris, the dulcet sounds of celebrating English colonists rang throughout the provinces, glorying—as New York City's "Cordial Address" to Amherst expressed it—in the knowledge that they were about to "reap the happy fruits" of victory. James Otis, perhaps Boston's most noteworthy lawyer and politician, remarked: "What God in his providence has united, let no man dare attempt to pull asunder." A dozen years later, Great Britain and America were at war. That the French and Indian War ended and the American Revolution began within a single generation was not coincidental.

Clearly, Britain's actions after 1763 precipitated the rebellion of its colonies, but some of London's problems and decisions in this era resulted from the long period of intercolonial warfare. The rejoicing brought by the peace was accompanied by the realization that Britain's national debt had soared to nearly 140 million pounds, the result of the huge expenditures entailed by almost twenty-five years of incessant warfare. Nor was that the end of the expense. The British government believed that it was necessary to leave a large army in the newly won West to pacify the region. Someone had to pay for the regiments that would remain in America.

The ministers of state believed that the colonists should bear a portion of the unavoidable tax burden that Britain faced. Not only had the wars been fought to protect and defend the provincials, London said, but the colonists would undeniably benefit from the great victory. Less charitably, some in the British government suggested that the colonists had not done all within their power to win the final victory. London recollected that some colonies had continued to trade with the French and Spanish sugar islands even while their fellow citizens fought and died on distant battlefields; indeed, so widespread had been the commerce that it seemed to have been sanctioned by provincial politicians, magistrates, and public opinion. The British government also remembered that not all provinces had met the troop quotas assigned by London, and that some colonies had only indifferently responded to the needs of Britain's military commanders in America. For instance, in 1757 three colonies provided no troops for the Earl of Loudoun, and four others raised only about one-half of their assigned quotas; in 1758, the northern colonies offered up fourteen hundred fewer men for Abercromby's campaign than they had promised, while in 1759 Connecticut not only fell short of its quota by two thousand men, but for the second consecutive year it delivered its soldiery later than Amherst desired. These shortfalls led some British officials to conclude that Britain's regulars had done far more to win the war than had their volunteer counterparts in the provinces. Given this outlook, it was not surprising that when Britain sought to raise a revenue to pay for the maintenance of an army in America, it levied taxes for the first time on its American colonies.

Whether London was aware of it, the colonists knew full well that the wars had been waged at a heavy cost to many in America. The colonies had raised about twenty thousand men annually through 1762, paying about half the cost themselves. Forty percent of the eligible men in New England had soldiered during this war; about 15 percent of those eligible to bear arms in Virginia had done so. Casualty rates were high. Approximately two thousand of Massachusetts's sons died in this war; in proportion to its population, this death rate was three times as high as the United States suffered in World War II. Nor was sacrifice limited to those who bore arms. Taxes rose everywhere. Massachusetts spent £818,000 on the French and Indian War, the equivalent of £14 per adult male, "the burden of which has been grievously felt by all orders of men," according to the royal governor. While illicit commerce persisted, trade with the French West Indies was embargoed between 1755 and 1757, with ruinous consequences for some merchants and their employees. An unprecedented number of bankruptcies occurred in Boston in the late 1750s, while throughout the urban north poor relief expenditures grew dramatically as great numbers of citizens were disabled and dislocated by the conflict.

During the wars tensions arose that undermined relations between England and America. The British often grew exasperated at the colonists' seeming inability to cooperate with one another, at their rivalries, profiteering, even apathy in some instances. Some Englishmen found it incomprehensible that a colony might balk at sending its militia beyond its borders or that provincial assemblies might resent—and resist—having to quarter British troops. The English never understood the mentality of the colonial soldiers who believed that they volunteered for a stated period of service at a stated rate of pay and for a stated purpose, and who refused to serve if the contract to which they had consented was violated. Nor could the British fathom the colonists' stinginess. London supplied the America troops with arms, artillery, provisions, and tents, leaving the colonists only to clothe and pay their men; many colonies found even that responsibility to be beyond their capacity. From Braddock to Loudoun, from Abercromby to Amherst, the British found the Americans' localism, greed, pertinacity, even mulishness, to be a costly impediment to waging war successfully.

Of course, the colonists harbored grievances, too. Assemblymen sometimes suggested that London's demands for American aid were unreasonable. Colonial officials bridled at the discriminatory policy that subordinated provincial officers to British regular officers. The fury of the colonials was aroused when they frequently were given duties such as building roads, clearing streams, and digging earthworks. Not only did such work require hard labor, but it was looked upon as unsoldierly, it brought no financial compensation, and it was a drudgery that the Americans were assigned repeatedly by British commanders who deemed the provincials to be poor soldiers and unfit for combat. Outraged by the contemptuous manner with which the British treated New England men, James Otis was moved to rail that redcoats considered the Americans to be little better than "hewers of wood and drawers of water." In addition, Britain's use of press gangs to fill the ranks of the Royal Navy provoked urban riots, and farmers and businessmen objected vigorously to the quartering of redcoats on their property.

By the end of the war each side had formed an opinion of the other's military capabilities, which proved to be important after 1763. Great Britain had come to see the provincials as ineffectual soldiers, as an undisciplined rabble prone to desertion, and as too poorly trained to excel in combat against an adversary consisting of professional soldiers. Braddock called the American soldiers "slothful and languid," Abercromby thought them "vagabonds," Loudoun berated them as "the lowest dregs . . . on which no dependence can be had" and insisted that they were "frightened out of their senses at the name of a Frenchman," Forbes charged that they were "the scum of the worst of people" and thought them a "bad collection of broken Innkeepers, Horse Jockeys, and Indian traders," Amherst seethed at their laziness, brashness, and impudence, and Wolfe fumed that they were "contemptible cowardly dogs" who "fall down dead in their own dirt and desert by battalions." These American "rascals," he went on, were "rather an encumbrance than any strength to an army."

Many colonists, on the other hand, were convinced that the British did not know how to wage an irregular war, the "American way of war," as it often was called. Braddock's defeat seemed to confirm that impression. Shortly after the debacle on the Monongahela, a Boston newspaper reported that the Iroquois "were not at all surprised to hear it, as [the British] were men who had crossed the Great Water and were unacquainted with the arts of war among the Americans." Young Washington spoke of the "dastardly behaviour" and "deadly panic" among the British regulars during Braddock's defeat. Of course, the colonists thought of themselves as experts when fighting under such conditions. Washington maintained that while "confusion and disobedience" had reigned among Braddock's redcoats, the Virginians had "behaved like men and died like soldiers." By 1763 the notion was prevalent that America's warriors were skilled in the deadly nuances of wilderness warfare. It was an art, many believed, that would stand them in good stead against a large, sluggish European army that allegedly remained inflexibly committed to the orthodoxy of European warfare. Such logic resulted in another concept: Colonial soldiers were superior to British regulars, the argument ran, because they fought "not, like the regulars, for pay," but "to revenge the blood of their nearest friends or relations or to redeem them from the miseries of a captive state."

Another idea appears to have crept into the outlook of many Americans by the end of the colonial wars. Many colonists believed that they were being dragged repeatedly into Britain's wars, conflicts, they were convinced, that the parent state unilaterally decided were worthwhile to enter or to terminate, irrespective of the colonists' interests. Having decided in 1775 to support the colonial rebellion against Great Britain,

Benjamin Franklin gave partial expression to this outlook. Great Britain, "that old rotten state," as he put it, would ever "drag us after them in all the plundering wars which their desperate circumstances, injustice and rapacity may prompt them to undertake." In *Common Sense* (1776), Thomas Paine boldly declared that British monarchs "hath little more to do than to make war," with the result that American dependence on Britain "tends directly to involve this continent in European wars and quarrels, and set us at variance with nations ... against whom we have neither anger nor complaint." America was "only a secondary object" to London, Paine went on, perhaps thinking of the British government's decision to return Louisbourg to France in the Treaty of Aix-la-Chapelle, or of those occasions in 1709 and 1746 when Great Britain had reneged on its promises to send forces to join the armies raised in the provinces. "England," he added, "consults the good of this country no further than it answers her own purpose."

Warfare, not just the French and Indian War, but two hundred years of periodic struggle in Britain's overseas provinces, had helped to shape American society. It would have been remarkable had the identity of the people who inhabited England's colonies not been touched by their experience with warfare, for wars were endemic, recurrent in America's early history. Through the long sweep of years that elapsed between the warm morning when Raleigh's men lugged their calivers onto the sandy beach of Roanoke Island and the chill September day in 1760 when New England soldiers dug artillery emplacements before Montreal, successive generations of colonists had been confronted with a violent, threatening world. During those two centuries warfare had ruined the lives of some and brightened the existence of others; but in some manner America's frequent wars had touched virtually everyone. Many had lived for a time in gut-wrenching fear. Many had been uprooted from their homes and families. Many had lost friends and relatives. Many had endured periods of austerity or groaned under higher taxes occasioned by warfare.

America's wars had affected America's political life. The powers of the central governments in the colonies were often enhanced as officials who waged war year after year sought the resources that would enable them to prosecute these conflicts successfully. In addition, tensions between royal governors and provincial assemblies deepened as bitter fights erupted over the recruitment, command, and disposition of armies.

A sense of an American identity had developed among many provincials during the eighteenth century, a trend stimulated more by war than by any other single factor, for the colonists gradually came to understand that their interests were not the same as those of the parent state. The New England colonies, drawn closer to London in the course of the wars between 1689 and 1713, discovered that the next two conflicts had just the opposite effect; the seeds of alienation had been sown between New England and Old England by the time of the Treaty of Paris.

Recurrent wars affected the way people thought of war, too. So commonplace and pervasive was the experience of war in some colonies that it was not unusual for provincials to exalt in the wars that confronted them, to volunteer in incredible numbers to bear arms, to lionize their warriors, and often to fight with a frightening savagery. But these same colonists had faced enough war by the mid-eighteenth century to hope desperately that repeated episodes of killing might be avoided. For the revolutionary generation, these dichotomous urges were given expression by Thomas Paine. On the one hand, *Common Sense* was a clarion call to arms, an inveighing of "Men of passive tempers" to shake off their "timidity" and march to battle, certain that victory would be achieved because Americans had acquired a "military ability" through their long experience with warfare. On the other hand, *Common Sense* held up the revolutionary sacrifice as the war to end wars. "We have it in our power to begin the world over again," Paine wrote, and at the forefront of that new world would be America's escape from English corruption, violence, and war.

After the fall of Quebec in 1759, British leaders, certain of a substantial victory, had begun to debate the issue of what territory the government should demand from defeated France. Some insisted that Britain must not retain Canada, over which so much national treasure and blood had been spent. These spokesmen suggested that if France was removed from North America, the colonists would no longer require British protection, and the day of American independence would be hastened. It was not a new idea. In 1755, only weeks after Braddock's defeat, John Adams, a nineteen-year-old law student, surmised that "if we can remove the turbulent French" from Canada, nothing could stop the inhabitants of America from "setting up for ourselves."

Many years later, after Great Britain had embarked upon a new colonial policy and after a long popular protest in the colonies against the policies of the parent state, that same John Adams led the fight for American independence in the Continental Congress. One month before independence was declared, he wrote to his friend Patrick Henry announcing the necessity "of an immediate Application to the French Court" for assistance. There was something ironic in the course that Adams recommended, which the United States soon pursued.

England had commenced its presence in America two hundred years before in the knowledge that it must "proceed with extremity, conquer . . . and in the end bring them all in subjection," as Richard Hakluyt had put it, in order to "plant in [America's] soils most sweet." In the end, Britain had nearly brought "them all in subjection." First, the Anglo-American citizenry had vanquished the peoples of the native tribes who had inhabited the lands east of the mountains. Next, after nearly a century of struggle, the Spanish empire east of the Mississippi River had been extirpated and France, too, had been subjected and expelled from North America. Great Britain had not subdued its own people in America, however, and in 1776 that citizenry reached out to France, long their bitter enemy, to help them separate from the British empire—an aim, they knew, that could be achieved only through still another long, bloody war.

BIBLIOGRAPHICAL ESSAY

Until recently, most historians shunned the study of warfare and military matters. The trained scholars who began to emerge from graduate seminars in late nineteenth-century America not only preferred to focus on political, economic, social, constitutional, and diplomatic concerns, but many appeared to disdain military history as an inconsequential pursuit. What, they seemed to ask, could possibly be learned from scrutinizing the course of a war? It was fine to study the cause of a war. The diplomacy that was part of a war was also a legitimate field of inquiry, as were the passions and dislocations wrought by a conflict. The war itself, however, was left to nonprofessionals who wrote for a wide, popular audience, or to the military profession. With a few exceptions, professional historians treated armies and battles, tactics and strategy, only when they wrote biographies of individuals who had borne arms before going on to some more worthy endeavor.

World War II, a massive conflict that touched every life and every aspect of life, altered such practices. Scholars of that generation came to realize that earlier wars had had a similarly pervasive impact. Soon a growing number of professional historians turned their attention toward wars, soldiers, armaments, fortifications, recruitment, logistics, armies, militia units, and partisan and guerrilla fighting. Shortly after World War II, moreover, two distinguished series, the Chicago History of American Civilization series, published by the University of Chicago Press, and the New American Nation series, issued by Harper and Row, included serious works by distinguished scholars that dealt with America's past wars.

America's involvement in the war in Vietnam not only energized another generation of trained historians to continue the work begun by their predecessors, but the nature of that war, and the domestic protest against the United States' participation in that distant conflict, led scholars down new paths of inquiry. Soon studies appeared that probed, among other things, the socialization of soldiers, the effect of service upon those who served, and combat motivation. Scholars now understood that a connection existed between military affairs and a nation's history; these historians wished to learn more about how war shaped society and, in turn, how war was shaped by society. For more on the evolution of these trends among historians, see: Peter Karsten, "The 'New' American Military History: A Map of the Territory, Explored, and Unexplored," *American Quarterly*, 36 (1984); Don Higginbotham, "American Historians and the Military History of the American Revolution," *American Historical Review*, 70 (1964); Edward M. Coffman, "The New American Military History," *Military Affairs*, 48 (1984); Walter Emil Kaegi, Jr., "The Crisis in Military Historiography," *Armed Forces and Society*, 7 (1981); and Richard H. Kohn, "War as Revolution and Social Process," *Reviews in American History*, 5 (1977).

Despite its relative infancy, the literature on the wars of early America has now begun to reach massive proportions. For that reason, students who are unfamiliar with the subject would be advised to begin by consulting two brief articles that deftly delineate the various schools of thought and the primary issues that scholars have highlighted. See Don Higginbotham, "The Early American Way of War: Reconnaissance and Appraisal," *William and Mary Quarterly*, 44 (1987), and E. Wayne Carp, "Early American Military History: A Review of Recent Work," *Virginia Magazine of History and Biography*, 94 (1986).

Students might also wish to read about the history of warfare before turning to America's wars. The literature is vast, but among the best works are two recent studies. One might consult either Robert L. O'Connell, *Of Arms and Men: A Military History of War, Weapons, and Aggression* (1989) or Larry H. Addington, *The Patterns of War through the Eighteenth Century* (1990). Each work has an excellent bibliography.

Few general histories of the colonial wars are available. Douglas Edward Leach, *Arms for Empire: A Military History of the American Colonies in North America, 1607–1763* (1973) is the most comprehensive treatment available. Leach and Howard H. Peckham, *The Colonial Wars, 1689–1762* (1964), a thin, somewhat dated volume, argue that America's military practices were consistent with European military thought and behavior. A good survey of the Anglo-French wars is I. K. Steele, *Guerrillas and Grenadiers: The Struggle for Canada, 1689–1760* (1969). A readable and informed popular account can be found in Edward P. Hamilton, *The French and Indian War: The Story of Battles and Forts in the Wilderness* (1962). The student who might wish to understand the conflict in a particular colony can turn to the relevant volume in two fine series: The States and the Nation series, edited by James M. Smith and published in the 1970s, and A History of the American Colonies in Thirteen Volumes, edited by Milton M. Klein and Jacob E. Cooke. This series also began publication in the 1970s.

The Indian warfare with which this study begins has, like the field in general, witnessed a recent explosion of important books and articles. Here, too, it might be best to begin with a bibliographical guide. The most comprehensive lists have been prepared by Francis Paul Prucha. See his *A Bibliographical Guide to the History of Indian-White Relations in the United States* (1977) and *Indian-White Relations in the United States: A Bibliography of Works Published, 1975–1980* (1982). Another good place to begin to acquire an understanding of the natives is through the essays on the various eastern tribes and their practices that can be found in Bruce G. Trigger, ed., *Handbook of North American Indians: Northeast*, 15 (1978).

In recent years historians have sought to rethink the meeting of Indian and white cultures that commenced with the first tragic occurrences at Roanoke Island. The day has passed when a scholar will describe what took place as a clash of an "advanced race with savages," as a distinguished historian wrote in 1958. Instead, increasing numbers of scholars have attempted to overcome the earlier propensity toward narrow Anglocentrism and better understand the life and thought of the Native Americans, necessary steps if a fresh view of interracial relations is to be forthcoming. J. Frederick Fausz in "The Invasion of Virginia. Indians, Colonialism, and the Conquest of Cant: A Review Essay on Anglo-Indian Relations in the Chesapeake," *Virginia Magazine of History and Biography*, 95 (1987), and also in "Anglo-Indian Relations in Colonial North America," in W. R. Swagerty, ed., *Scholars and the Indian Experience: Critical Reviews of Recent Writing in the Social Sciences* (1984), surveys the recent literature and concludes that progress has been made in escaping the mythopoeic cant and racist stereotypes that flavored earlier studies. In addition, any of the following historiographical essays should prove to be a valuable time-saver for the individual beginning to study the conflicts between colonists and Indians: Bernard W. Sheehan, "Indian-White Relations in Early America: A Review Essay," *William and Mary Quarterly*, 26 (1969); James Axtell, "The Ethnohistory of Early America: A Review Essay," *William and Mary Quarterly*, 35 (1978); and Alden T. Vaughn, "From White Man to Redskin: Changing Perceptions of the American Indian," *American Historical Review*, 87 (1982).

The English mind at the time of first settlement is more easily penetrated than that of the Indians. Bernard W. Sheehan, *Savagism and Civility: Indians and Englishmen in Colonial Virginia* (1980), and Karen Ordahl Kupperman, *Settling with the Indians: The Meeting of English and Indian Cultures in America, 1580–1640* (1980), delineate English predispositions and discoveries with regard to the natives, showing how each influenced subsequent relations. Gary B. Nash, in "The Image of the Indian in the Southern Colonial Mind," *William and Mary Quarterly*, 29 (1972), found that the English arrived with a dual image of the Indians; seen as backward but amicable on the one hand, and as hostile savages on the other. The settlers' prejudicial preconceptions usually won out and clearly gained ascendance after Opechancanough's sudden attack in 1622. It is not enough to understand the English outlook toward Indians at the time of settlement. Nicholas Canny, in *The Elizabethan Conquest of Ireland: A Pattern Established, 1565–1576* (1976) demonstrates that through their military activities in Ireland the English learned how to subject an alien people before stepping foot on Roanoke Island.

Much has been written about the English experience in the environs of Roanoke Island. Karen Ordahl Kupperman, *Roanoke: The Abandoned Colony* (1984), fully comprehends the mindset of Elizabethan expansionism and stresses the militaristic nature of Sir Walter Raleigh's attempts to succeed in America. In *Set Fair for Roanoke: Voyages and Colonies, 1584–1606* (1985), David Beers Quinn provides a more detailed analysis and is more charitable than Kupperman with regard to the behavior of the English. An excellent narrative account of Raleigh's failures in North America is that of David Stick, *Roanoke Island: The Beginnings of English America* (1983).

As one would imagine, the literature on the early years of Virginia is even more voluminous. The best surveys of the initial century of contact between Europeans and natives in Virginia can be found in Wesley Frank Craven, *White, Red, and Black: Seventeenth-Century Virginians* (1971) and Richard L. Morton, *Colonial Virginia*, 2 vols. (1960). An excellent way to approach the earliest years of the colony is through biographies of John Smith. The best and most detailed is Philip L. Barbour, *The Three Worlds of Captain John Smith* (1964), but other satisfactory accounts are those of Bradford Smith, *Captain John Smith* (1953) and Alden T. Vaughn, *American*

Genesis: Captain John Smith and the Founding of Virginia (1975). In recent years, perhaps the most exciting work on early Virginia has come from the pen of J. Frederick Fausz. His "An 'Abundance of Blood Shed On Both Sides': England's First Indian War, 1609–1614," *Virginia Magazine of History and Biography*, 98 (1990), shows how the relative harmony that characterized early settler-native relations deteriorated as increased contacts heightened tensions and misunderstandings on both sides, resulting in English bellicosity and a Powhatan response to the sudden threat within their midst. His "Opechancanough: Indian Resistance Leader," in David Sweet and Gary B. Nash, eds., *Struggle and Survival in Colonial America* (1981), convincingly demonstrates the reasons for the Indian attack in 1622 from the point of view of the beleaguered natives. Another provocative attempt to see things through the eyes of the natives can be found in Nancy Oestrich Lurie, "Indian Cultural Adjustment to European Civilization," in James Morton Smith, ed., *Seventeenth-Century America: Essays in Colonial History* (1959), while Alden T. Vaughn, " 'Explusion of the Savages': English Policy and the Virginia Massacre of 1622," *William and Mary Quarterly*, 35 (1978) shows how English prejudice and ethnocentrism resulted in short-sighted policies that destroyed whatever chance existed for harmony between the two peoples.

The war triggered by Opechancanough's assault in 1622 is detailed in William S. Powell, "Aftermath of the Massacre: The First Indian War, 1622–1632," *Virginia Magazine of History and Biography*, 66 (1958). On the later wars in seventeenth-century Virginia, one might consult Stephen Saunders Webb, *1676: The End of American Independence* (1984), which castigates Gov. William Berkeley for a flawed Indian policy and romanticizes Nathaniel Bacon, or Wilcomb E. Washburn, *The Governor and the Rebel: A History of Bacon's Rebellion in Virginia* (1957), which is more defensive of the governor and critical of the leader of the rebellion and his Indian policies. The evolution of an organized fighting force among the settlers is traced in William L. Shea, *The Virginia Militia in the Seventeenth Century* (1983).

If historians have busily chronicled the clashes between settlers and natives in early Virginia, they have been even more active in studying the confrontations in seventeenth-century New England. The most detailed survey of relations in this century, as well as the best treatment of the Pequot War, can be found in Alden T. Vaughn, *New England Frontier: Puritans and Indians, 1620–1675* (1965). What Vaughn does for the Pequot War is done for King Philip's War by Douglas Edward Leach in *Flintlock and Tomahawk: New England in King Philip's War* (1958). Russell Bourne, *The Red King's Rebellion: Racial Politics in New England, 1675–1678* (1990) is a popular narrative history. A challenge to Leach's Anglocentricism is Philip Ranlet, "Another Look at the Causes of King Philip's War, *New England Quarterly*, 61 (1988), which depicts Philip as an unwilling warrior. Students should additionally consult Francis Jennings, *The Invasion of America: Indians, Colonialism, and the Cant of Conquest* (1975), an angry but illuminating and provocative survey of Puritan-Indian relations that places the burden of responsibility for the recurrent warfare and the ultimate destruction of the Indians squarely upon the backs of the English settlers in New England. Native culture, from before the European arrival through the Pequot War, is the subject of Neal Salisbury, *Manitou and Providence: Indians, Europeans, and the Making of New England, 1500–1643* (1982).

To understand the Puritan mind at the moment of settlement, one might consult Charles M. Segal and David C. Stineback, *Puritans, Indians, and Manifest Destiny* (1977) or William S. Simmons, "Cultural Bias in the New England Puritans' Perception of Indians," *William and Mary Quarterly*, 38 (1981), contributions that reveal an outlook that made a collision between settlers and Indians virtually certain. Adam J. Hirsch, however, in "The Collision of Military Cultures in Seventeenth-Century New England," *Journal of American History*, 74 (1988), demonstrates that misunderstandings on both sides contributed to the Pequot War. The Pequots, who were seen by contemporary Englishmen as a bloodthirsty and violent people, are cast in a quite different light in Alfred A. Cove, "The Pequot Invasion of Southern New England: A Reassessment of the Evidence," *New England Quarterly*, 62 (1989). Steven T. Katz, who believes that much of what has been written on this topic in recent years was skewed by scholarly "outrage at the treatment of the Indians," is more defensive of the colonists' actions in "The Pequot War Reconsidered," *New England Quarterly*, 64 (1991).

In recent years scholars have probed the nature of Indian warfare. Patrick M. Malone, "Changing Military Technology among the Indians of Southern New England, 1600–1677," *American Quarterly*, 25 (1973) and James Axtell, *The School Upon a Hill: Education and Society in Colonial New England* (1974), demonstrate how contact with the English altered native practices in time of war, particularly as European firearms came into their possession. A recent challenge to those who have suggested that Indian warfare was waged in a more modest manner and resulted in less damage than European conflicts is Leroy V. Eid, " 'National' War among Indians of Northeastern North America," *Canadian Review of American Studies*, 16 (1985). Also important is Wendell S. Hadlock, "War among the Northeastern Woodland Indians," *American Anthropologist*, 49 (1947). For more general surveys on this topic, see Wilcomb E. Washburn, "Seventeenth-Century Indian Wars" and Douglas E. Leach, "Colonial Indian Wars," in Bruce G. Trigger, ed., *Handbook of North American Indians*, Vols. 15 (1978) and 4 (1988), respectively. Some Indians fought alongside the English against other Native Americans. This phenomenon in New England is assayed in Richard R. Johnson, "The Search for a Usable Indian: An Aspect of the Defense of Colonial New England," *Journal of American History*, 64 (1977–78).

The late seventeenth century witnessed the advent of the intercolonial warfare among Great Britain, France, and Spain, their colonists, and their Native American allies. Scholarly activity has been even more pronounced in this area than in the realm of the conflicts between the natives and the Anglo-American settlers. In addition to the general histories of colonial warfare mentioned earlier, the student entering this vast field might wish to begin with the brilliant essay by John Shy, "Armed Force in Colonial America: New Spain, New France, and Anglo-America," in Kenneth J. Hagan and William R. Roberts, eds., *Against All Enemies: Interpretations of American Military History from Colonial Times to the Present* (1986). Another good place to start is with the work of W. J. Eccles. He offers a masterful overview of the history of New France, including its wars, in *France in America* (1972). His works are judicious and serve as an antidote to the Anglocentrism that prevails in so many works published by American scholars. Also valuable are Eccles's *The Canadian Frontier, 1534–1760* (1969), *Frontenac: The Courtier Governor* (1959), *Canada under Louis XIV, 1663–1701* (1964), and "Frontenac and the Iroquois, 1672–1682," *Canadian Historical Review*, 36 (1955). During the nineteenth century Francis Parkman published voluminous accounts of the struggle for America. A tireless researcher and masterful writer, Parkman unfortunately reflected the racism of his time. Seven of his classic narratives have recently been combined and reissued as *France and England in North America*, 2 vols. (1983). Excellent surveys of the European phase of these wars, including information on the causes and settlements of the various conflicts, can be found in John B. Wolf, *The Emergence of the Great Powers, 1685–1715* (1951), Penfield Roberts, *The Quest for Security, 1715–1740* (1947), and Walter L. Dorn, *Competition for Empire, 1740–1763* (1940).

Much work has been done on both the impact of the colonial wars on frontier residents and the role of the Native Americans in these clashes. One of the best and most readable accounts is that of Richard I. Melvoin, *New England Outpost: War and Society in Colonial Deerfield* (1989). An informative survey of the northern backcountry is Douglas Edward Leach, *The Northern Colonial Frontier, 1607–1763* (1966). An especially good study of the seemingly endless struggle for Acadia and the bloodletting that resulted on the frontiers of New England and New France is provided by George A. Rawlyk, *Nova Scotia and Massachusetts: A Study of Massachusetts—Nova Scotia Relations* (1973); the author treats Massachusetts as the aggressor in these recurrent conflicts. On the South, see W. Stitt Robinson, *The Southern Colonial Frontier, 1607–1763* (1979), a sweeping history that includes sections on early warfare, and Verner Crane, *The Southern Frontier, 1670–1732* (1928), which focuses more on diplomacy and war. Caught between the European belligerents, the Iroquois found it difficult to escape involvement in their wars. A sympathetic treatment of their plight, and of the diplomacy and warfare that resulted, can be found in Francis Jennings, *The Ambiguous Iroquois Empire: The Covenant Chain Confederation of Indian Tribes with English Colonies from its Beginning to the Lancaster Treaty of 1744* (1984). The Iroquois are also treated in George T. Hunt, *The Wars of the Iroquois* (1940) and Allen W. Trelease, *Indian Affairs in Colonial New York: The Seventeenth Century* (1960); the former emphasizes economic factors in explaining the Iroquois ties to the English, whereas the latter suggests a cultural motivation behind their policy. The policy of the English is the emphasis of Arthur Buffinton, "The Policy of Albany and English Westward Expansion," *Mississippi Valley Historical Review*, 8 (1922) and Helen Broshar, "The First Push Westward of the Albany Traders," also in the *Mississippi Valley Historical Review*, 7 (1920), each of which focuses upon New York's Indian diplomacy and Anglo-American expansionism.

Much of the literature on the earliest intercolonial wars is now dated. Indeed, as a result of the paucity of sources, little has been written on King William's War, although a good general treatment of its successor, Queen Anne's War, can be found in Wesley Frank Craven, *The Colonies in Transition, 1660–1713* (1968). The political fallout in New England from these two wars is covered in Philip Haffenden, *New England in the English Nation, 1689–1713* (1974) and Richard Johnson,

Adjustment to Empire: The New England Colonies 1675–1715 (1981); the latter develops the argument that these wars had the effect of reintegrating New England into Britain's imperial network. W. J. Eccles's "Frontenac's Military Policies, 1689–1698: A Reassessment," *Canadian Historical Review*, 37 (1956) is critical of the French leader and remains the best work on the subject. New France's prewar campaign on the Illinois prairie is ably treated in George B. Selden, Jr., "The Expedition of the Marquis de Denonville against the Seneca Indians: 1687," in Rochester Historical Society *Publication Fund Series*, 4 (1925). The tragedy that sometimes befell frontier residents in these wars is graphically described in C. E. Bennett, "The Burning of Schenectady," *New York History*, 13 (1932). For the larger picture in this war, one might consult William T. Morgan, "The British West Indies during King William's War (1689–97), *Journal of Modern History*, 2 (1930) and John Ehrman, *The Navy in the War of William III, 1689–1697; Its State and Direction* (1953). No first-rate biography of the intrepid Sir William Phips exists. In its absence, one has to make do with Alice Lounsberry, *Sir William Phips: Treasure Fisherman and Governor of the Massachusetts Bay Colony* (1941). Three important studies that cover a broad sweep commence their journeys with this conflict. The son of Col. Benjamin Church published an important work that chronicled the actions of his father on the Maine and Acadian frontier in two wars. Likely based on a long lost diary kept by Church, *The History of the Eastern Expeditions of 1689, 1692, 1696, 1704*, edited by H. M. Dexter (1867), reveals the harshness of this kind of warfare. William Pencak, *War, Politics, and Revolution in Provincial Massachusetts* (1981) elucidates the forces that led to warfare and shows the impact of conflict on life and politics in the province, while Harry M. Ward, *"Unite or Die": Intercolony Relations, 1690–1763* (1971) traces the colonists fatal inability to cooperate during warfare.

The best-remembered action in Queen Anne's War is the abortive Anglo-American campaign for Quebec in 1711. Indispensable on that episode is Gerald S. Graham, ed., *The*

Walker Expedition to Quebec, 1711 (1953). Also useful is William Thomas Morgan, "Queen Anne's Canadian Expedition of 1711," *Queen's University Bulletin*, 56 (1928). The role of the businessman-imperialist in this and other operations can be found in G. M. Waller, *Samuel Vetch: Colonial Enterpriser* (1960). On New York in this war, see Waller's "New York's Role in Queen Anne's War, 1702–1713," *New York History*, 33 (1952). The Iroquois in this conflict are considered in William Thomas Morgan, "The Five Nations and Queen Anne," *Mississippi Valley Historical Review*, 13 (1926) and Anthony F. C. Wallace, "Origins of Iroquois Neutrality: The Grand Settlement of 1701," *Pennsylvania History*, 24 (1957). The literature on the war in the South is especially thin. Charles W. Arnade's *The Siege of St. Augustine in 1702* (1959) and "The English Invasion of Spanish Florida, 1700–1706," *Florida Historical Quarterly*, 41 (1962) are good.

The best treatment of the Tuscarora and Yamassee wars remains the previously cited books on the southern frontier. To place those conflicts in their proper context, however, one might consult Hugh T. Lefler and William S. Powell, *Colonial North Carolina: A History* (1973) and Robert M. Weir, *Colonial South Carolina: A History* (1983). Important contributions to an understanding of southern tribes can be found in two works by David H. Corkran, *The Creek Frontier, 1540–1783* (1967) and *The Cherokee Frontier: Conflict and Survival, 1740–1762* (1962).

The final intercolonial wars have attracted more attention than the initial conflicts. The literature on the fighting along the Georgia-Florida border is considerable. One might start with one of two good studies on the founder of Georgia. The best biography available is that of Phinizy Spalding, *Oglethorpe in America* (1977). Rodney M. Baine and Mary E. Williams, "James Oglethorpe in Europe: Recent Findings in His Military Life," in Phinizy Spalding and Harvey H. Jackson, eds., *Oglethorpe in Perspective: Georgia's Founder after Two Hundred Years* (1989) makes clear the military necessities that existed in leading a fledgling frontier colony. Broader treatments of

Georgia in the war with Spain can be found in Larry E. Ivers, *British Drums on the Southern Frontier* (1974), Trevor R. Reese, "Britain's Military Support of Georgia in the War of 1739–1748," *Georgia Historical Quarterly*, 43 (1959), and John Tate Lanning, *The Diplomatic History of Georgia: A Study in the Epoch of Jenkins' Ear* (1936).

For a wider view of the war with Spain in the 1740s, see Albert Harkness, Jr., "Americanism and Jenkins' Ear," *Mississippi Valley Historical Review*, 37 (1950), John Tate Lanning, "American Participation in the war of Jenkins' Ear," *Georgia Historical Quarterly*, 11 (1927), and Francis L. Berkeley, Jr., "The War of Jenkins' Ear," in the volume of essays, *The Old Dominion* (1964), edited by Darrett Rutman. The best source on the background of the colonials who enlisted for the Cartagena campaign is William A. Foote, "The Pennsylvania Men of the American Regiment," *Pennsylvania Magazine of History and Biography*, 87 (1963). For a provocative essay that stresses how the Cartagena expedition resulted in mutually unfavorable perceptions among Americans and British, see Douglas E. Leach, "The Cartagena Expedition, 1740–1742, and Anglo-American Relations," in Maarten Ultee, ed., *Adapting to Conditions: War and Society in the Eighteenth Century* (1986). The latter stages of the war in the South are the subject of Norman W. Caldwell, "The Southern Frontier during King George's War," *Journal of Southern History*, 7 (1941).

No American official played a greater role in King George's War than Gov. William Shirley of Massachusetts. A judicious biography of his career is that by John Schutz, *William Shirley: King's Governor of Massachusetts* (1961). A good study of the British naval commander during the siege of Louisbourg is Julian Gwyn, *The Enterprising Admiral: The Personal Fortune of Sir Peter Warren* (1974). The leader of New England's army at Louisbourg is profiled in Byron Fairchild, "Sir William Pepperrell: New England's Pre-Revolutionary Hero," *New England Historical and Genealogical Register*, 130 (1976), although no satisfactory biography exists. The literature on the siege of Louisbourg is vast. The best brief treatment is Robert Emmet Wall, Jr., "Louisbourg, 1745," *New England Quarterly*, 37 (1964); the best detailed narrative is that of George Rawlyk, *Yankees at Louisbourg* (1967), a work that also demonstrates how anti-Catholicism could serve as a recruiting device in raising a New England army. Britain's failure to cooperate in the projected campaign against New France in 1746 is the subject of Arthur H. Buffinton, "The Canadian Expedition of 1746: Its Relation to British Politics," *American Historical Review*, 55 (1940). Britain's controversial decision to return the post to France is treated in Jack Sosin, "Louisbourg and the Peace of Aix-la-Chapelle," *William and Mary Quarterly*, 14 (1957); his article demonstrates that Great Britain returned Louisbourg to France in order to reacquire its position in Flanders. The naval warfare in the intercolonial conflicts is detailed in Gerald S. Graham, *Empire in the North Atlantic: The Maritime Struggle for North America* (1950). On naval matters in this war, see Herbert Richmond, *The Navy in the War of 1739–48*, 3 vols. (1920), although privateering is best covered by Howard Chapin in *Privateering in King George's War, 1739–1748* (1928) and in *Privateer Ships and Sailors: The First Century of American Colonial Privateering, 1625–1725* (1926).

Historians have been concerned not only with specific wars, but also with the nature of warfare in the colonial era. Some scholars have stressed the uniqueness of American warfare, arguing that because it often appeared to be unlimited or total warfare, and because it was fought beyond the limits of the formal rules of war by an armed citizenry, the wars of early America differed significantly from their counterparts in Europe. See the essay on war in Daniel Boorstin, *The Americans: The Colonial Experience*(1958) and John E. Ferling, *A Wilderness of Miseries: War and Warriors in Early America* (1981). The impact on European warfare wrought by the American environment and its native inhabitants is the subject of John K. Mahon, "Anglo-American Methods of Indian Warfare, 1676–1794," *Mississippi Valley Historical Review*, 45 (1958). There can be no doubt that there was a formalized manner of warfare in Europe. To understand what was at least the theory that undergirded warfare on the continent, and which was described in the numerous military manuals available in the eighteenth century and read by both American and English soldiers, two essays by Ira Gruber are important. See "Classical Influences on British Strategy in the War of Independence," in John Eadie, ed., *Classical Traditions in Early America* (1976) and "British Strategy: The Theory and Practice of Eighteenth-Century War," in Don Higginbotham, *Reconsiderations on the Revolutionary War* (1978). On the intellectual underpinnings of American war and warriors, see John Dederer, *War in America to 1775: Before Yankee Doodle* (1990). Those wishing to read about the nature of war in Europe might see Theodore Ropp, *War in the Modern World* (1962).

Who bore arms in America's early wars? Few topics have attracted greater interest among scholars than the early militia system. Recent studies have riddled the old myth that the militia system alone provided for the defensive needs of the colonists. Historians now understand that militia units seldom took to the field. When mobilized, the trainbands served primarily as a home defense system, or as a source of draftees for the army that the province had raised for longer service, perhaps even for service beyond the colony's limits. The most important works in this area are those of Don Higginbotham, "The Military Institutions of Colonial America: The Rhetoric and the Reality," in Higginbotham, *War and Society in Revolutionary America: The Wider Dimensions of Conflict* (1989), Higginbotham, "The American Militia: A Traditional Institution with Revolutionary Responsibilities," in the previously cited Higginbotham, *Reconsiderations on the Revolutionary War*, John K. Mahon, *History of the Militia and the National Guard* (1983), and John Shy, "A New Look at the Colonial Militia," in his collection, *A People Numerous and Armed: Military Aspects of the American Revolution* (1976).

For essays on the militia in specific provinces and regions, see Timothy Breen, "The Covenanted Militia of Massachu-

setts Bay: English Background and New World Development,"
in Breen, *Puritans and Adventurers: Change and Persistence
in Early America* (1980); Allen French, "The Arms and Military Training of Our Colonizing Ancestors," in Massachusetts
Historical Society, *Proceedings*, 67 (1945), which focuses pri-
marily on the New England experience; Robert W. Kenny,
"The Beginning of the Rhode Island Train Bands," *Rhode
Island Historical Society Collections*, 33 (1940); Douglas Ed-
ward Leach, "The Military System of Plymouth Colony," *New
England Quarterly*, 24 (1951); H. Telfer Mook, "Training Day
in New England," *New England Quarterly*, 24 (1951); Jack
Radabaugh, "The Militia of Colonial Massachusetts," *Military
Affairs*, 18 (1954); Louis Dow Scisco, "Evolution of Colonial
Militia in Maryland," *Maryland Historical Magazine*, 35
(1940); Morrison Sharp, "Leadership and Democracy in the
Early New England System of Defense," *American Historical
Review*, 50 (1945); E. Milton Wheeler, "Development and Or-
ganization of the North Carolina Militia," *North Carolina Historical Review*, 41 (1964). Also see William Shea on Virginia,
cited previously. The role of African-American soldiers is the
subject of Benjamin Quarles, "The Colonial Militia and Negro
Manpower," *Mississippi Valley Historical Review*, 45 (1959).

In the intercolonial wars, America's primary fighting force
consisted of volunteer armies supplemented with some militia
conscripts. Several recent studies have challenged the old notion that these armies were composed almost solely of men
from the bottom rung of society. It now appears that even in
the volunteer armies America's soldiers were broadly representative of American society. On Massachusetts's army during the French and Indian War, see Fred Anderson, *A People's
Army: Massachusetts Soldiers and Society in the Seven Years'
War* (1984). Harold E. Selesky, *War and Society in Colonial
Connecticut* (1990), has produced a study with similar findings
for Connecticut. On Virginia, see John Ferling, "Soldiers for
Virginia: Who Served in the French and Indian War?" *Virginia
Magazine of History and Biography*, 94 (1986).

Were these men in reality the wretched soldiers that Great Britain's professional officers thought them to be? The most thoughtful analysis of the quality of America's soldiers can be found in Fred Anderson, "Why Did Colonial New Englanders Make Bad Soldiers? Contractual Principles and Military Conduct during the Seven Years' War," *William and Mary Quarterly*, 38 (1981). Whatever their quality, by the eighteenth century American society lionized its warriors. John Ferling, "The New England Soldier: A Study in Changing Perceptions," *American Quarterly*, 33 (1981) shows how society's views toward war and warriors changed in the course of the transition to the more secular eighteenth century. In John Ferling, " 'Oh that I was a Soldier': John Adams and the Agony of War," *American Quarterly*, 36 (1984), one can see how an individual who did not bear arms could come to see himself as a failure.

Of course, the British army also fought in these eighteenth-century wars. The standard source is John Fortescue, *A History of the British Army*, 13 vols. (1889–1930). Volume 2 deals with the intercolonial conflicts. Life in the British army is the subject of Sylvia Frey, *The British Soldier in America: A Social History of Military Life in the Revolutionary Period* (1984). The dispatch of the British army to Virginia during Bacon's Rebellion is covered in Dallas Irvine, "The First British Regulars in North America," *Military Affairs*, 9 (1945). Three important essays survey how the British army sought to adjust to American conditions. See Eric Robson, "British Light Infantry in the Mid-Eighteenth Century: The Effect of American Conditions," *Army Quarterly*, 63 (1952), Peter E. Russell, "Redcoats in the Wilderness: British Officers and Irregular Warfare in Europe and America, 1740–1760," *William and Mary Quarterly*, 25 (1978); and Daniel J. Beattie, "The Adaptation of the British Army to Wilderness Warfare, 1755–1763," in the previously cited Ultee, *Adapting to Conditions*. Russell and Beattie focus on the creation and nature of British ranger forces. On the provincials who served in Britain's army, see Stanley Pargellis, "The Four Independent Companies of

New York," in *Essays in Colonial History Presented to Charles McLean Andrews by his Students* (1931).

Those who wish to learn of the weaponry of this age should begin with Harold L. Peterson, *Arms and Armor in Colonial America, 1526–1783* (1956), which traces the evolution of muskets, sidearms, and artillery. The evolution of small arms is the subject of Charles W. Sawyer, *Firearms in American History*, 3 vols. (1910–1920). The variety of artillery available to commanders is covered in B. P. Hughes, *British Smooth-Bore Artillery: The Muzzle Loading Artillery of the 18th and 19th Centuries* (1969). On the weapons used by the initial generations of settlers, see Harold Peterson, "The Military Equipment of the Plymouth and Bay Colonies, 1620–1690, *New England Quarterly*, 20 (1947).

The final intercolonial conflict, the French and Indian War, has been the most thoroughly studied of the four struggles. So much has been written about it that it alone among the wars is the subject of a bibliographical reference work, a compilation and brief summary of over fifteen hundred titles that runs nearly three hundred printed pages. This guide is a convenient starting point for any student. See James G. Lydon, *Struggle for Empire: A Bibliography of the French and Indian War* (1986). An excellent popular history of the war can be found in Harrison Bird, *Battle for a Continent* (1965). The view from Paris, including a good analysis of France's ultimate failure, is provided by Lee Kennett, *The French Armies in the Seven Years' War: A Study in Military Organization and Administration* (1967). A monumental study from the Anglo-American viewpoint, which also succeeds in placing the war in America in its worldwide context, is that of Lawrence H. Gipson, *The British Empire before the American Revolution*, 15 vols. (1935–70).

Many explanations have been put forward with regard to the origin of this war. Charles M. Andrews, "Anglo-French Commercial Rivalry, 1700–1750," *American Historical Review*, 20 (1915), emphasizes the rivalry over the fur, sugar, and slave trades. European factors are emphasized by Patrice

Louis-Rene Higonnet, "The Origins of the Seven Years' War," *Journal of Modern History*, 40 (1968) and Elizabeth Malcolm-Smith, *British Diplomacy in the Eighteenth Century, 1700–1789* (1937). To understand the role of Virginia in the coming of this conflict, as well as during the course of the war, see Hayes Baker-Crothers, *Virginia and the French and Indian War* (1928) and Charles Ambler, *George Washington and the West* (1936).

Most of the major participants in this war have found biographers. Owen A. Sherrard, *Lord Chatham*, 3 vols. (1952–58) is the best study of the architect of British victory, but Hubert Hall, "Chatham's Colonial Policy," *American Historical Review*, 5 (1900) is good on the ultimate British victory. For the British commanders, see Lee McCardell, *Ill-Starred General: Braddock of the Cold-Stream Guards* (1958), and Stanley M. Pargellis, *Lord Loudoun in North America* (1933). General Abercromby awaits his biographer, but several good studies of Jeffery Amherst exist. John Cuthbert Long, *Lord Jeffery Amherst, A Soldier of the King* (1933) is somewhat romantic, Lawrence Shaw Mayo, *Jeffery Amherst: A Biography* (1916) is more balanced but less scholarly, and Louis de Cognets, *Amherst and Canada* (1962) is scholarly but not a true biography. William T. Waugh, *James Wolfe: Man and Soldier* (1928) lionizes the conqueror of Canada, while Frederick E. Whitton, *Wolfe and North America* (1929) is more balanced. Thomas Gage, an important officer of lower rank, is ably treated in the early chapters of John R. Alden, *General Gage in America* (1948). To understand the British rangers and their American leader, see John R. Cuneo, *Robert Rogers of the Rangers* (1959). Britain's Indian superintendent and military commander is treated in Milton W. Hamilton, *Sir William Johnson: Colonial American, 1715–1763* (1976) and James Thomas Flexner, *Lord of the Mohawks: A Biography of Sir William Johnson* (1959).

Among the American soldiers only George Washington has received much attention. On this Virginia soldier, see the encyclopedic Douglas Southall Freeman, *George Washington:*

A Biography, 7 vols. (1948–1957), especially the first two volumes. James Thomas Flexner, *George Washington: The Forge of Experience* (1965) deals with his subject before the American Revolution and John E. Ferling, *The First of Men: A Life of George Washington* (1988) accents personal and emotional factors in Washington's behavior. Although not a biography, Bernard Knollenberg, *George Washington: The Virginia Period, 1732–1775* (1964), is valuable on the French and Indian War.

The Marquis de Montcalm deserves a good biography. In the meantime, there are the excessively laudatory works of Thomas Chapais, *Le Marquis de Montcalm* (1911) and William C. H. Wood, *The Passing of New France: A Chronicle of Montcalm* (1915). These older works should be contrasted with the views of W. J. Eccles in his history of France in America, cited earlier.

Great Britain's first action in the war, Braddock's ill-fated campaign, has resulted in numerous studies. The best works are those of Paul E. Kopperman, *Braddock at the Monongahela* (1977), which exonerates the British general and also contains a useful bibliography, and Stanley M. Pargellis, "Braddock's Defeat," *American Historical Review*, 41 (1936). Governor Shirley's problems on the New York frontier are blamed on the internecine fighting among the province's politicians in Theodore Thayer, "The Army Contractors for the Niagara Campaign, 1755–1756," *William and Mary Quarterly*, 14 (1957). Ian K. Steele, *Betrayals: Fort William Henry and the "Massacre"* (1990) is a brilliant revisionist study of Montcalm's campaign in New York in 1757, one that reassesses the magnitude of the butchery that followed the British defeat. The debacle that befell Abercromby at Ticonderoga the following year could benefit from a similar study. Robert F. Berkhofer, "The French and Indians at Carillon," *Fort Ticonderoga Museum Bulletin*, 9 (1956) stresses the role of the Native Americans, while British logistical problems are the emphasis of John A. Schutz, "The Disaster of Fort Ticonderoga: The Shortage of Muskets during the Mobilization of 1758," *Hun-*

tington Library Quarterly, 14 (1951). A brief, popular narrative of the engagement is that of Richard F. Snow, "The Debacle at Fort Carillon," *American Heritage,* 23 (1972). The best treatments of the British seizure of Niagara are those of Wilfred B. Kerr, "Fort Niagara, 1759–1763" and John Cuthbert Long, "Amherst in 1759," both in *New York History,* 15 (1934).

More has been written on the campaign for Quebec than on any other battle in this war. Good popular accounts are by Henri Raymond Casgrain, *Wolfe and Montcalm* (1905), Christopher Hibbert, *Wolfe at Quebec* (1959), and Charles C. Lloyd, *The Capture of Quebec* (1959). Nevertheless, an invaluable starting point should be the sound introduction provided by W. J. Eccles, "The Battle of Quebec: A Reappraisal," French Colonial Historical Society, *Proceedings,* 3 (1978), which is critical of Montcalm's strategy, and the lengthier reassessment of the undertaking in the extremely important Charles P. Stacey, *Quebec, 1759: The Siege and the Battle* (1959). The battle is assayed by a famous military historian in Basil H. Liddell Hart, "The Battle that Won an Empire," *American Heritage,* 11 (1959).

The frontier in wartime is the subject of Dale Van Every, *Forth to the Wilderness: The First American Frontier, 1754–1774* (1977). A good start toward understanding the bloody occurrences in frontier Pennsylvania can be made with Ralph L. Ketchum, "Conscience, War, and Politics in Pennsylvania, 1755–1757, *William and Mary Quarterly,* 20 (1963), Leonard W. Labaree, "Benjamin Franklin and the Defense of Pennsylvania, 1754–1757," *Pennsylvania History,* 29 (1962), and Theodore G. Thayer, *Pennsylvania Politics and the Growth of Democracy, 1740–1776* (1953), which contains an excellent chapter on the war in this province. Britain's conquest of Fort Duquesne is best treated in the biographies of Washington and the general works cited elsewhere, but Niles Anderson, "New Light on the 1758 Forbes Campaign," *Western Pennsylvania History Magazine,* 50 (1967) focuses on the role of colonial gunsmiths in this endeavor, and James L. Stokesbury, "John Forbes and the Wilderness Road," *American History Illus-*

trated, 9 (1974) has written an accurate and readable account for a popular audience. Otherwise, the war in the Virginia backcountry is ably covered in James Titus, *The Old Dominion at War: Society, Politics and Warfare in Late Colonial Virginia* (1991). Virginia's most remote frontier is treated in Otis Rice, "The French and Indian War in West Virginia," *West Virginia History*, 24 (1963). The limited military role played by African-Americans—limited because of fear of a slave insurrection—is the subject of Larry Bowman, "Virginia's Use of Blacks in the French and Indian War," *Western Pennsylvania Historical Magazine*, 53 (1970).

On the role of the Five Nations in this war, see John Wolfe Lydekker, *The Faithful Mohawks* (1938). Alden T. Vaughn and Daniel K. Richter, *Crossing the Cultural Divide: Indians and New Englanders, 1605–1763* (1981) and L. F. S. Upton, *Micmacs and Colonists: Indian-White Relations in the Maritimes, 1713–1867* (1979) treat Indian relations in other regions over a long period.

A fascinating article on the captives taken in this and other wars is that of James Axtell, "The White Indians of Colonial America," *William and Mary Quarterly*, 32 (1975), which explains why many white prisoners refused to return to their pre-war society.

The best study available on the peace settlement is that of Zenab Esmat Rashed, *The Peace of Paris, 1763* (1951). For good essays on Britain's decision to keep Canada, see William Lawson Grant, "Canada versus Guadaloupe, An Episode of the Seven Years' War," *American Historical Review*, 17 (1912), which surveys the pamphlet literature on the topic, and Marjorie G. Reid, "Pitt's Decision to Keep Canada in 1761," *Canadian Historical Association, Report* (1926).

For a thoughtful, interpretive essay on this long period of warfare, one should see Howard H. Peckham, "Speculations on the Colonial Wars," *William and Mary Quarterly*, 17 (1960). Historians have been especially intrigued with the meaning of the final war, the French and Indian War. Several scholarly works have linked the war to the coming of the American Revolution. Lawrence Henry Gipson, "The American Revolution as an Aftermath of the Great War for the Empire, 1754–1763," *Political Science Quarterly*, 45 (1950) suggests that Britain's indebtedness and the very totality of its victory led to subsequent problems. Jack P. Greene, "The Seven Years' War and the American Revolution: The Causal Relationship Reconsidered," *Journal of Imperial Commonwealth History*, 8 (1980) argues that the war helped shape the manner in which imperial leaders viewed the colonial relationship. John M. Murrin, "The French and Indian War, the American Revolution, and the Counterfactual Hypothesis: Reflections on Lawrence Henry Gipson and John Shy," *Reviews in American History*, 1 (1973), scrambles facts in order to understand the significance of this war. The wartime evolution of Britain's postwar actions toward America is traced in Thomas C. Barrow, "Background to the Grenville Program, 1757–1763," *William and Mary Quarterly*, 22 (1965). The linkage between the war and the colonists' resistance against Britain's new colonial policies after 1763 is explored by Fred Anderson, "The Colonial Background to the American Victory," in John Ferling, ed., *The World Turned Upside Down: The American Victory in the War of Independence* (1988). Imperial relations deteriorated as a result of Britain's arbitrary treatment of the Americans according to J. Alan Rogers, *Empire and Liberty: American Resistance to British Authority, 1755–1763* (1974). Douglas Edward Leach, *Roots of Conflict: British Armed Forces and Colonial Americans, 1677–1763* (1986) explores the antagonism that developed between the colonists and British military leaders in the course of the eighteenth century, with particular emphasis on the events of the final war. The ties between this war and the origin of American ideas of independence is explored in J. M. Bumstead, "'Things in the Womb of Time': Ideas of American Independence, 1633 to 1763," *William and Mary Quarterly*, 31 (1974).

INDEX

Struggle for a Continent:
   The Wars of Early America
Copy editor: Claudia Lamm Wood
Production editor: Lucy Herz
Proofreader: Urban Editorial Services
Indexer: Catherine Fox
Cartographer: James Bier
Typesetter: Impressions, Inc.
Printer: Edwards Bros., Inc.
Book designer: Roger Eggers